Soft Circuits

THE JOHN D. AND CATHERINE T. MACARTHUR FOUNDATION SERIES ON DIGITAL MEDIA AND LEARNING

Engineering Play: A Cultural History of Children's Software, by Mizuko Ito

Hanging Out, Messing Around, and Geeking Out: Kids Living and Learning with New Media, by Mizuko Ito, Sonja Baumer, Matteo Bittanti, danah boyd, Rachel Cody, Becky Herr-Stephenson, Heather A. Horst, Patricia G. Lange, Dilan Mahendran, Katynka Martínez, C. J. Pascoe, Dan Perkel, Laura Robinson, Christo Sims, Lisa Tripp, with contributions by Judd Antin, Megan Finn, Arthur Law, Annie Manion, Sarai Mitnick, David Schlossberg, and Sarita Yardi

The Civic Web: Young People, the Internet, and Civic Participation, by Shakuntala Banaji and David Buckingham

Connected Play: Tweens in a Virtual World, by Yasmin B. Kafai and Deborah A. Fields

The Digital Youth Network: Cultivating New Media Citizenship in Urban Communities, edited by Brigid Barron, Kimberley Gomez, Nichole Pinkard, and Caitlin K. Martin

Connected Code: Children as the Programmers, Designers, and Makers for the 21st Century, by Yasmin B. Kafai and Quinn Burke

The Interconnections Collection: Understanding Systems through Digital Design, developed by Kylie Peppler, Melissa Gresalfi, Katie Salen Tekinbaş, and Rafi Santo

   Gaming the System: Designing with Gamestar Mechanic, by Katie Salen Tekinbaş, Melissa Gresalfi, Kylie Peppler, and Rafi Santo

   Script Changers: Digital Storytelling with Scratch, by Kylie Peppler, Rafi Santo, Melissa Gresalfi, and Katie Salen Tekinbaş

   Short Circuits: Crafting e-Puppets with DIY Electronics, by Kylie Peppler, Katie Salen Tekinbaş, Melissa Gresalfi, and Rafi Santo

   Soft Circuits: Crafting e-Fashion with DIY Electronics, by Kylie Peppler, Melissa Gresalfi, Katie Salen Tekinbaş, and Rafi Santo

Inaugural Series Volumes

Six edited volumes were created through an interactive community review process and published online and in print in December 2007. They are the precursors to the peer-reviewed monographs in the series. For more information on these volumes, visit http://mitpress.mit.edu/books/series/john-d-and-catherine-t-macarthur-foundation-series-digital-media-and-learning.

Soft Circuits
Crafting e-Fashion with DIY Electronics

by Kylie Peppler, Melissa Gresalfi,
Katie Salen Tekinbaş, and Rafi Santo

The MIT Press
Cambridge, Massachusetts
London, England

MIT Press books may be purchased at special quantity discounts for business or sales promotional use. For information, please email special_sales@mitpress.mit.edu.

This book was set in Melior LT Std 9.5/13pt by Toppan Best-set Premedia Limited. Printed and bound in the United States of America.

Library of Congress Cataloging-in-Publication Data
Peppler, Kylie A.
    Soft circuits: crafting e-fashion with DIY electronics / by Kylie Peppler, Melissa Gresalfi, Katie Salen Tekinbaş, and Rafi Santo.
pages cm. — (Interconnections: understanding systems through digital design) (The John D. and Catherine T. Macarthur Foundation series on digital media and learning)
    Includes bibliographical references and index.
    ISBN 978-0-262-02784-7 (hardcover: alk. paper) 1. Electronic circuits—Study and teaching (Middle school)—Activity programs. 2. Dress accessories. 3. Activity programs in education. I. Gresalfi, Melissa, 1977- II. Tekinbaş, Katie Salen. III. Santo, Rafi, 1982- IV. Title.
    TK7862.P475 2014
    646.40028'4—dc23
                                    2014003841

10   9   8   7   6   5   4   3   2

CONTENTS

SERIES FOREWORD

In recent years, digital media and networks have become embedded in our everyday lives and are part of broad-based changes to how we engage in knowledge production, communication, and creative expression. Unlike the early years in the development of computers and computer-based media, digital media are now *commonplace* and *pervasive*, having been taken up by a wide range of individuals and institutions in all walks of life. Digital media have escaped the boundaries of professional and formal practice, and of the academic, governmental, and industry homes that initially fostered their development. Now they have been taken up by diverse populations and noninstitutionalized practices, including the peer activities of youth. Although specific forms of technology uptake are highly diverse, a generation is growing up in an era when digital media are part of the taken-for-granted social and cultural fabric of learning, play, and social communication.

This book series is founded upon the working hypothesis that those immersed in new digital tools and networks are engaged in an unprecedented exploration of language, games, social interaction, problem solving, and self-directed activity that leads to diverse forms of learning. These diverse forms of learning are reflected in expressions of identity, in how individuals express independence and creativity, and in their ability to learn, exercise judgment, and think systematically.

The defining frame for this series is not a particular theoretical or disciplinary approach, nor is it a fixed set of topics. Rather, the series revolves around a constellation of topics investigated from multiple disciplinary and practical frames. The series as a whole looks at the relation between youth, learning, and digital media, but each contribution to the series might deal with only a subset of this constellation. Erecting strict topical boundaries would exclude some of the most important work in the field. For example, restricting the content of the series only to people of a certain age would mean artificially reifying an age boundary when the phenomenon demands otherwise. This would become particularly problematic with new forms of online participation where one important outcome is the mixing of participants of different ages. The same goes for digital media, which are increasingly inseparable from analog and earlier media forms.

The series responds to certain changes in our media ecology that have important implications for learning. Specifically, these changes involve new forms of media *literacy* and developments in the modes of media *participation*. Digital media are part of a convergence between interactive media (most notably gaming), online networks, and existing media forms. Navigating this media ecology involves a palette of literacies that are being defined through practice but require more scholarly scrutiny before they can be fully incorporated pervasively into educational initiatives. Media literacy involves not only ways of understanding, interpreting, and critiquing media, but also the means for creative and social expression, online search and navigation, and a host of new technical skills. The potential gap in literacies and participation skills creates new challenges for educators who struggle to bridge media engagement inside and outside the classroom.

The John D. and Catherine T. MacArthur Foundation Series on Digital Media and Learning, published by the MIT Press, aims to close these gaps and provide innovative ways of thinking about and using new forms of knowledge production, communication, and creative expression.

FOREWORD

When I was a girl and a young woman, my favorite thing to do was to make stuff. I especially loved making fashion: clothes, handbags, shoes, and jewelry. I spent endless hours sketching, sewing, crocheting, cutting, and gluing. One summer, I spent over a month painstakingly weaving together a set of sparkly gloves from tiny seed beads. Though I haven't worn them in years, they still occupy a special place in my jewelry box. I always prided myself in doing things that were hard. I loved making beautiful and utterly unique pieces.

I gave my creations away to my friends, relatives, and mentors. I also wore them proudly. It was a special thrill to have my handiwork admired, to hear people say things like: "What a lovely necklace!" "You could sell those!" or "How long did it take you to make that!?"

Making things was how I spent much of my free time through young adulthood. It also formed a core of my identity. I was a designer, an artist, and a craftsperson. I could make interesting and desirable things. I had knowledge and skills that other people appreciated.

Meanwhile, in school, my favorite subjects were art and math. Art I loved for what are probably obvious reasons—its use of different materials, its emphasis on aesthetics, and the time and space it allowed for independence. Math, on the other hand, was all about the delight of solving puzzles—the notion that, from a few basic principles, you could figure out nearly anything. Math was wonderfully simple and structured—precise, clean, and clear. I also liked math because I was good at it.

It was an Important School Subject. All the adults in my life—my teachers, my parents, and other smart people I admired—thought it was terrific that I excelled at math, so I did too.

I never spent time on mathematics at home, though. I never sought out geometry brain teasers or algorithmic riddles in my free time. I never read or worked beyond my school textbooks. I was never *obsessed* with math.

One short semester in high school, I took a programming class (it was only offered that one time). I briefly intuited that computers—despite their disappointing virtuality—might provide a "mathland" I could obsess over. It seemed to me that programming was like crafting: an open-ended creative enterprise, only with mathematics as raw material. But I didn't learn enough in that class to be able to explore computers on my own, so though the thought stayed stashed away in the back of my mind, it was almost 10 years before I revisited it.

In the early 2000s, I impulsively—and, it turns out fortuitously—decided to pursue my old hunch and go back to school to study computer science. It was in graduate school that I learned I was right. I also discovered the wondrous world of electronics and learned that programming and electronics could be blended with art, design, and even fashion. In my late twenties, I became as joyously absorbed by programming and electronics as I was by crafts.

I suspect that lots of young women and young men are like me. They are drawn to arts and crafts for a complex range of personal and social reasons. They excel in math, science, computing, or similar disciplines at school. But they don't see these disciplines as creative or meaningful, and they don't personally identify with the cultures of these disciplines.

Soft circuits and e-textiles present one powerful way to change this pattern. By situating technology in a creative, artistic (feminine) context, e-textiles invite new audiences to the table to tinker and play.

There are a number of terrific e-textile books. Many of these (including my recent contribution, *Sew Electric*) are collections of instructions for DIY projects. There are also beautiful design compilations, like *Textile Visionaries*, and a recent scholarly survey, *Textile Messages*.

Soft Circuits: Crafting e-Fashion with DIY Electronics is the first e-textile book designed for and by educators. By reaching out directly to teachers, it promises to make the field much more visible, especially to young people. It presents a thoughtful and practical framework that elementary, middle, and high school teachers can use to introduce e-textiles in their classrooms. The projects in this book are delightfully fun and grounded in Common Core science and language arts standards.

Had I discovered e-textiles earlier, I have no doubt I would have embraced programming and electronics as a girl, and I would be a more skilled and knowledgeable engineer than I am today. This book will undoubtedly open pathways that will enable other young people to fall in love with technology and design. I can't wait to see what they make!

Leah Buechley, designer and engineer, inventor of the LilyPad Arduino toolkit, and author of *Sew Electric*

ACKNOWLEDGMENTS AND PROJECT HISTORY

ACKNOWLEDGMENTS

This book collection would not have been possible without the involvement of so many people, who were as inspired as we were by the idea of having youths develop powerful new ways for seeing and acting in the world. It's the result of years of collaboration with research and design partners across the United States, cycles of testing and feedback from teachers, and helpful insights from advisors and friends. In particular, we'd like to thank the following:

- Connie Yowell (Director of Education for U.S. Programs at the John D. and Catherine T. MacArthur Foundation), for the ongoing support provided to this project through the MacArthur Foundation's Digital Media and Learning (DML) initiative. The project would have been impossible without not only the funding provided, but also the incredible networks of colleagues within the DML field that she has done so much to foster.

- This material also is based in part upon work supported by the National Science Foundation under Grant No. 0855886, awarded to Kylie A. Peppler.

- Nichole Pinkard (Associate Professor of Interactive Media, Human Computer Interaction, and Education, DePaul University), for seeing the need for the project from the beginning and catalyzing this incredible group of partners to come together to work on it.

- The hard-working team of graduate research assistants at Indiana University who have contributed to this project over the years, including Sinem Siyyahan, Diane Glosson, Charlene Volk, Mike Downton, Leon Gordon, Jackie Barnes, Sophia Bender, and Kate Shively, not to mention the broader Learning Sciences student body, who have all engaged in conversations with us around this work one way or another.

- Our colleagues and teacher leaders at the National Writing Project (NWP), who worked with us to pilot the activities in this book and helped us integrate their valuable insights into the final manuscript: Christina Cantrill, Paul Oh, Steve Moore, Lori Sue Garner, Janie Brown, Deidra Floyd, Laura Beth Fay, Carol Jehlen, Travis Powell, Laura Lee Stroud, Eric Tuck, Kevin Hodgson, Janelle Bence, Laura Fay Beth, Cliff Lee, Chad Sansing, and Trina Williams.

- The many institutions in Bloomington, Indiana, that have worked with us to pilot the activities in these books, including the Boys and Girls Club, under the leadership of Matthew Searle; and the Bloomington Project School, under the leadership of Daniel Baron.

- Our advisory board, which has provided valuable feedback both on the treatment of the ideas in these books and how they fit into the broader field: Linda Booth Sweeney, Natalie Rusk, Amon Millner, and Cindy Hmelo-Silver.

HISTORY OF THE GRINDING NEW LENSES PROJECT

One of the important lessons to be learned from working on systems thinking is that nothing is created in a vacuum; the same is true of all the work shared in this book. In this section, we briefly share the background on the Grinding New Lenses (GNL) project, which has led to this book collection and shaped its focus.

Taking a systems perspective, it's somewhat challenging to tell a linear story about what led to this work. But a good place to start might be a school called Quest to Learn (Q2L; q2l.org), which was opened by Katie Salen and Institute of Play in New York City in 2009 (www.instituteofplay.org) with support from the MacArthur Foundation's Digital Media and Learning initiative (Salen et al., 2010). The school was designed as a proof of concept to answer a unique question: How can school-based learning be designed based on powerful learning principles found in the best games—ones that inspire engagement, collaboration, critical thinking, and, of course, systems thinking?

In answering this question, Q2L did a number of things differently from traditional schools. To begin with, it reorganized the curriculum so that disciplines with natural intersections that were usually kept separate were joined together. Mathematics and

English language arts became "Codeworlds," a class that focused on symbolic and representational systems. Another class called "The Way Things Work," taught science and math combined, and still another class called "Being, Space, and Place" was put together to teach history and English literature. Assessment and testing also was done differently—instead of finals at the end of each semester, each class broke up into teams that needed to work collaboratively on a week-long "boss level," which challenged the youths to integrate insights from the rest of the course. More broadly, the school made the idea of youths as designers and makers of systems central to the overall setup of Q2L's learning environment an idea that was reflected in the after-school activities, the course design, the boss levels, and the school's integration of design thinking throughout the curriculum. All the different parts of the school aimed to have kids use what they were learning to make or design something concrete.

While the Q2L school represented great innovations in learning and was lucky to have the freedom to do a lot of things differently, it was just one school. How could what was being learned there be shared, tested, and added to by the wealth of innovative educators and schools in the world already doing great work? In many ways, the GNL project, titled from idea that systems thinking offers a powerful new "lens" to see the world, came from a desire to do just this. In the initiative, Kylie Peppler and Melissa Gresalfi, researchers and educational designers from Indiana University's Learning Sciences program (**education.indiana.edu/learnsci**), began to work with Katie Salen from Institute of Play (**instituteofplay.org**), Nichole Pinkard from DePaul University, and the Digital Youth Network (DYN; **digitalyouthnetwork.org**) to develop a series of modular toolkits that used the design of digital media as a means to develop systems thinking skills, all based on the existing approaches taken in the Q2L school. With the financial support of the MacArthur Foundation and the help of additional partners like the NWP (**www.nwp.org**) (a network of educators and local writing project sites that serve up to 100,000 teachers annually), the initiative worked for three years to make this idea a reality.

The main goal of the initiative was twofold: to create a series of scalable modular toolkits that used the power of designing with new media to promote engagement in design and systems thinking dispositions in young people; and to conduct research on what kind of curricular supports lead to the development of systems thinking dispositions through design activities.

Ultimately, four sets of modular curricula were developed in close coordination with teachers in the NWP network at every step of the process. Each of these uses a different technology and provides unique ways to engage in design with various approaches to understanding systems. The *Gaming the System* curricula involves game design with the Gamestar Mechanic (G*M) platform (Salen, 2007) and focuses on understanding games as systems and young people as designers of those systems. A second set of curricula, *Script Changers* focuses on the idea of using narrative and stories to understand systems, and uses the Scratch programming environment (Resnick et al., 2009) as a way to tell digital stories about systems by way of a computational system. The final two sets of curricula, *Short Circuits* and *Soft Circuits,* use physical computing technology like light-emitting diodes (LEDs), sensors, and the wearable technology controlled by the LilyPad Arduino (Buechley, 2006) to show how youths can create electronics embedded in paper, clothing, and other everyday objects and understand how these creations operate as systems.

Using an approach called Design-Based Research (DBR) (Brown, 1992), which employs approaches found in the world of engineering to engage in an iterative and cyclical design process around learning activities in which each implementation yields lessons that are incorporated into final designs, we piloted and tested the modules in many contexts. A particularly positive benefit of DBR is that it acknowledges that you're not necessarily going to get things right the first time (we certainly didn't!) but trusts a process of embracing failures and missteps as learning opportunities that are really gifts in disguise. For us, the process of being active learners about what worked and why was a central part of the work that we did in developing the activities being shared here.

Many of the activities were, as mentioned, initially developed and tested in New York City at Q2L; others were developed and piloted at local schools like the Bloomington Project School in Indiana, as well as at a local Boys and Girls Club that serves a wide range of youths from varied ethnic and socioeconomic backgrounds. A significant amount of testing was done in close coordination with our NWP partners in sites across the United States and through extended, project-specific summer workshops hosted at DePaul University in Chicago and elsewhere. Testing and refinement also was done in Chicago in schools affiliated with partners at the DYN. Additionally, DYN's parent institution, DePaul University, hosted a summer camp that served as a major testing ground for the curricula. Over the course of four weeks in the summer of 2011, expert teachers from across the United States affiliated with the NWP worked with researchers from Indiana University and designers from Institute of Play to refine the modules based on lessons born of implementing them with almost 100 youths native to Chicago, again with a mix of kids from different backgrounds. These educators are too numerous to list here, but their voices and contributions to this volume are recognized both in our list of contributors and in the "Voices from the Field" sections that you will see throughout all three of these volumes. The exercises, ideas, and guiding pedagogical ideas throughout these books are infused with their perspectives.

In developing the volumes, we wanted to ensure that the work was grounded both in insights from the academic literature on systems thinking and the learning sciences, and also in the lived experiences of educators. The research team contained a number of members who had worked as educators for many years in both formal learning contexts like public schools and informal ones like after-school programs, libraries, and museums. Most importantly, though, the initiative's partnership with the NWP meant that the kind of educators interested in the sort of innovative approaches that we were developing were kept at the center of our designs. They played important roles in testing and refining the modules as previously described, as well as serving on an editorial advisory board (including, most prominently, the assistance of Christina Cantrill, Paul Oh, and Steve Moore) that offered insights, made substantial edits, gave productive feedback, and helped to create many of the activities and materials found in these volumes. They were indispensable to the core design team throughout the project. Through this partnership, we hope that the current volumes are useful to educators in a wide variety of settings to engage youths in design activities that will help them to become systems thinkers, with the ultimate goal of transforming the world that we live in today.

As you might have already noticed, this project brought together many different participants with divergent backgrounds, including game designers from Institute of Play; researchers with backgrounds in the arts, mathematics, and civic education at Indiana University; out-of-school educators at DYN; and professional teachers from the NWP. So, what common threads brought all of these partners together? While there was certainly a common interest in systems thinking as a critical skill for an increasingly complex world, the group also shared a common belief that kids in the twenty-first century had new opportunities for learning as a result of the changing technological landscape. Like many forward-thinking educators, we all saw that the ways that we've been educating young people as a society, through focusing on skill and drill rather than innovation and exploration, and through teaching to the test rather than teaching to youths' interests, were doing a major disservice to young people.

Each of these partners was involved in a broader movement started by the MacArthur Foundation in 2006 to investigate the ways that digital media was changing how kids learn and how these technologies might be leveraged to create new opportunities for learning that might have been previously unimaginable. The Digital Media and Learning (DML) initiative has supported over $80 million in grants to research and develop innovations in digital learning at the time of this writing. It has focused on youth-interest-driven activity in digital spaces as a source of inspiration for creating new learning environments that incorporated the kinds of engagement and higher-order skill development found in places like massively multiplayer online games or do-it-yourself online creative communities like those centered around fan fiction, video blogging, and many other forms of making, tinkering, and designing. The Q2L school and the G*M platform used in the game design module were two examples of learning environments that came out of the DML initiative. Both aimed to build off of interests that youths already brought to school with them, as well as focus on the kinds of twenty-first-century skills they'll need to thrive in the world.

We share this background to enable the reader to think about the activities and resources in this collection not as an isolated approach to teaching, but rather as part of a larger movement to rethink learning in a digital age. There is an incredible amount of innovation happening at the edges of education, and in places that people tend not to think of as learning spaces. We see youths learning in new ways connected to pursuing their interests, engaging deeply, and solving problems through engagement with technology. We want to bring that kind of learning into more formal learning spaces, and we know that we're not alone in this desire. If you're reading this, it's probably because you agree with us that education can be done differently, that youths can engage in problems that are meaningful for them, are connected to their lives, and prepare them for lifelong learning in a changing and complex world.

A TEACHER'S REFLECTION

In concluding this section on the history of the project, we wanted to share the voice and experience of one of the many talented educators that worked on this project. Laura Lee Stroud—a secondary teacher and English language arts instructional coach in the Round Rock Independent School District, as well as a member of the Central Texas Writing Project—reflected on her experience as a maker and learner while engaging with the GNL curriculum during the GNL summer camp in 2011. As part of a playtesting moment, Stroud joined a number of other teachers to construct her own understanding of tools like G*M, Scratch, and e-textiles, as well as facilitate understanding for youths at the camp:

> The Grinding New Lenses camp experience was unlike any experience I'd ever had the opportunity to engage in. NWP teachers from all over the nation gathered for one month in Chicago, away from our homes and families, hoping to learn about systems thinking concepts and internalize them into our existing teaching repertoires. The only thing that we all knew about each other and the work was that we believed in the lifelong learning process and that we had the NWP in common.

The group of educators, in partnership with researchers from Indiana University, Institute of Play, and the DYN, participated in conversations and activities that would evolve into the challenges described in these volumes. As the teachers explored platforms and tools in the service of systems thinking by doing what they soon would be asking youths to do, they also provided feedback, suggestions, and their own mods, contributing to the overall development of the modules as they exist today. As Stroud says, "As a professional, I was viewed as a professional and asked to help edit and revise the curriculum." This feedback and response process with the educators continued throughout the camp experience:

> After we were comfortable with the first layers of the curriculum we were to learn, we split into the modules we were to teach. We were partnered with another teacher and reviewed the materials, learned new vocabulary, and tried to familiarize ourselves with this newfound systems thinking perspective. Every day, in preparation for the summer camp youths, we processed the modules as learners and created the products—be it games, digital narratives with sprites as characters, or e-textile clothing and accessories.

Stroud was a facilitator of the *Soft Circuits* curriculum with youths, but also saw herself as a learner. By entering this brand new world of e-textiles (though it easily could have been a "brand new world of game development" or "brand new world of the programming of a digital story"), she discovered the gaps that existed in her own knowledge—about circuits and circuitry, for instance. This made her that much more sympathetic to the needs of her youths, which in turn allowed her to support them in relating the e-textiles work to their life experiences:

> As the youth entered the camps, for the most part not one teacher assumed the comfortable position of "expert" with our novice youths learning under us. Instead, we were positioned as learners alongside our campers. In some cases, our campers knew more about the content than did we the teachers. We had to remember our new value of supporter, encourager, observer, and researcher. We provided scaffolds for the new concepts, such as an immersion into the new vocabulary, and created a space in the modules for explicit vocabulary instruction. For example, the youths needed to know how to sew a "running stitch" before they could complete a circuit with conductive thread. In fact, in creating the e-cuff, we realized that many of the youths had never made a hem, which is created with a running stitch. As we tried to explain to them how we teachers learned to sew a running stitch, a previously disinterested camper had a light bulb moment as she realized she in fact knew how to sew. She'd worked with her mother in a beauty shop in which they sewed in extra hair for clients. She not only knew how to create a running stitch, she was able to teach the other children how to do it, too! This experience reinforced for me the iterative process of discovering the

strengths available within our classrooms that in turn make our instructional systems most productive.

Stroud concluded by saying:

> When we teachers had group time to reflect on our experience, we found that we all struggled in one way or another and as a result we had a newfound level of respect for our youths' learning processes and struggles, as well as a wonderful glimpse into our own learning process.

LIST OF CONTRIBUTORS

Jackie Barnes, Indiana University
Lori Sue Bell, Great Bear Writing Project
Sophia Bender, Indiana University
Christina Cantrill, National Writing Project
Leah Gilliam, Institute of Play
Diane Glosson, Indiana University
Leon Gordon, Indiana University
Paola Guimerans, Institute of Play
Carol Jehlen, Great Bear Writing Project
Don Miller, Institute of Play
Steve Moore, Greater Kansas City Writing Project
Melissa Morgenlander, Institute of Play
Paul Oh, National Writing Project
Nichole Pinkard, DePaul University
Laura Lee Stroud, Central Texas Writing Project
Eric Tuck, Oregon Writing Project
Janis Watson, Indiana University

SYSTEMS THINKING CONCEPTS IN THIS BOOK COLLECTION

The goal of the *Interconnections: Understanding Systems through Digital Design* book collection is to make available an accessible set of activities that can help youths develop a "systems lens" for seeing the world—a lens they can use to make sense of problems around them. Our hope is that youths will be able to see, anticipate, and understand patterns in the systems that make up that world, and use those understandings to eventually design better systems.

In these modules, we share a range of practices and concepts related to systems thinking. These concepts by no means represent a comprehensive list of every major idea in systems thinking—instead, we have chosen to focus on a subset of key ideas that focus centrally on *understanding systems,* and, in some of the volumes, on more complex ideas related to *system dynamics.* Understanding systems involves recognizing the elements that structure a system, and, more important, the ways that those elements interconnect to impact each other and the overall function of a system. These understandings are mostly oriented toward analyzing a system at a particular point in time, which is a common focus in these modules. In contrast, the study of system dynamics is fundamentally concerned with understanding the behavior of systems *over time.* Examining how a system changes and the kinds of patterns that emerge over time is crucial to understanding how to intervene effectively in systems. As is detailed next, not all the modules deal with these ideas in the same way—the *Gaming the System* module focuses almost exclusively on supporting youths' understanding of systems, while the *Script Changers* module is more fundamentally concerned with understanding (and orchestrating) system changes over time.

The choices made about which concepts and practices to include were driven by the kinds of design activities that we envisioned for youths, and those ideas that are particularly easy to see via the tinkering and iteration processes associated with design. For example, all modules spend a significant amount of time helping youths to see the kinds of *interconnections* that take place among components of a system and the kinds of system dynamics that emerge through these interconnections. This focus is easily revealed through design work because youths can define interconnections, observe the functioning of the system, and then, through iterations on their designs, change the nature of these interconnections and immediately observe the resulting changes in system function. For example, when youths are designing a videogame (in *Gaming the System),* they can see immediately how changing the behavior of a single component (such as the health of an avatar, or the damage that an enemy can do) can immediately change how challenging the game is (the overall *function* of the game— the way it works). Likewise, in *Short Circuits* and *Soft Circuits,* youths can observe how changing the structure of light-emitting-diode (LED) connections (i.e., the ways that they're linked to each other) can immediately affect the number of LEDs that can light up.

Although there is a lot of overlap among the concepts covered in the four books, each one tackles these ideas uniquely, and there are some particular systems thinking concepts that are covered only in some modules. In the following sections, we describe and define the "big ideas" that are addressed in the modules. In the table that follows, the specifics of those big ideas and where they are addressed in each book and module are portrayed.

1. IDENTIFY SYSTEMS.

A *system* is a collection of two or more components and processes that interconnect to function as a whole. For example, speed and comfort in a car are created by the interactions of the car's parts, so they are "greater than the sum" of all the separate parts of the car. The way that a system works is not the result of a single part; rather, it is produced by the *interactions* among the components and/or individual agents within it. A key way to differentiate whether something is a system or not is to consider whether the overall way that it works in the world will change if you remove one part of it.

2. USE LANGUAGE THAT REVEALS A SYSTEM'S CHARACTERISTICS AND FUNCTION.

A key indicator of youths' understanding of systems involves listening for the ways that they describe and make sense of a system. When using a systems thinking approach effectively, youths will be able to identify a system's *components*, the *behaviors* of those components, how those behaviors are shaped by the *system's structure*, and how these behaviors *interconnect* to form broader *system dynamics* that move the system toward a particular *function*. At times, a system is designed to meet a particular *goal,* which can be (but is not always) aligned with the actual function of the system.

3. MAKE SYSTEMS VISIBLE.

When we learn to "make the system visible"—whether through a system model drawn on the back of a napkin, a computer simulation, a game, a picture, a diagram, a set of mathematical computations, or a story—we can use these representations to communicate about how things work. At their best, good pictures of systems help both the creator and the "reader" or "audience" to understand not only the parts of the system (the components), but also, how those components work together to produce the whole.

4. SEEK OUT COMMON SYSTEM PATTERNS.

Beyond the core aspects of a system (i.e., components, behaviors, interconnections, dynamics, and function), there are a number of common patterns that are important for young people to look for when engaging with systems. Specifically, systems often have *reinforcing feedback loops* that cause growth or decline, as well as *balancing feedback loops* that create stability in a system. These loops are directly related to the *stocks and flows* of a system—what is coming into a system and what is going out. In particular, when more is flowing out of a system than is coming in, there begins to be a concern about *limited resources* within a system. Sometimes patterns in systems can be seen best by examining the ways that systems are *nested* within each other.

5. DESIGN AND INTERVENE IN SYSTEMS.

A key practice of a systems thinker involves both designing new systems and fixing systems that are out of balance. These interventions allow youths to go beyond simply interrogating existing systems in the world to use their understanding of how systems work to actually change the world around them, while doing so in a conscious way that respects the complexity of systems. The process of *designing* a system involves thinking deeply about the state of the system that you have envisioned, and how the particular components you have to work with might interconnect with other components for that state to be realized. This process of design involves more than understanding interconnections, however; it is also about considering what to do when things go wrong—the most productive *leverage point* to intervene or change a system, why a proposed solution might *fail*, and what *unintended consequences* might occur based on your design.

6. SHIFT PERSPECTIVES TO UNDERSTAND SYSTEMS.

Systems thinkers regularly shift perspectives as they look at systems to get the full picture of what's happening. They think about the actors in a system and what *mental models* they bring to the system that affect the way that they participate. They shift among different *levels of perspective*—from events, to patterns, to structures, and finally to the mental models that give rise to a system—to better understand that system. And finally, they change the *time horizon* associated with looking at a system in order to find *time delays* from prior actions in a system.

Concept	Gaming the System: Designing with Gamestar Mechanic						Script Changers: Digital Storytelling with Scratch						Short Circuits: Crafting e-Puppets with DIY Electronics				Soft Circuits: Crafting e-Fashion with DIY Electronics			
	CH 1	CH 2	CH 3	CH 4	CH 5	CH 6	CH 1	CH 2	CH 3	CH 4	CH 5	CH 6	CH 1	CH 2	CH 3	CH 4	CH 1	CH 2	CH 3	CH 4
1. Identify systems	x	x	x	x	x	x	x	x	x	x	x	x	x	x	x	x	x	x	x	x
2. Use language that reveals a system's characteristics and function																				
Identifying the way that a system is functioning	x	x	x	x	x	x	x	x	x	x	x	x	x	x	x	x	x	x	x	x
Distinguishing the goal of a system	x	x	x	x		x		x					x	x		x	x	x	x	x
Identifying components	x	x	x	x	x	x	x	x	x	x	x	x	x	x	x	x	x	x	x	x
Identifying behaviors	x	x	x	x	x	x	x	x	x	x	x	x	x	x	x	x	x	x	x	x
Identifying interconnections	x	x	x	x	x	x	x	x	x	x	x	x	x	x	x	x	x	x	x	x
Perceiving dynamics							x		x	x	x		x	x			x			
Considering the role of system structure			x						x			x			x	x		x	x	x
3. Make systems visible			x			x	x	x	x	x	x	x	x	x	x	x	x	x	x	x
4. Seek out common system patterns																				
Reinforcing feedback loops										x										
Vicious cycles										x										
Virtuous cycles										x										
Balancing feedback loops						x												x		
Stocks and flows																				x
Limited resources in systems													x	x						x
Nested systems								x											x	
Dynamic equilibrium																				x
5. Design and intervene in systems																				
Designing a system	x	x	x	x	x	x	x	x		x	x	x	x	x	x	x	x	x	x	x
Fixes that fail											x									
Leverage points											x	x		x		x		x		
Unintended consequences												x								x
6. Shift perspectives to understand systems																				
Mental models									x											
Levels of perspective									x											
Time horizons and delays								x												

ALIGNMENT TO COMMON CORE STATE STANDARDS

The following tables represent an at-a-glance view of the alignment of Design Challenges from all four books in the *Interconnections: Understanding Systems through Digital Design* collection to relevant Common Core State Standards (CCSS) for English Language Arts and Literacy in History/Social Studies, Science and Technical Subjects. Only relevant standards are included in these tables. (For the complete list of standards, go to www.corestandards.org/ELA-Literacy.)

The Common Core State Standards for English Language Arts and Literacy in History/Social Studies, Science, and Technical Subjects are the result of an initiative to provide a shared national framework for literacy development to prepare youths for college and the workforce. The CCSS span kindergarten through twelfth grade, divided into three bands: K–5, 6–8, and 9–12. The CCSS may be thought of as a "staircase" of increasing complexity that details what youths should be expected to read and write, both in English and in targeted content areas. The CCSS are built upon a set of guiding "anchor standards" that evolve through grade-level progression and emphasize informational text and argumentative writing, particularly at the middle and high school levels. In addition, the CCSS include a strand that emphasizes literacy skills associated with production and distribution via technology.

For newcomers, a useful way to enter into the English Language Arts standards is to read the online About the Standards page at the CCSS website (www.corestandards.org/about-the-standards), and then read the anchor standards for each grade band, as well as for the content areas.

Through the Design Challenges, youths are introduced to a range of core skills and information that stretch their learning potential and build on prior knowledge. Expect them to encounter material described in the English Language Arts standards for reading informational text for key ideas and detail, as well as the integration of knowledge and ideas; for producing and distributing writing with technology; and for speaking and listening tasks that prepare youths for college and careers through comprehension and collaboration, as well as the presentation of knowledge and ideas.

Because the *Interconnections* collection presents curricula that engage youths in literacy practices that fall in the English Language Arts domain, as well as the domains of History/Social Studies and Science and Technical Subjects, the letter-number designation that accompanies each standard in the table aligns with the CCSS letter-number designation as follows:

- R—Reading Literature
- RI—Reading Informational Text
- W—Writing
- SL—Speaking & Listening
- RST—Reading in Science and Technical Subjects
- WHST—Writing in History/Social Studies, Science and Technical Subjects

The standards included in these tables serve as a guide through which the Design Challenges can be understood in conjunction with the CCSS. They do not represent an exhaustive list of all possible alignments, but rather those most prevalent and immediate to the central tasks.

Common Core English Language Arts Standards	Gaming the System: Designing with Gamestar Mechanic					
	CH 1	CH 2	CH 3	CH 4	CH 5	CH 6
R.6-12.7 (anchor standard) Integrate and evaluate content presented in diverse formats and media, including visually and quantitatively, as well as in words.	x					x
RI.7.3 Analyze the interactions between individuals, events, and ideas in a text (e.g., how ideas influence individuals or events, or how individuals influence ideas or events).						x
RI.7.7 Compare and contrast a text to an audio, video, or multimedia version of the text, analyzing each medium's portrayal of the subject (e.g. how the delivery of a speech affects the impact of the words).						x
RI.7.9 Analyze how two or more authors writing about the same topic shape their presentations of key information by emphasizing different evidence or advancing different interpretations of facts.	x			x	x	
W.6-8.3 Write narratives to develop real or imagined experiences or events using effective technique, relevant descriptive details, and well-structured event sequences.	x	x	x	x	x	
W.7.6 Use technology, including the Internet, to produce and publish writing and link to and cite sources as well as to interact and collaborate with others, including linking to and citing sources.						x
RST.6-8.3 Follow precisely a multistep procedure when carrying out experiments, taking measurements, or performing technical tasks.	x	x	x	x	x	
RST.6-8.4 Determine the meaning of symbols, key terms, and other domain-specific words and phrases as they are used in a specific scientific or technical context relevant to grades 6–8 texts and topics.						
RST.6-8.7 Integrate quantitative or technical information expressed in words in a text with a version of that information expressed visually (e.g., in a flowchart, diagram, model, graph or table).	x	x	x	x	x	x
RST.6-8.9 Compare and contrast the information gained from experiments, simulations, video, or multimedia sources with that gained from reading a text on the same topic.	x	x	x	x	x	x
RST.11-12.9 Synthesize information from a range of sources (e.g., texts, experiments, simulations) into a coherent understanding of a process, phenomenon, or concept, resolving conflicting information when possible.						x
SL.6-12.4 (anchor standard) Present information, findings, and supporting evidence such that listeners can follow the line of reasoning and the organization, development, and style are appropriate to task, purpose, and audience.	x	x	x	x	x	x
SL.7.5 Include multimedia components and visual displays in presentations to clarify claims and findings and emphasize salient points.	x	x	x	x	x	

Common Core English Language Arts Standards	Script Changers: Digital Storytelling with Scratch					
	CH 1	CH 2	CH 3	CH 4	CH 5	CH 6
R.6-12.3 (anchor standard) Analyze how and why individuals, events and ideas develop and interact over the course of a text.			x	x	x	x
R.6-12.7 (anchor standard) Integrate and evaluate content presented in diverse formats and media, including visually and quantitatively, as well as in words.	x	x	x	x	x	x
RI.7.3 Analyze the interactions between individuals, events, and ideas in a text (e.g., how ideas influence individuals or events, or how individuals influence ideas or events).		x	x	x	x	x
W.6-12.2 (anchor standard) Write informative/explanatory texts to examine and convey complex ideas and information clearly and accurately through the effective selection, organization, and analysis of content.		x	x	x	x	
W.6-8.3 Write narratives to develop real or imagined experiences or events using effective technique, relevant descriptive details, and well-structured event sequences.	x					
W.8.6 Use technology, including the Internet, to produce and publish writing and present the relationships between information and ideas efficiently as well as to interact and collaborate with others.	x	x	x	x		x
W.8.7 Conduct short research projects to answer a question (including a self-generated question), drawing on several sources and generating additional related, focused questions that allow for multiple avenues of exploration.				x		x
W.6-12.7 (anchor standard) Conduct short as well as more sustained research projects based on focused questions, demonstrating understanding of the subject under investigation.		x		x	x	x
W.6-12.9 (anchor standard) Draw evidence from literary or informational texts to support analysis, reflection and research.			x	x	x	x
RST.6-8.3 Follow precisely a multistep procedure when carrying out experiments, taking measurements, or performing technical tasks.	x	x	x	x	x	x
RST.6-8.4 Determine the meaning of symbols, key terms, and other domain-specific words and phrases as they are used in a specific scientific or technical context relevant to grades 6–8 texts and topics.						

Common Core English Language Arts Standards	Script Changers: Digital Storytelling with Scratch					
	CH 1	CH 2	CH 3	CH 4	CH 5	CH 6
RST.6-8.7 Integrate quantitative or technical information expressed in words in a text with a version of that information expressed visually (e.g., in a flowchart, diagram, model, graph or table).		x	x	x		x
RST.11-12.9 Synthesize information from a range of sources (e.g., texts, experiments, simulations) into a coherent understanding of a process, phenomenon, or concept, resolving conflicting information when possible.						x
SL.7.2 Analyze the main ideas and supporting details presented in diverse media and formats (e.g., visually, quantitatively, orally) and explain how the ideas clarify a topic, text or issue under study.		x	x	x	x	x
SL.7.4 Present claims and findings, emphasizing salient points in a focused, coherent manner with pertinent descriptions, facts, details, and examples; use appropriate eye contact, adequate volume, and clear pronunciation.						
SL.6-12.4 (anchor standard) Present information, findings, and supporting evidence such that listeners can follow the line of reasoning and the organization, development, and style are appropriate to task, purpose, and audience.		x	x	x	x	x
SL.7.5 Include multimedia components and visual displays in presentations to clarify claims and findings and emphasize salient points.			x	x		x
WHST.6-8.4 Produce clear and coherent writing in which the development, organization, and style are appropriate to task, purpose, and audience.						x
WHST.6-8.5 With some guidance and support from peers and adults, develop and strengthen writing as needed by planning, revising, editing, rewriting, or trying a new approach, focusing on how well purpose and audience have been addressed.						x
WHST.6-8.6 Use technology, including the Internet, to produce and publish writing and present the relationships between information and ideas clearly and efficiently.						x
WHST.6-8.7 Conduct short research projects to answer a question (including a self-generated question), drawing on several sources and generating additional related, focused questions that allow for multiple avenues of exploration.			x			x

Common Core English Language Arts Standards	Short Circuits: Crafting e-Puppets with DIY Electronics				Soft Circuits: Crafting e-Fashion with DIY Electronics			
	CH 1	CH 2	CH 3	CH 4	CH 1	CH 2	CH 3	CH 4
R.6-12.7 (anchor standard) Integrate and evaluate content presented in diverse formats and media, including visually and quantitatively, as well as in words.								X
RI.7.3 Analyze the interactions between individuals, events, and ideas in a text (e.g., how ideas influence individuals or events, or how individuals influence ideas or events).			X	X		X		
RI.7.4 Determine the meaning of words and phrases as they are used in a text, including figurative, connotative, and technical meanings; analyze the impact of a specific word choice on meaning and tone.			X			X		X
RI.7.5 Include multimedia components and visual displays in presentations to clarify claims and findings and emphasize salient points.			X				X	
RI.8.5 Analyze in detail the structure of a specific paragraph in a text, including the role of particular sentences in developing and refining a key concept							X	
RI.8.7 Evaluate the advantages and disadvantages of using different mediums (e.g., print or digital text, video, multimedia) to present a particular topic or idea.							X	X
W.6-12.2 (anchor standard) Write informative/explanatory texts to examine and convey complex ideas and information clearly and accurately through the effective selection, organization, and analysis of content.	X				X			X
W.6-8.3 Write narratives to develop real or imagined experiences or events using effective technique, relevant descriptive details, and well-structured event sequences.	X	X			X			
W.7.6 Use technology, including the Internet, to produce and publish writing and link to and cite sources as well as to interact and collaborate with others, including linking to and citing sources.								X
W.8.6 Use technology, including the Internet, to produce and publish writing and present the relationships between information and ideas efficiently as well as to interact and collaborate with others.			X					X
W.8.7 Conduct short research projects to answer a question (including a self-generated question), drawing on several sources and generating additional related, focused questions that allow for multiple avenues of exploration.							X	

Common Core English Language Arts Standards	Short Circuits: Crafting e-Puppets with DIY Electronics				Soft Circuits: Crafting e-Fashion with DIY Electronics			
	CH 1	CH 2	CH 3	CH 4	CH 1	CH 2	CH 3	CH 4
RST.6-8.3 Follow precisely a multistep procedure when carrying out experiments, taking measurements, or performing technical tasks.		X		X		X	X	X
RST.6-8.4 Determine the meaning of symbols, key terms, and other domain-specific words and phrases as they are used in a specific scientific or technical context relevant to grades 6–8 texts and topics.	X	X			X			X
RST.6-8.7 Integrate quantitative or technical information expressed in words in a text with a version of that information expressed visually (e.g., in a flowchart, diagram, model, graph or table).	X				X			X
RST.6-8.9 Compare and contrast the information gained from experiments, simulations, video, or multimedia sources with that gained from reading a text on the same topic.						X		X
RST.11-12.9 Synthesize information from a range of sources (e.g., texts, experiments, simulations) into a coherent understanding of a process, phenomenon, or concept, resolving conflicting information when possible.	X		X		X			
SL.6-12.4 (anchor standard) Present information, findings, and supporting evidence such that listeners can follow the line of reasoning and the organization, development, and style are appropriate to task, purpose, and audience.	X		X		X		X	
SL.7.2 Analyze the main ideas and supporting details presented in diverse media and formats (e.g., visually, quantitatively, orally) and explain how the ideas clarify a topic, text, or issue under study.						X		
SL.7.4 Present claims and findings, emphasizing salient points in a focused, coherent manner with pertinent descriptions, facts, details, and examples; use appropriate eye contact, adequate volume, and clear pronunciation.				X				
SL.7.5 Include multimedia components and visual displays in presentations to clarify claims and findings and emphasize salient points.			X			X		
WHST.6-8.4 Produce clear and coherent writing in which the development, organization, and style are appropriate to task, purpose, and audience.			X					X
WHST.6-8.6 Use technology, including the Internet, to produce and publish writing and present the relationships between information and ideas clearly and efficiently.							X	

NEXT GENERATION SCIENCE STANDARDS

Because the *Interconnections* book collection presents curricula that engage youths in design activities that embrace the sciences, the standards included in this table serve as a guide through which the challenges can be understood in conjunction with the Next Generation Science Standards (NGSS; found at **www.nextgenscience.org/next -generation-science-standards**). They do not represent an exhaustive list of all possible alignments, but rather those most prevalent and immediate to the central tasks.

As the NGSS are explicit in assigning specific scientific topics and learning to specific grade levels, the correlations in these tables range from third grade to high school. The following tables were created to help identify which national science standards align to our Design Challenges, to what grade, and in which challenge each is addressed. Please note, however, that all the Design Challenges have been tested in a wide range of ability, grade, and age groups.

NGSS CODE DESIGNATIONS

- 3–5: Upper elementary grades
- MS: Middle school grades 6–8
- HS: High school grades 9–12
- ESS = Earth and Space Science
- ETS = Engineering, Technology, and Applications of Science
- PS = Physical Sciences

Next Generation Science Standards	Gaming the System: Designing with Gamestar Mechanic					
	CH 1	CH 2	CH 3	CH 4	CH 5	CH 6
ETS1 Engineering Design						
3-5-ETS1-1. Define a simple design problem reflecting a need or a want that includes specified criteria for success and constraints on materials, time, or cost.	x	x	x	x	x	x
3-5-ETS1-2. Generate and compare multiple possible solutions to a problem based on how well each is likely to meet the criteria and constraints of the problem.	x	x	x	x	x	x
3-5-ETS1-3. Plan and carry out fair tests in which variables are controlled and failure points are considered to identify aspects of a model or prototype that can be improved.	x	x		x	x	x
MS-ETS1-1. Define the criteria and constraints of a design problem with sufficient precision to ensure a successful solution, taking into account relevant scientific principles and potential impacts on people and the natural environment that may limit possible solutions.			x	x	x	x
MS-ETS1-2. Evaluate competing design solutions using a systematic process to determine how well they meet the criteria and constraints of the problem.	x	x	x	x	x	x
MS-ETS1-3. Analyze data from tests to determine similarities and differences among several design solutions to identify the best characteristics of each that can be combined into a new solution to better meet the criteria for success.				x	x	x
MS-ETS1-4. Develop a model to generate data for iterative testing and modification of a proposed object, tool, or process such that an optimal design can be achieved.	x	x	x	x	x	x

Next Generation Science Standards	Script Changers: Digital Storytelling with Scratch					
	CH 1	CH 2	CH 3	CH 4	CH 5	CH 6
ETS1 Engineering Design						
3-5-ETS1-1. Define a simple design problem reflecting a need or a want that includes specified criteria for success and constraints on materials, time, or cost.	x	x	x	x	x	x
3-5-ETS1-2. Generate and compare multiple possible solutions to a problem based on how well each is likely to meet the criteria and constraints of the problem.			x	x	x	x
3-5-ETS1-3. Plan and carry out fair tests in which variables are controlled and failure points are considered to identify aspects of a model or prototype that can be improved.				x	x	x
MS-ETS1-1. Define the criteria and constraints of a design problem with sufficient precision to ensure a successful solution, taking into account relevant scientific principles and potential impacts on people and the natural environment that may limit possible solutions.	x	x	x	x	x	x
MS-ETS1-2. Evaluate competing design solutions using a systematic process to determine how well they meet the criteria and constraints of the problem.			x	x	x	x
MS-ETS1-3. Analyze data from tests to determine similarities and differences among several design solutions to identify the best characteristics of each that can be combined into a new solution to better meet the criteria for success.					x	x
MS-ETS1-4. Develop a model to generate data for iterative testing and modification of a proposed object, tool, or process such that an optimal design can be achieved.			x	x	x	x
ESS3 Human Impacts						
MS-ESS3-3. Apply scientific principles to design a method for monitoring and minimizing a human impact on the environment.		x	x	x	x	x

Next Generation Science Standards	Short Circuits: Crafting e-Puppets with DIY Electronics				Soft Circuits: Crafting e-Fashion with DIY Electronics			
	CH 1	CH 2	CH 3	CH 4	CH 1	CH 2	CH 3	CH 4
PS2 Motion and Stability: Forces and Interactions								
3-PS2-3. Ask questions to determine cause and effect relationships of electric or magnetic interactions between two objects not in contact with each other.	x	x	x	x	x	x	x	x
MS-PS2-3. Ask questions about data to determine the factors that affect the strength of electric and magnetic forces.	x	x	x	x	x	x	x	x
PS3 Energy								
4-PS3-2. Make observations to provide evidence that energy can be transferred from place to place by sound, light, heat, and electric currents.	x	x	x	x	x	x	x	x
4-PS3-4. Apply scientific ideas to design, test, and refine a device that converts energy from one form to another.		x		x		x	x	x
MS-PS3-2. Develop a model to describe that when the arrangement of objects interacting at a distance changes, different amounts of potential energy are stored in the system.		x				x	x	x
HS-PS3-3. Design, build, and refine a device that works within given constraints to convert one form of energy into another form of energy.								x
ETS1 Engineering Design								
3-5-ETS1-1. Define a simple design problem reflecting a need or a want that includes specified criteria for success and constraints on materials, time, or cost.	x	x	x	x	x	x	x	x
3-5-ETS1-2. Generate and compare multiple possible solutions to a problem based on how well each is likely to meet the criteria and constraints of the problem.	x	x	x	x	x	x	x	x
3-5-ETS1-3. Plan and carry out fair tests in which variables are controlled and failure points are considered to identify aspects of a model or prototype that can be improved.	x	x	x	x	x		x	x
MS-ETS1-1. Define the criteria and constraints of a design problem with sufficient precision to ensure a successful solution, taking into account relevant scientific principles and potential impacts on people and the natural environment that may limit possible solutions.								x
MS-ETS1-2. Evaluate competing design solutions using a systematic process to determine how well they meet the criteria and constraints of the problem.	x	x	x	x	x	x	x	x
MS-ETS1-4. Develop a model to generate data for iterative testing and modification of a proposed object, tool, or process such that an optimal design can be achieved.		x		x		x	x	x

INTRODUCTION

You think that because you understand "one" that you must therefore understand "two" because one and one make two. But you forget that you must also understand "and."

—Sufi teaching

Few would argue with the idea that the world is growing more complex as the twenty-first century unfolds. We live in a time that not only requires us to work across disciplines to solve problems, but also one in which these problems are of unprecedented scale, coming from a world that is more interconnected than ever. In such a context, power rests in the hands of those who understand the nature of the interdependent systems that organize the world, and, more important, can identify where to act or how to intervene in order to change those systems. Effective intervention requires considering not just simple causal relations, but also the complex interconnections that work together in often-unexpected ways to produce an outcome. Taking action in our complex world requires a set of twenty-first century skills and competencies called "systems thinking."

Systems thinking is best characterized by the old dictum that the whole is always greater than the sum of its parts. It's an approach that involves considering not just the behavior of individual components of a system, but also the complex interconnections between multiple parts that work together to form a whole. Systems are ubiquitous in our world—which includes natural systems that deal with climate and biodiversity, economic systems that drive production and labor trends, and political systems that enact governance of communities and nations. And, of course, these systems are themselves connected to one another in important ways, so understanding the nature of these interconnections, not just within but also across systems, is becoming ever more vital. The promise of learning to reason about how systems work is that of creating a new and effective lens for seeing, engaging with, and changing the world.

Systems thinking allows one not just to understand better how systems function, but also to decide the best way to intervene to *change* systems. Systems thinkers have the potential to have a significant impact on the world around them—an impact that is often denied to those who think in simple cause-and-effect terms. As a consequence, we believe that to effectively and ethically educate children to thrive in the twenty-first century, we must create contexts in which young people are supported in learning to be creative and courageous about making changes to systems in the world and to understand that those changes will always have an impact on other parts of the system—everything is interconnected. It's not enough to instill this competency in current leaders—we must prepare the next generation to be effective and thoughtful stewards of the world that they will inherit soon. Helping young people to understand how systems work, how they are represented, and how they change—via direct or indirect means—is critically important to this larger project. Furthermore, it's important that young people learn about systems not in a distant and unfamiliar context, but in contexts that have meaning to today's youth—those rooted in popular culture, design, and new technologies. This approach is the basis of this collection.

Digital media are central in almost every aspect of daily life, most notably in how we communicate, understand political issues, reflect, produce, consume, and share knowledge. We are living in an era in which digital media is rapidly becoming a driving force in globalization, scientific advances, and the intersection of cultures. The growing accessibility of digital tools and networks, the prevalence of many-to-many distribution models, and the large-scale online aggregation of information and culture are leading to profound changes in how we create and access knowledge. Perhaps nowhere is this digital influence contested more than in education, where questions arise about the ability of traditional systems to prepare young people for the social, economic, and political demands of a complex and connected new century.

This collection, *Interconnections: Understanding Systems through Digital Design,* builds on the existing work of educators, management theorists, designers, and learning scientists who are aiming to promote systems thinking in young people. The project uses a design-based approach to learning and offers up a toolkit for supporting systems thinking in ways that are aligned to current Common Core State Standards (CCCS) and relevant to youth interests in digital culture. Through a collaborative effort across a leading group of designers and educators from Institute of Play, Indiana University's Creativity Labs, the Digital Youth Network (DYN), and the National Writing Project (NWP), we've developed an innovative approach to supporting the development of systems thinking in young people; one that allows them to see how systems are at play in the digital contexts that they regularly engage with and one that puts them in the position of designers of those systems. Most prior work on teaching systems thinking has focused on the biological, physical, and social sciences. By contrast, this collection aligns itself with a growing body of work emerging from the fields of game design, digital storytelling, and do-it-yourself (DIY) electronics as contexts for engaging in systems thinking. Creating animated digital stories about aspects of their community they would like to see changed, for example, provides young people with rich opportunities for observation, analysis, and problem solving.

Each of the four books in the collection is rooted in *constructionist* learning theory, which positions young people as active creators of their own understanding by engaging in the design, iteration, and sharing of media artifacts within communities of interest (Papert, 1980; Kafai, 2006). Each book teaches systems thinking concepts and skills in the context of a specific digital media platform and includes an average of six design "challenges" totaling between 25 and 40+ hours of project time.

The first book in the collection, *Gaming the System: Designing with Gamestar Mechanic*, orients readers to the nature of games as systems, how game designers need to think in terms of complex interactions between game elements and rules, and how to involve systems concepts in the design process. The core curriculum uses Gamestar Mechanic (G*M), an online game design environment with a strong systems thinking focus. *Script Changers: Digital Storytelling with Scratch*, focuses on how stories offer an important lens for seeing the world as a series of systems and provides opportunities for young people to create interactive and animated stories about the systems around them. The projects in this book use the Scratch visual programming environment as a means to tell stories about how to affect change in youths' local communities. The two final books, *Short Circuits: Crafting e-Puppets with DIY Electronics* and *Soft Circuits: Crafting e-Fashion with DIY Electronics,* both explore the fields of electronics and "e-textiles," which involves physical computing projects making fabrics and other everyday materials, including incorporating microprocessors into these materials and programming them with accessible tools like Modkit or ArduBlock.

WHAT IS SYSTEMS THINKING?

It has become increasingly clear that youths' experiences in school do not match the kinds of experiences that they are likely to have once they have completed school. The push to support "twenty-first-century" skills stems from this mismatch, and many have advocated for ensuring that young people learn to think about the world not as a simple set of cause-and-effect experiences, but rather as a set of complex systems. *Systems thinking* generally refers to a way of understanding the world as a set of systems that are made up of many components, each of which has distinct behaviors that change and interact, giving rise to emergent behavior. There are many advantages to understanding the world as a set of systems, but a chief one is that systems thinking allows youths to understand and interpret the world across content areas (Goldstone & Wilensky, 2008). Unfortunately, supporting youths to develop systems thinking has proven to be a significant challenge. First, systems thinking ideas are difficult (Hmelo-Silver & Pfeffer, 2004) and also can be counterintuitive (Wilensky & Resnick, 1999). Systems thinking requires youths to look for myriad contributions to system behaviors as opposed to simple cause-and-effect. Indeed, a key concept of systems thinking involves understanding that a small change can lead to a significant outcome—an idea that flies in the face of many core assumptions that we have about the world. Linda Booth Sweeney (2001) points out that most of our experiences in the world, particularly those we have as children, are explained in terms of linear causality. As a consequence, we have limited opportunities to practice talking about or interpreting our experience of the world as a set of systems.

While linking systems thinking to digital media and learning may seem novel, an integration of systems thinking in K–12 education began in the late 1980s and continues today through the efforts of many organizations and individuals, including the Waters Foundation, the Creative Learning Exchange, the Society for Organizational Learning Education Partnership, and various research groups at institutions like the Massachusetts Institute of Technology (MIT), Northwestern University, Rutgers, and Indiana University. There are also many passionate educators across the United States who have been informed by these initiatives, as well as by leaders in the field of systems dynamics, including Jay Forrester, Linda Booth Sweeney, Peter Senge, and George Richardson. According to Debra Lyneis of the Creative Learning Exchange, the field first began to take root in classrooms when Gordon Brown, a retired MIT dean of engineering, introduced a piece of modeling software called STELLA to a middle school teacher at Orange Grove Junior High School in Tucson, Arizona. That teacher, Frank Draper, and his principal, Mary Scheetz, worked for years to integrate systems thinking across grades in their school. The work was transformative, as Draper writes of his classroom experience:

> Since October 1988 our classrooms have undergone an amazing transformation. Not only are we covering more material than just the required curriculum, but we are covering it faster (we will be through with the year's curriculum this week and will have to add more material to our curriculum for the remaining five weeks) and the students are learning more useful material than ever before. "Facts" are now anchored to meaning through the dynamic relationships they have with each other. In our classroom, students shift from being passive receptacles to active learners. They are not taught about science per se, but learn how to acquire and use knowledge (scientific and otherwise). Our jobs have shifted from dispensers of information to

producers of environments that allow students to learn as much as possible.

We now see students come early to class (even early to school), stay after the bell rings, work through lunch, and work at home voluntarily (with no assignment given). When we work on a systems project—even when the students are working on the book research leading up to system work—there are essentially no motivation/discipline problems in our classrooms. (Draper, 1989)

At the same time, other initiatives rooted in digital media have used computer-based modeling and simulations as a powerful approach to teaching about systems. Leading designers have produced other kid-friendly modeling software packages such as Star-Logo, NetLogo, and other tools to study the ways that these sorts of technologies can be used in the context of small and large groups in classrooms (Colella, Klopfer, & Resnick, 2001; Wilensky, 1999; Goldstone & Wilensky, 2008). The field also has extended its use of simulations to include participatory simulations (Colella, 2000) that use technology to allow youths to act as agents in simulations of complex systems. In addition, it has found ways to use simulation software to teach even children in early elementary classrooms the properties of complex systems (Danish et al., 2011).

Systems education now can be found in such diverse places as an elementary school in the Netherlands, public middle and high schools in New York City and Chicago, a private elementary day school in Toledo, a charter school in Chelmsford, Massachusetts, rural schools in northern Vermont and Georgia, suburban schools in Carlisle and Harvard, Massachusetts, and an entire school district in Tucson, Arizona. Some people believe that the middle school level is a good place to begin because of the developmental level of the youths and the flexibility of the middle school structure, but many (including Sweeney, 2001) advocate that both stories and simulations can be used to bring systems thinking to elementary schools, and others (including Lyneis, 2000) have developed robust systems thinking programs in high schools as well.

Throughout the process of coming to know something about their own capacity as systems thinkers, this book collection encourages educators and youths alike to manage and reflect on their evolving identities as learners, producers, peers, researchers, and citizens. The resulting focus is on learning how to *produce meaning*—both for themselves and for external audiences—within complex, multimodal, and systems-rich contexts. Creativity, expression, and innovation underlie this learning as learners practice and apply systems thinking concepts through the coding and decoding of linguistic, computational, social, and cultural systems. This approach challenges traditional barriers between consumer and producer/viewer and designer, allowing youths to gain the skills to act as full citizens within a connected, participatory landscape (Salen et al., 2010).

WHAT IDEAS ABOUT SYSTEMS WILL YOUTHS LEARN IN *SOFT CIRCUITS*?

Although typically systems thinking curricula are concerned with encouraging youths to describe the behavior of systems, the goal of the *Soft Circuits* module is for youth to experience the internal structure and interconnections within systems. This is accomplished by creating design experiences that allow youths to tweak components of systems and examine the impact of those tweaks on other components of the system and on the overall function of the system as a whole. Specifically, our goal is that, by the end of the module, youths will have had opportunities to deeply engage with the following practices:

- **Identifying a system:** Understanding that systems are a collection of parts, or components, which interconnect to function as a whole

- **Identify the way a system is functioning:** Understanding what a system is actually doing—the "state" it is moving toward.

- **Distinguishing the goal of a system:** Identifying the ideal state or function of a system from the particular perspective of the designer.

- **Identifying components:** Considering what a system is made of—what are the parts that work together to make a system function as it does?

- **Identifying behaviors:** Identifying the different ways that each component can act.

- **Identifying interconnections:** Identifying the different ways that a system's parts, or components, interact with each other through their behaviors and, through those interactions, change the behaviors of other elements.

- **Considering the role of system structure:** Understanding that the way the system works (i.e., what it actually does) is the product of a set of complex interconnections between components that cannot simply be reduced to an account of the components themselves—these sorts of system dynamics emerge from the way the components interconnect, and these interconnections largely are determined by the way that the system's structure sets them up in relation to one another.

- **Designing systems:** Students are participating in an iterative design process that involves designing systems, tweaking elements of those designs, creating new iterations, and then reflecting on how changes they made fundamentally shape the ways that those systems function and whether they satisfy their own goals for the system.

- **Modeling systems:** Students create versions of existing systems as designed games; that creation involves the act of translating what they understand about the target system to a new domain with new representations.

These are just a subset of the ideas relevant to systems thinking that are covered in the *Soft Circuits* module. Each challenge details the ideas about systems thinking that are specifically covered. In addition, these ideas are explored in more depth in the "Delving Deeper into Systems Thinking" chapter that appears at the end of the Design Challenges.

WHAT IS DESIGN THINKING?

To know the world one must construct it.

—Cesare Pavese

When a young person creates a video, a poster, an animation, a customized T-shirt, or a digital app, she is operating within the space of design. Design is a particularly important activity for learning because it positions the learner as an active agent in the creation process. As learners construct a public artifact, they externalize their mental models and iterate on them throughout the design process (Papert, 1980; Kafai, 2006). In contrast to prescriptive approaches to design, where youths all construct the same artifact in parallel or arrive at an idealized solution through design, the challenges in this book strike a balance between structure and free exploration (Colella, Klopfer, & Resnick, 2001). The activities presented here engage youths in design activities to encourage them to learn key systems thinking concepts. We also acknowledge that learning happens best when it's done in a collaborative setting and there are purposeful moments for reflection. As such, the challenges in each volume share a common structure of activities, based on the creative design spiral proposed by Rusk, Resnick, and Cooke (2009).

Resnick (2007) describes the creative process of design as an idea that is realized by iteratively imagining, creating, playing, sharing, and reflecting on the work. *Imagining* begins with youths' open exploration of the materials to ignite their creativity and imagination to take the work in unexpected and personally meaningful directions. *Creating* places an emphasis on building, designing, and making artifacts that can be shared with a broader community. The act of construction not only provides opportunities to develop and enrich creative thinking, but also presents youths with the chance to experience disciplinary content through hands-on reconstruction of their prior knowledge. *Play*, the next step in the design cycle, is where playful experimentation with ideas is done in a low-risk environment to explore and test the boundaries of the materials. The public presentation or *sharing* of work in progress or completed work is also critical to the learning and motivation in the design process, where youths become more engaged and find new inspiration and an audience for their ideas. Resnick also argues for systematic *reflection* on both the design and learning process, where youths discuss and reflect on their thinking. Making the thinking process visible through easy access to the design artifacts from various parts of the creative process is crucial to learning. Finally, Resnick describes this pathway through the design process as a spiral that is then iteratively repeated.

To this work, we add two more steps to the design cycle: Research and Publish. *Research* encapsulates the information gathering that is critical to high-quality teaching and learning. This includes the introduction and definition of key terms and vocabulary, the introduction of key concepts that are important to systems thinking and disciplinary content, and the activities used to gather this information (including the use of videos, diagrams, and other information sources). We also disentangle the sharing of the final product, which we call *Publish*, from more informal moments where sharing is done within the local community to assist in iteration. Current research has demonstrated that this is an important moment for learning and community building, and that there are some crucial differences in who is likely to post in the informal, interest-driven hours (Lenhart and Madden, 2007).

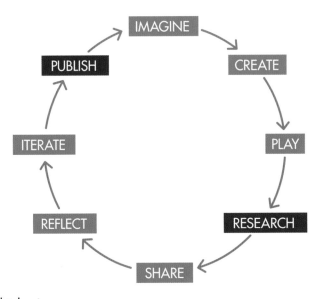

Design-based approach to learning.

As a methodology for learning about systems, design is all about providing constructive contexts in which to explore ideas, interactions, and expressions. Linking design to digital media tools expands this context further: digital tools often make it easier, faster, and less risky to test ideas. There is no need to worry about wasting expensive materials, and erasing a mistake is as easy as clicking a mouse. The act of designing incorporates complex technical, linguistic, and symbolic elements from a variety of domains, at a variety of different levels, and for a variety of different purposes. Designers explicate and defend design ideas, describe design issues and user interactions at a meta-level, imagine new possibilities, create and test hypotheses, and reflect on the impact of each of their creations as a distinctive medium in relation to other media. And each of these involves a melding of technological, social, communicational, and artistic concerns in the framework of a form of scientific thinking in the broad sense of the term. Designers make and think about complex interactive systems, a characteristic activity today, both in the media and in science.

The challenges included within this book emphasize a process of prototyping and iteration based on a design methodology: youths envision new solutions to open-ended problems, work through multiple versions of any idea, integrate ongoing feedback into the learning process, and identify the strengths and weaknesses of both their processes and solutions. In some cases, youths may choose to build on previous solutions or approaches of their peers, seeing themselves as contributors to a larger body of collaboratively generated knowledge.

DESIGNING A SUPPORTIVE LEARNING ENVIRONMENT

Before sharing the Design Challenges that we've developed, it's important to provide a set of guiding design principles for creating a supportive learning environment that are never stated explicitly, but form the base assumptions about what kind of pedagogy they're aiming to promote. As you adapt (and appropriate, of course), the activities in this book, we hope that the principles here might help guide you.

A design-oriented experience, particularly one created to support systems understandings has to be … well, designed. The curriculum modules shared in this book focus on activity structures and learning outcomes—what learners might be doing, with what tools, and in what kinds of configurations. Young people must experience the activities robustly when they take into account a set of larger principles defining the qualities of the learning context itself. The principles outlined next help to structure a learning setting that is itself understood as a dynamic system—one where the interactions among learners and mentors, peers, resources, and social contexts has been considered and where specific attention has been paid to the ways in which these different relationships reinforce or amplify each other.

The principles are intended to offer suggestions for how the experience of learning might be designed to support the learning resources offered later in the book. Please note that the principles should be understood as working together within a system—that is, no single principle does much on its own. It is in the relationships between principles that the robustness of the system resides. For example, creating learning experiences where a challenge is ongoing likely will fail miserably if it doesn't also include feedback that is immediate and ongoing. Organizing a classroom environment where authority is shared, expertise is distributed, and a broad range of ways to participate is allowed matters only if there are also visible ways for learners to share and exchange expertise and discover resources. The whole is far greater than the sum of its parts. The fact that the principles are listed separately should be understood as a limitation of the page, not as a feature of the principles.

1. Everyone is a participant.

Create a shared culture and practice where everyone contributes. Design learning experiences that invite participation and provide many different ways for individuals and groups to contribute. Build in roles and supports for teachers, mentors, and instructors to act as translators and bridge-builders for learners across domains and contexts. Make sure that there are opportunities for participants (especially new participants) to lurk and leech (i.e., observe and borrow), and that peer-based exchange, like communication and sharing, is easy and reciprocal. Provide a diverse set of resources to support teaching and peer-to-peer mentorship activities, allowing youths with various forms of expertise to take on leadership roles.

2. Feedback is everywhere; iteration is assumed.

Encourage youths to assume that their first draft is never the final version—they should make something and then gather feedback, rather than waiting to share their creation until they "get it right." Feedback should include structures for guidance and mentorship, which may take place via the online communities associated with the modules, or in classroom, after-school, or home settings. Make sure that there are plenty of ways for participants to share their work in progress with their peers, solicit feedback, teach others how to do things, and reflect on their own learning. Provide opportunities for participants to incorporate feedback in iterative design cycles. One key aspect of this latter element is allowing every participant's contribution to be visible to everyone else in the group through frequent posting, sharing, group discussion, or a combination of the three. Utilize the tools associated with the module platform to enable communication and exchange between peers who may or may not be part of the same program or setting to broaden the kind of feedback that youths receive.

3. Create a need to know.

One of the more powerful features of challenge-based experiences is that they create a *need to know* by challenging youths to solve a problem whose resources are accessible but require work to find. They must develop expertise in order to access the resources, and they are motivated to do so either because they find the problem context itself engaging or because it connects to an existing interest or passion. Make sure that challenges are implemented within learning environments that support situated inquiry and discovery so that youths have rich contexts within which they can practice using concepts and content. As participants advance through a challenge, provide a diverse array of opportunities for them to build social and cultural capital around their progress. Allow youths to collaborate in many different ways as they explore different roles or identities related to the design project at hand.

4. Learning happens by doing.

Modules emphasize performance-based activities that give rise to authentic learning tasks. These experiences provide opportunities for participants to develop knowledge and understanding through direct discovery and engagement with a complex but well-ordered problem space. These spaces often require participants to figure out the nature of the problem space itself, rather than proposing a specific problem to be solved.

Make sure that learners have access to robust mechanisms for discoverability; a number of resources to support this type of inquiry are included in this volume (on Systems Thinking Concept cards and Gaming the System Challenge cards), while additional resources—peer-produced tutorials and other materials—should be easy to find, use, and share. Think of ways to situate challenges within a context that has meaning or relevance for participants, whether in peer, interest-driven, or academic contexts. Provide participants with multiple, overlapping opportunities to interact with experts and mentors who model expert identities associated with the problem space. Explore teaming and competing structures like competitions and collaborations that mix collaborative and competitive elements in the service of problem discovery and solving.

5. Create meaningful public contexts for sharing.

In addition to sharing and receiving feedback during the design and iteration cycles, encourage the sharing of final products and projects with both local and global audiences. Knowing that there will be an audience, especially one that youths care about, is motivating, but also promotes a sense of creating something with a particular audience in mind. This contrasts with creating things in a vacuum, which is too often the case in educational contexts.

Create infrastructures for youths to share their work, skills, and knowledge with others across networks. These channels might take the form of online public portfolios, streamed video or podcasts, student-led parent conferences, or public events where work is critiqued and displayed, to name only a few options. Allow participants to develop identities in contexts of their own choosing; create opportunities for acquiring status via achievements that are visible in a range of home, school, workplace, and peer group settings. Provide diverse forms of recognition and assessment, which might take varied forms, including prizes, badges, ranking, ratings, and reviews.

6. Encourage play and tinkering.

Youths often learn best by experimentation, tinkering, and doing things that might look like they're "wasting time." As much as possible, build in open-ended spaces for playing and tinkering with the tools, materials, and platforms in addition to more structured challenges. Invite interaction and inquiry into the limits and possibilities of the platform, media, or form in which youths are working. Support learners in defining goals that structure the nature of their interaction and inquiry from moment to moment, as well as over a longer term.

7. Position youths as change agents.

The whole process of design implies agency—that people are able to create innovative solutions in the face of problems, be they large or small. And a big idea behind a pedagogy of systems thinking is that young people who bring this lens to complex problems can envision better solutions than those who don't. Help youths reflect on the choices that they are making in the design or transformation of a system—empower them to see themselves as agents of change.

WHO IS THIS COLLECTION FOR?

These materials were designed for both in- and out-of-school spaces. Educators and mentors using the materials and tools in this book, such as conductive thread and sewable battery holders, do not need to be experts in sewing or needlework. The activities in this book are designed to spur a range of interactions between young people and the digital platform or tool, as well as between peers. Educators should serve as facilitators for youth discussion, reflection, and ideation. The principles of systems thinking encourage young people to figure things out, put puzzle pieces together, look for similar patterns, and work together to ask questions and find answers across disciplines. The activities have been designed to invite young people to teach one another, because the act of playing and making products for each other, be they games, stories, or physical objects, moves learning into a collaborative context. Youth can show others what they've discovered as they work on their projects, which provides an opportunity for them to act as experts. We recommend that educators try and support youth taking on these roles in the classroom, serving as teachers and mentors to their peers.

APPROACH TO CONVERSATION AND CRITIQUE IN THIS VOLUME

With the aim of creating a participatory environment where feedback is welcomed and iteration is assumed, several processes and protocols have been included that support productive conversation and critique within groups. For example, there are many points where youths share their work with each other, with the goal of getting feedback to refine and improve their designs. This can be a tricky endeavor, as they might be reluctant to let others see their work, and not all youths are practiced at offering feedback that goes beyond being simply laudatory or critical, to hit a point of being *constructively critical.* Although there are many ways to help them learn to find this "sweet spot" of feedback, in these Design Challenges, we encourage them to give a balance of "warm" and "cool" feedback to each other, taking turns as presenter and responder. In any community that does not have much experience providing constructive feedback and critique, the warm and cool feedback protocol can be a really effective tool. Next, we give details about this process, as well as a few related suggestions. All of these could be modeled and discussed beforehand with youths to support familiarity and ease of use.

Warm/cool feedback: This type of feedback begins with a few minutes of warm feedback from the responder, which should include comments about how the work presented seems to meet the desired goals. Next, the responder provides a few minutes of cool feedback, sometimes phrased in the form of reflective questions. Cool feedback may include perceived disconnects, gaps or problems in attaining the goal. This is an opportunity to include suggestions for making changes as well. You might note that people feel encouraged to improve something that they have worked on when they feel *good* about it. A young designer especially can become discouraged without some positive feelings and compliments about the design.

Consider role-playing this, with you—the teacher or mentor—taking on the part of the partner receiving feedback. Ask for a volunteer to give you examples of feedback, starting with warm feedback and then moving to cool. When processing the results afterward, focus first on what felt like helpful feedback. Then explore with the group what types of feedback seemed unhelpful. Provide examples of several feedback sentence starters that might lead to more constructive conversation. (e.g., "Have you thought about …?" "What were you thinking when you …?" "I was confused when … Can you help me understand?")

WARM FEEDBACK

elements that work well
goals that were met
things to build on

COOL FEEDBACK

areas of wondering
gaps or disconnects
suggestions for improvement

"Yes, and ..." feedback: Another way to support youths in developing ideas together is to have them generate "Yes, and ..." feedback as opposed to "Yes, but ..." or negative feedback. This type of feedback reserves judgment, challenge, or dismissal, and instead focuses on refining the original idea that the youths generated. It is a technique often used in supporting iteration in a design process.

One way to demonstrate the difference between these two types of feedback is to create a silly or neutral situation in which one person presents an idea (such as "I think we should get rid of all money. We don't need it."), and then a larger group answers only with "Yes, but ..." feedback (e.g., "Yes, but how can we buy things online without money?"). Then ask the presenter to present the same idea again and have the larger group answer only with "Yes, and ..." feedback (e.g., "Yes, and then maybe we could then use [suggestion] when we want to buy something online."). Ask the presenter, and then the group, to describe the differences between the two experiences.

Response starters: At any given moment, not everyone in any community will agree completely about what's working or not working in a creative project. Sometimes this means that debate is necessary to clarify ideas, and healthy debate can support the development of critical thinking skills around systems at play in their communities. To help youths respond to each other civilly while still disagreeing—during both formal response times and informal collaborative work periods—you may want to post in the room a range of possible response starters that introduce disagreement respectfully, such as the following:

- "I see your point, and …"

- "I am wondering about …"

- "I understand that you see this as a way to … , and from my perspective …"

- "What if …?"

- "Yes, and …"

APPROACH TO ASSESSMENT IN THIS VOLUME

Assessment is designed to happen in three ways in these modules: informally, through *embedded discussions* within challenges, and formally; as *structured reflections* and design feedback in the challenges; and as *written assessments,* which can be administered as pre- and post-tests. Of course, all assessments can and should be used at the discretion of the educator. All of the assessment opportunities that we included here were designed to be formative, serving not just as an important opportunity for the educator to get information on how youths are learning, but for the youths themselves to gain insight into their own understanding of the key ideas being explored and the areas that they might want to work to improve.

With the goal of helping to prepare you to listen for and evaluate youths' understanding, we also include rubrics that offer an overview of what "novice" versus "expert" understanding of the concepts in each section would look like. These rubrics are intended to be used for instructional decision making, so that the educator can determine whether students are ready to move on, must talk more about a particular idea, or need more chances to show what they know.

Informal assessments are marked with this "Let's talk" icon. These assessments are designed to be formative and informal, in that they take place within the context of the Design Challenge as small-group or whole-group conversations. These conversations should serve both to help youths formalize some of the ideas that they've been working on and to create an opportunity for the educator to gauge what they understand about a particular idea.

Structured assessments indicated by the "hands on" icon, are times when youth write down and document what they understand about a particular idea. Structured assessments come in a variety of forms. For example, this might a piece of peer feedback about another person's design, a sketch or diagram about their own design, or perhaps a paragraph in which they reflect on a particular idea. These assessments are intended to help youth formalize their understanding of a particular idea, but are also designed to provide educators with a formal representation (i.e., a hard copy!) of what youth understand about a particular idea at a particular time. If desired, these assessments can be graded and returned to youth as a means of tracking performance toward a grade in the context of classroom use.

Written assessments are given only at the end of the module (and perhaps at the beginning, if the educator is interested in pre- and post-change information). The written assessment is designed to measure what youths have learned across the entire module, and it targets both youths' understanding of key systems-thinking content and what they've learned about a particular technology platform.

Information about ways that students might reason about the content can be found in the *What to Expect* sections of each Design Challenge. We share the end points of student reasoning (novice and expert) but, of course, rarely are youth novices or experts at everything at the same time. The goal of these rubrics is for the educator to be able to determine how students are thinking about the content to inform decisions about how to proceed, review, or intervene.

COMMON CORE STATE STANDARDS (CCSS) AND TIPS FOR INTEGRATION

You might be asking yourself: Why focus on the Common Core State Standards for English Language Arts in a book designed to support understanding of systems thinking concepts through the use of circuitry? What do electronic artifacts and literacy have in common?

On a basic level, the challenges in this book involve literacy practices related to narrative development. Youths will create a shadow puppet and then write a script for that puppet. They will need to understand nuances of character development and dialogue, skills that are featured in the CCSS.

Dig a little deeper and you'll see that youths will also need to read and create technical subject texts: the ability to create an e-puppet, for instance, is predicated on youths' ability to understand complex, step-by-step directions. Dig deeper still—not only are youths consuming these technical subject texts, but they're doing so within the context of thinking systemically. In addition, youths in these challenges are asked to learn while they design, with the goal and gaining and understanding science content knowledge. Knowing, for instance, the way in which electrical circuits function is crucial. The CCSS, in fact, build upon the layer of English Language Arts standards to create guidelines for literacy skills and knowledge specific to Science and Technical Subjects.

Literacy in the content areas like Science is critical, in the eyes of the CCSS, to support youths as they progress down a path toward college and career readiness. Creating with e-textiles, therefore, clearly involves a number of key literacy arenas—narrative writing, speaking and listening, analyzing technical subject texts—as outlined in the CCSS through standards such as:

- Writing 6–8.3: Write narratives to develop real or imagined experiences or events using effective technique, relevant descriptive details, and well-structured event sequences.

- Speaking and Listening 6–12.4: Present information, findings, and supporting evidence such that listeners can follow the line of reasoning and the organization, development, and style are appropriate to task, purpose, and audience.

- Reading and Science in the Technical Subjects 6–8.3: Follow precisely a multistep procedure when carrying out experiments, taking measurements, or performing technical tasks.

In addition, technology is woven throughout the standards—as a way to gain knowledge, as something to be understood through critical media analysis, and as a means to produce and disseminate work. The challenges in this book touch upon many of these areas. But perhaps most important, in these challenges youths use technology tools to *produce*, to create electronic artifacts. And during an age when composing means everything from writing text to producing a YouTube video, they may in fact be helping to shape a broader definition of "writing" today.

TOOLKIT

In this chapter, we transition from talking about the ideas and principles behind this book to share more about how they can be realized in practice. Here, we offer a toolkit and various tips on how to foster a productive climate of making with Do-It-Yourself (DIY) electronics.

Throughout this volume, we encourage instructors to follow the spirit, rather than the letter, of the upcoming Design Challenges. Every learning environment is different——a classroom is dramatically different from a library space, which is also different from an after-school program. Every group of youths is different—tweens are not teens, youths who grew up in a city are different from ones who grew up in rural areas, immigrant youths are different from youths born in their country of residence. And every educator is different in terms of style, history, and relationships to youths. So we don't assume that the activities we share will (or should) ever be implemented in the exact same way in every context. We assume that these materials will be adapted, reinvented, and even improved in your own classroom. This is part of why we spent a good deal of space talking about the "big ideas"—the concepts and principles that drove this work—in the first section of this book. We didn't simply see this sort of background as something interesting and informative (though we hope it is); rather, we offered it up as tools that you could use to bring this work to life. We hope that when you inevitably adapt our activities to fit your context and interests, you have a sense of what the spirit behind them is, and you have the opportunity to adapt the lessons (and even create new activities) with these key principles in mind.

This book contains a sequence of four crafting Design Challenges with DIY electronics that both build an early understanding of electronics and introduce core systems thinking concepts. Each of the Design Challenges builds off of the last, deepening and extending youths' understanding of systems thinking and electronics. The bulk of the Design Challenges follow a similar curricular trajectory (see the table on p. 22). Typically, youths will experience a short systems thinking activity followed by a mini-Maker Design Challenge, which is designed to introduce both the big ideas of systems thinking and the tools and materials needed for the Design Challenge. Youths then are invited to take part in a thematic activity to construct gadgets such as electronic cuffs and T-shirts or solar-powered backpacks. The final part of most of the Design Challenges involves youths' reflecting on and sharing their work with a larger community by posting it online.

PLANNING YOUR TRAJECTORY IN SOFT CIRCUITS

Instructors can augment the learning experiences in this volume by offering complementary Design Challenges from another book in this collection, *Short Circuits: Crafting e-Puppets with DIY Electronics*. Both volumes share a common introductory challenge ("Design Challenge 1: Introduction to the Electronic Circuit") and then branch into three unique Design Challenges in line with that volume's theme.

- **Crafting e-puppets:** In *Short Circuits*, youths begin by exploring thematic projects around electronic hand puppets (e-puppets) in "Design Challenge 2: It's Alive! Making e-Puppets"; then they create storyboards with an embedded recordable sound module in "Design Challenge 3: Speaking Stories"; and finally, they create an LED flashlight to facilitate putting on a unique shadow puppet show in "Design Challenge 4: DIY Flashlights and Shadow Puppets." Each of these challenges involves circuitry concepts that range in difficulty from understanding a simple circuit with a switch to creating circuits with multiple light-emitting diodes (LEDs) both in series and parallel.

- **Crafting e-fashion:** The projects in this volume explore wearable electronic textiles (e-textiles), including creating an electronic cuff/bracelet with a simple circuit and multiple LEDs in "Design Challenge 2," fashioning a T-shirt embedded with a small wearable computer called the LilyPad Arduino that controls the LEDs in "Design Challenge 3," and making a solar-powered backpack in "Design Challenge 4."

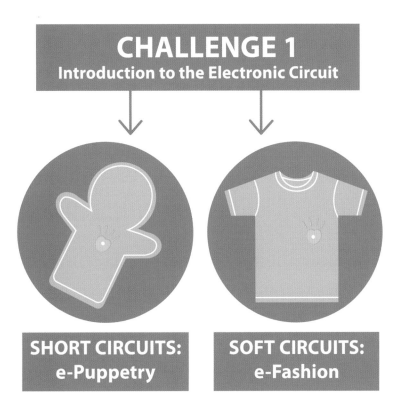

CHALLENGE 1
Introduction to the Electronic Circuit

SHORT CIRCUITS:
e-Puppetry

SOFT CIRCUITS:
e-Fashion

This volume focuses on a series of e-fashion Design Challenges. Each of these challenges is designed with unique systems thinking and circuitry content. We suggest beginning with Design Challenge 1 and then deciding which of the remaining Design Challenges best suits your setting. All Design Challenges can be used independently, but be warned: They were created with the assumption that you have read or introduced prior Design Challenges, so you will need to make some limited modifications if you use the Design Challenges out of order or in isolation.

Note   For more information on the connections within each Design Challenge to the Common Core State Standards (CCSS) and Next Generation Science Standards (NGSS), please see the Preface. For more information on the circuitry concepts, targeted systems thinking concepts, estimated costs of consumable materials per child, and the relative technical difficulty captured in each Design Challenge, see the table on p. 22. This information is meant to help guide your larger decisions about which Design Challenges are right for your setting, influence your decision-making process, and inform the trajectory that you're planning.

Soft Circuits Challenges at a Glance

	Strand	Estimated Cost per Child*	Technical Difficulty Rating	Targeted Systems Thinking Concepts Introduced	Other Targeted Concepts
Design Challenge 1: Introduction to the Electronic Circuit (Time: 105 minutes)	General introduction	$5	1	Circuits as systems Components Behaviors Functioning Goals Interconnections Limited resources Balancing feedback loops	Simple circuits Resistance Conductivity Electric current Short circuits
Design Challenge 2: e-Textile Cuffs (Time: 310 minutes)	e-Fashion	$12	2	System's structure Interconnections Leverage points Limited Resources	Series circuit Parallel circuit Voltage e-Textiles
Design Challenge 3: ElectriciTee (Time: 345–435 minutes)	e-Fashion	$35	3	Nested Systems Subsystems System's structure Interconnections	Microcontroller Programming Code Scripts
Design Challenge 4: Solar-powered backpack (Time: 490 minutes)	e-Fashion	$60	4	Stocks and flows Balance Limited resources Dynamic equilibrium	Solar panel Amp Voltage Microcontroller Programming Code Scripts

*Note that estimated costs per child only include those costs for the basic project materials. Materials that are general start-up supplies are not included in these estimates. This is also calculated without factoring in price reductions for larger quantities. There are many ways to cut costs significantly; see suggestions throughout these materials.

WHAT ARE DIY ELECTRONICS?

The DIY movement has been popularized by *Make* magazine, and today there is a growing number of Makerspaces across the United States to promote personalized fabrication outside traditional manufacturing. These spaces promote a DIY approach to electronics that most often include physical materials and electronics in a project of one form or another. Our focus on e-textiles and other forms of merging papercrafts and electronics in this volume places an equal emphasis on both high- and low-tech materials, as well as merging the materials and activities from both traditionally female and male maker cultures (i.e., sewing/crafting and shop/electronics). The e-textiles introduced in Design Challenge 2 (and used widely in this volume) are electronically enhanced garments, accessories, and other fabric-based items that are designed to combine traditional aspects of textile crafts with elements of embedded computing, conductive sewing/craft materials such as conductive thread or fabrics, sensors for light and sound, and actuators such as LEDs and speakers.

We see an additional benefit to exploring e-textiles and DIY electronics: namely, that they reveal insights about the production or design of technology itself and cultural assumptions that nowadays are often hidden or invisible to youths. Creative production with e-textiles encourages both youths and instructors to question their current under-standing of functionality and aesthetics, make explicit their gender assumptions about crafts, and master the fundamentals of a new field by learning the visual, aural, and technological literacies necessary to inscribe themselves into the larger DIY and fashion culture. All in all, what takes place during such creative production becomes a critical reflection on how technology design decisions are made, how they are interrelated with craft production and engineering functionality, and how they intersect with personal decisions and cultural assumptions.

WHY USE DIY ELECTRONICS IN A SYSTEMS THINKING CURRICULUM?

These curricular Design Challenges involve a range of activities including role playing, small games, and group discussions to engage youths in ideas and practices of systems thinking. However, the core activities in which systems thinking is used are ones where youths create tangible design projects that incorporate DIY electronics, as we believe that the process of designing systems provides an important context for understanding how systems work.

To begin with, each DIY electronics project can be understood, in and of itself, as a *system*. Every project comprises interdependent elements—batteries, LEDs, conductive thread or wire, and sometimes even microcomputers—that take on specific roles as they work together to accomplish a goal. If any of these parts are removed, that has an impact on the whole system. These projects allow an educator to provide opportunities for youths to ground the ideas and practices of systems thinking in a real-world, tangible context where they can see things like interconnections and stocks and flows come to life.

Another important aspect of DIY electronics and e-textiles projects is that they allow youths to engage in personally meaningful creative activity. These projects let them bring in many of their own ideas, styles, and interests, whether by allowing them to tell stories they care about or by giving them avenues for exploring their own sense of aes-thetics. Being able to make things that have personal relevance deepens engagement and learning outcomes.

DIY electronics also promote collaboration and peer-to-peer learning through online global communities such as those suggested at the Interconnections website (**digitalis .nwp.org/gnl**) where youths share, learn from one another, and give feedback on projects. Creating personally meaningful objects is certainly an important way to learn, but when youths can share them in a community context, it increases the likelihood that they'll persist and iterate on a project, gives them an audience to keep in mind when they're authoring, and lets their voice be heard on a global scale. Importantly, such a community is also a place where youths can be inspired by each other and even teach one another techniques and practices to improve their ability to be creators of technologies and crafts.

Finally, we like using these materials because DIY electronics and e-textiles have been linked to a host of other twenty-first-century skills beyond systems thinking, including computational thinking and design thinking. Specifically, when projects like those featured in the *Soft Circuits* volume incorporate the LilyPad Arduino, they support youths in exploring a range of computational thinking *concepts* (sequence, loops, conditionals), *practices* (working iteratively and incrementally, testing and debugging, reusing and remixing), and *perspectives* (expressing, connecting, questioning). In a world where interactions between digital and physical spaces are growing ever more fluid, these competencies become increasingly important. More broadly, these sorts of maker projects provide opportunities for youths to engage in design thinking, wherein they go through cycles of research, tinkering, iteration, feedback, revision, and publication. These design-thinking competencies are applicable to a range of creative, production-oriented activities that are becoming ever more ubiquitous in our information society.

For all these reasons, we believe that DIY electronics and e-textiles provide a strong avenue for developing systems thinking and twenty-first-century skills in youths.

The next sections are intended to help orient you to the tools and materials that you'll put to use in the Design Challenges in this book and give you suggestions for organizing your space, as well as how to pack general toolboxes to hold materials common across most Design Challenges so as to minimize setup/cleanup time.

TOOLS AND MATERIALS

The following sections are organized into general families of tools and materials used in all the Design Challenges in both volumes, including those for sewing and crafting, conductive crafting, electronics, and e-textiles. It might be a good idea to ask youths whether they have any crafting experience—knitting, crocheting, weaving, etc.—because it might be useful for engaging in and extending many of the projects in this volume in creative ways, although such activities are not supported in these books. This section is meant to give you a sense of things that you'll need to have on hand, as well as general instructions for their use.

TOOLS

BASIC SEWING AND CRAFTING TOOLS

The ability to sew is crucial to many of the Design Challenges in this volume. Helpful guides throughout the book can be copied onto construction paper to help youths learn the basics of hand stitching, tying knots, threading a needle, and sewing a button, sequin, or other objects. In addition to sewing, the activities and Design Challenges contained in this book connect deeply to the traditions of crafting both in and out of school. For most of these tools, you only need a few per group, as they can be shared easily among four to eight youths.

(1) Sewing needles will be some of the most important tools for your e-textile Design Challenges; they come in a variety of lengths and eye sizes. Look for some that have larger eyes (like those labeled as "crewel" or "embroidery" needles), but note that they still must be small enough to fit through the e-textile components in your circuit. If you're worried about threading needles for larger groups, **(2) needle threaders** are inexpensive and can be used to help thread regular sewing needles, or try **(3) self-threading needles**. Although self-threading needles come in a variety of sizes and brands, not all self-threading needles will work with conductive thread. We recommend the Clover Self-Threading needles, which come in a five-pack. Note that the largest and smallest needles in this pack may prove difficult to use with e-textile components. **(4) Beeswax** (one or two for a large group) is also useful, particularly when working with conductive thread because the ends of the thread tend to fray.

(5) Straight pins, while not necessary for any of the Design Challenges in this volume, can be useful to help keep multiple layers of fabric in place while sewing.

Straight pins with pearl heads are easier to see if dropped or placed in a garment while sewing; they also are easier on the fingers. **(6) Embroidery hoops** (we suggest the 10" size) are frames made of two hoops and make sewing or embroidery easier by creating a taut, flat surface for stitching. **(7) Pincushions** hold sewing needles and straight pins when not in use. We recommend placing sewing needles in pincushions to help in setup and cleanup with larger groups. They also help to hold self-threading needles steady during threading.

(8) Fabric scissors (also called *dressmaker's shears*) typically have handles that bend upward so that the blades can sit flat along a surface while cutting. They are also sharper (and can be resharpened), but they also are more expensive than household paper scissors. For this reason, you'll want to keep these scissors clearly labeled and out of reach when working on paper-based projects. **(9) Embroidery scissors** are smaller and less expensive and are particularly useful for cutting thread and more precise cuts.

(10) Tailor's chalk can easily mark and be easily brushed off most fabrics. Such a tool, or something like a fabric pencil or a water- or air-soluble pen, is useful when you want to sketch out sewing lines that you don't want to be visible on the final project. **(11) Retractable measuring tape** is useful to have in the toolbox to make measurements, and it retracts neatly into its shell to avoid the rolling-up tendency of classic dressmaker's tape or the inflexibility of a standard ruler. Note that there are versions made from both metal and fabric (which adds more flexibility around curved surfaces). **(12)** A **seam ripper** can make it easier to tear out knotted pieces of thread or misplaced stitching. **(13) Tweezers** can be useful for fine detail work in sewing and beadwork.

(14) A **mini-iron** is a small iron designed for use in interior spaces, corners, or small areas when you want to avoid objects that will melt under high heat. It can be useful as a way to press fabric before sewing or to affix iron-on adhesives to your T-shirt, backpack, or other item. A full-size iron and ironing board also can be useful if you have the space.

In addition, you'll need at least one method to seal knots made with conductive thread. Because of the thread's thickness, knots in conductive thread can easily come undone over time. To prevent this, use **(15) clear nail polish**, **(16) fabric glue**, or a **(17) low-temperature glue gun with glue sticks**. Fabric glue and a low-temperature glue gun are also useful for affixing decorative elements to your garments and craft projects. (We recommend a low-temperature glue gun to prevent burns and melting plastic, but any type of glue gun will work.)

A few additional tools are useful for the instructor to have on hand to precut large amounts of fabric (and are not listed as supplies needed in the individual Design Challenges), including a **(18) gridded ruler**, which is a translucent, wider-than-usual ruler with markings to aid in the precise measuring and cutting of straight edges or sharp corners. It can be used to cut down felt or other fabrics to a specific size across a variety of projects. Be careful not to cut into the ruler, as it can be damaged easily. To aid cutting, you also can use larger metal rulers that won't be as easily damaged. **(19)** A **self-healing sewing mat** is marked out with centimeter or inch increments and is used as a protective surface for cutting with a rotary cutter or utility knife. **(20)** A **rotary cutter** is designed to be used in conjunction with a self-healing mat and has a straight edge for cutting large amounts of materials with a good deal of precision. Alternatively, **(21) pinking shears** have zigzag blades that cut a unique edge and reduce fraying. These shears can be used to create an attractive edge or to cut fabric that might easily fray (conductive or nonconductive woven fabrics) and can be useful when cutting large quantities of fabric.

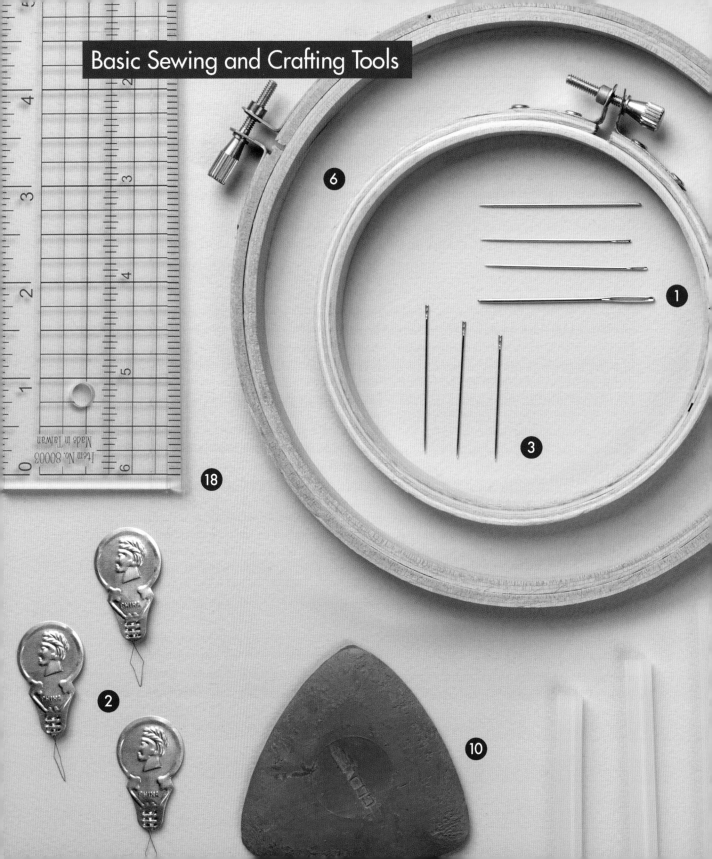

Basic Sewing and Crafting Tools

BASIC ELECTRONICS TOOLS

There are a host of useful basic tools to have around to help with electronics. For most of these tools, except for the multimeter and alligator clips, it will be sufficient to have one or two of them for the entire group. Most of these supplies can be found at your local hardware or electronics supply store.

(1) Digital multimeters are handheld devices with a negative and a positive probe that measure electric current, voltage, and resistance to help determine whether a material or artifact is conductive or nonconductive. While it's possible to create many of these projects without multimeters, they help to make some of the invisible properties of electricity more tangible. We recommend getting digital multimeters with Continuity mode settings to aid in the debugging process.

(2) Diagonal wire cutters (also known as *side cutters*) easily cut copper wire, but they should not be used to cut harder metals. Some have spring-loaded handles to ease hand strain.

(3) Needlenose pliers are named for their long, thin shape and are useful for crafts or in electrical projects to bend wire, for fine detail work, or for bending the pins of two-pronged LEDs to make them sewable.

(4) Wire strippers are used to remove the plastic coating from insulated wires. Wire strippers typically have different gauge settings that can be used to strip wires of various widths.

(5) A **utility knife** is an all-purpose blade useful for cutting holes in thick material. We suggest that the instructor assist in using the utility knife for safety reasons.

(6) Alligator clips (also called *alligator test leads* and named for their resemblance to the jaws of an alligator) are electrical connectors attached to an electric cable for making a temporary connection to a battery or other component. The ones depicted here are vinyl-insulated, but noninsulated alligator clips will work well and may be easier to use when you're hooking up multiple clips to a single component. Use them with caution, though, as the teeth on the clips can damage electronics and also can slip off e-textile components.

Basic Electronics Tools

DIGITAL MULTIMETER 830

0.00

Ω 20MΩ OFF 200mV V⎓
200kΩ   2V
20kΩ   20V
2kΩ   200V
200Ω   600V
                         600V
⊶·))   200V V~
10A
200mA   20μA
20mA 2mA 200μA CE
A⎓
10A   COM   mAVΩ

10sec M   MAX 600
10A   200mA
FUSED   FUSED

⑤

①

⑥

MATERIALS

SEWING AND CRAFTING

More than accessories or decorative accents for these design challenges, crafting supplies allow for a good deal of personalization and adding meaning to the projects. While shopping, be sure to look around for other materials that might be meaningful to your youths or community, and consider using recycled goods in your designs as well. Here are a few suggestions for starter supplies to get the creativity flowing! Most of these supplies can be found at your local crafting supply store.

There are a host of everyday craft items, some of which you may already have on hand, including **(1) glitter**, **(2) feathers**, and **(3) paint** that could be used to embellish projects. We recommend having a large supply of **(4) googly eyes** (which can be affixed to almost any surface using your low-temperature glue gun) to instantly transform a project. **(5) Yarn** in a variety of colors can be cut to create "hair," to make ties or bows on clothing, or for many other possible uses in your projects. **(6) Assorted gems, rhinestones, and sequins** add extra light reflection and to embellish the work. **(7) Pipe cleaners** can be bent into various shapes to cast interesting shadows, twisted into a mustache, or cut and affixed to an e-puppet as hair.

(8) Assorted beads can be particularly useful in e-textile projects. **(9) Glass beads**, for example, can be used to insulate the conductive thread, prevent shorts, or embellish designs. Look for beads with larger holes so that they can be incorporated easily into projects without fraying the conductive thread. In addition, try to avoid bugles (small tubelike beads), as these can fray the thread easily. **(10) Indian glass beads** are larger and relatively inexpensive, and they come in a variety of shapes and colors. **(11) Puffy paint** (also called *dimensional fabric paint*) is useful both to insulate conductive thread to keep it from slowly corroding over time and to decorate T-shirts, backpacks, and other items.

Keep on hand **(12) assorted fabrics**, including quilting squares and scraps of fabrics. Look for a variety of patterns because youths like to cut out motifs to iron or glue onto designs. Also look for fabrics with a tight weave (to minimize stretch in the project, which will strain the sewn circuit) and fabrics that are medium in weight to allow for the needle to move in and out easily. To check the weave, pull on the fabric horizontally, vertically, and diagonally and look for fabrics that have little stretch in at least two of the three directions. **(13) Assorted colors of felt** (in 9" x 12" squares or larger bolts) are also useful for most projects. Because felt is a thicker

Sewing and Crafting

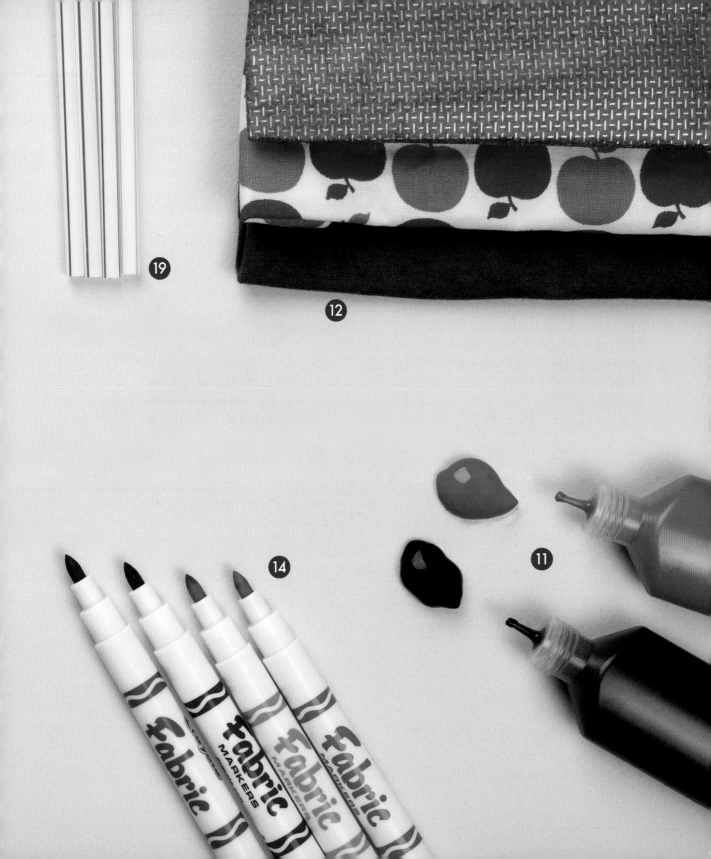

fabric and is not woven, it won't fray on the edges when cut. Felt is inexpensive and has some weight to it, but it allows a needle to pass through easily and allows for smooth sewing.

(14) Fabric markers leave permanent or semipermanent marks on fabric and are useful for drawing outlines before making cuts or for drawing designs into projects. They are easy to use and a great alternative to puffy paint or fabric glue, which take longer to dry.

(15) Sewing thread comes in a rainbow of colors and can be made from a variety of materials, including polyester, cotton, and viscose. While any thread that is suitable for hand-stitching will work, we recommend purchasing a polyester thread set in a variety of colors, as it's an all-purpose thread with a durable "give" and silky feel. Polyester thread also doesn't tangle easily.

(16) Assorted buttons can be a practical form of fastening, or they can be glued onto a creation to become an integral part of the design. Buttons come in a variety of shapes and sizes—be sure to gather a variety so that the color, size, shape, and quantity can be considered in the final design decisions. Due to the expense of these items, consider holding a button collection: Have youths bring in spare buttons from home over time for upcoming projects.

(17) Decorative duct tape, a new line of duct tape for crafters that retains the same properties as regular duct tape but comes in an array of colors and patterns. While not easy to sew through, duct tape is useful for personalizing projects and can also be functional. **(18) Brads** (paper fasteners) come in a variety of colors and sizes and can be added to your paper projects to create movement for arms and legs, among other uses. **(19) Bamboo skewers, plastic straws,** and **wooden sticks** are particularly useful in shadow puppet projects.

Throughout these design challenges, you'll see suggestions to include other everyday crafting items, including craft foam sheets, poster board, 8.5" x 11" sheets of cardstock, hole punches or dowels for making holes, colored plastic, as well as cotton cloths, cardboard, and wax paper needed to create a shadow puppet stage.

CONDUCTIVE CRAFTING

In DIY electronics, you can use the conductive properties of everyday materials as well as incorporate other specialty crafting items to inspire your electronic designs. While many of the things listed here are specialty items, just look around your environment to see if there are any items that are conductive and could be incorporated into your designs. Some of these items can be made (e.g., homemade Play-Doh) or picked up from your local general or craft store (e.g., magnets, metal fasteners, fine-steel wool, or aluminum foil, which can be ironed on fabric with fusible backing), but other items (e.g., conductive paints, ribbon, pens, or yarns) will need to be purchased through a special vendor. Even the antistatic foam that electronics are shipped in can be reused as a pressure sensor! For more ideas, look at KOBAKANT's web-based resource on "How to Get What You Want" (www.kobakant.at/DIY). Throughout this book, you will find shopping lists with suggested retailers to help you locate these and other specialty materials.

(1) Paperclips are one example of an everyday item that might be conductive and which can be bent into new shapes and creatively incorporated into your circuit designs. Use your multimeter's Continuity mode to test things out! **(2) Sewable metal snaps** can act as switches and typically are good conductors of electricity. It is important to look for snaps that are conductive (i.e., not covered in a protective coating)—take your multimeter with you to the store to help you check for this aspect. **(3) Sewable metal magnetic snaps** can be substituted for sewable metal snaps, but they offer a magnetic clasp instead of a simple snap. Note that magnets are also good conductors!

(4) Conductive metal beads are also useful, as they can be incorporated into e-textile designs for a switch, as well as for decorative purposes. Be careful, as not all metallic-looking beads are good conductors. **(5) Conductive thread** has many of the qualities of typical thread and can be used in hand sewing, but it also conducts electricity because it is plated with silver or stainless steel. Similar to wire or cables, conductive thread can carry current to power your e-textiles. It comes in both two-ply and four-ply. **(6) Conductive Velcro®** is similar to the regular product, but it has a conductive silver coating. Conductive Velcro can be sewn in or glued.

(7) Conductive fabric tape is a flexible fabric tape with conductive adhesive made from a blend of nickel-, copper-, and cobalt-coated nylon ripstop fabric. This tape is conductive on both sides (although not all conductive tapes are), making it easy to incorporate into e-textiles or other crafting projects. Other types of fabric tape made out of copper or aluminum are less flexible but are a little less expensive. **(8) Conductive fabric** is woven with

Conductive Crafting

conductive metal strands. There are a variety of conductive fabrics available that range in color, nonconductive materials (like bamboo), the conductive materials used (like silver, stainless steel, or copper), and their degree of stretchiness. Keep in mind that some of the fabrics will tarnish (making them resistant fairly quickly). For that reason, we recommend fabrics made with silver or stainless steel over copper taffeta, which will tarnish more quickly. Some retail companies, like LessEMF, sell a sample set of fabric swatches so that you can see and test various types. Keep in mind that most projects benefit from using a 1" square of fabric or smaller, so one piece of fabric will likely be enough for your entire group. For the purposes of the projects included in this volume, any of the conductive fabrics will work, but we suggest nonwoven fabrics (as they won't fray or whisker, causing shorts) or Lycra, which can be cut into small pieces and affixed using fabric glue.

If you're curious about the resistance of any these materials, you can measure it with your multimeter and calculate per meter (see the tips on using your multimeter in Continuity mode found in Design Challenge 1). In general, remember that the length of the thread or material will increase the resistance. Shorter threads or pieces of material have less resistance. Additionally, note that the greater the surface area of a material, the less resistance it will have, so thicker threads or wider strips of conductive fabric with more surface area will have less resistance than thinner ones. Note that conductive thread has more resistance than wire or cable, but that shouldn't present any problems at the size and scale of projects in these Design Challenges.

ELECTRONICS

Of the vast range of hardware options available to DIY and electronics hobbyists, we present a subset of materials that provide a good entry point into the domain of electronics. These include **(1) two-pin LEDs** (also referred to as *simple LEDs*) are small devices that light up when electric current passes through them. They are relatively inexpensive, produce a tremendous amount of light, and can last a very long time before burning out. Most LEDs are powered with about 3.3V and come in an assortment of colors and sizes. LEDs also can be incorporated into e-textile projects by bending the legs into two circles to make them sewable. To learn how to make your own DIY sewable LED, see the "DIY Sewable Electronics" section at the end of this chapter. **(2) Super Bright LEDs** are brighter than normal LEDs and useful in projects where you want to cast a shadow or illuminate a larger area.

You will encounter a variety of prefabricated circuits in everyday toys and materials, like electronic greeting cards. There are also a number of preassembled modules that can be used across a variety of projects, such as a **(3) recordable sound module**, which records sound and plays it back when a button is pressed. For early explorations, we recommend a 20-second recording module with a 9V battery connector. A **(4) miniature slide switch** can be used as a simple on/off switch in a project.

(5) Spools of insulated hook-up wire come in a variety of colors and sizes and can be cut into smaller pieces and incorporated in your projects or used for prototyping. Note that when purchasing wire, certain colors have connotations in the field of electronics. Red wire will typically denote the power (or positive connection to the battery), and black wire will typically indicate the ground (or negative connection to the battery). **(6) Electrical tape** provides an insulating barrier to any exposed wires, helping to prevent shorts. **(7) Flexible solar panels** are thin semiconductor wafers specially treated to form an electric field when struck by light. The solar panel can be used to charge a separate battery as well as run electricity directly from the solar panel through a circuit.

(8) 9V batteries (alkaline batteries) are energy sources that convert chemical energy to electricity. **(9)** A **9V battery snap connector** is a clip designed to attach to a 9V battery. There are two wires (red wire = positive; black wire = negative) that can attach easily to alligator clips or to other wires in your design. If your map connector has an unwanted plug at one end, simply use your wire cutters and strippers to expose the ends of the two wires and use them in your project.

In electronics, two-pin LEDs are normally paired with "resistors," electronic components designed to slow or oppose an electric current. In this case, resistors prevent the LED from being overwhelmed by the battery and burning out. However, throughout the projects in this volume,

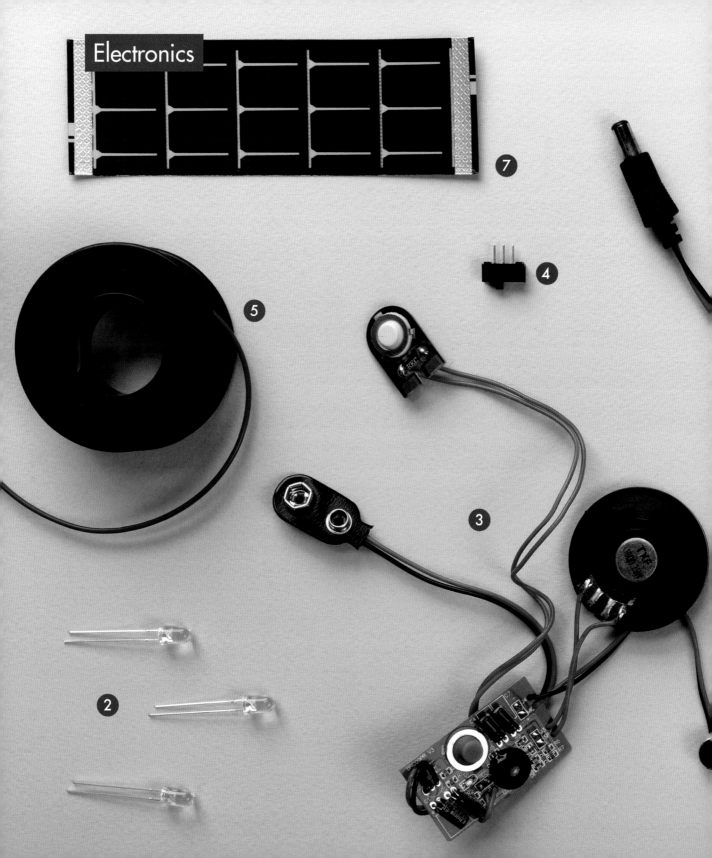

Electronics

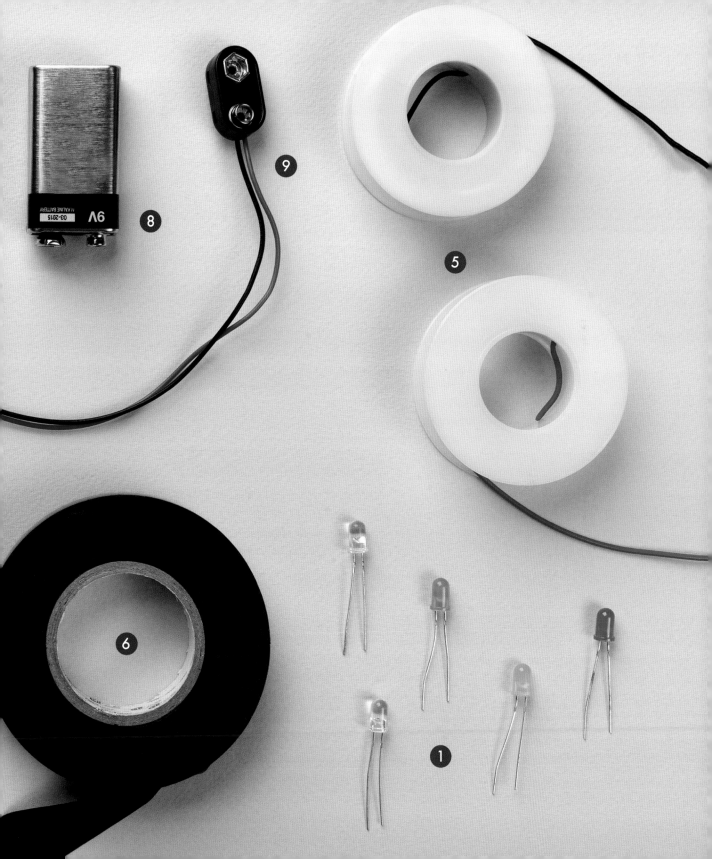

you probably won't find a need for a resistor, as the LEDs recommended here often have a built-in resistor, and the conductive thread also poses enough resistance for two-pin LEDs (more so than wires), which is usually enough to prevent the LEDs from being overwhelmed by the battery.

Note It can actually be a good learning moment for your youths to overwhelm an LED on purpose. Unlike batteries, very little heat will be released, but you can expect a small amount of smoke and fumes when an LED is burned out. To check whether an LED has burnt out, you can use a 3V battery that you know is working and test your LED by pressing its two pins on the appropriate sides of the battery.

If you find a need for resistors in your circuit, use the following information to determine the resistor needed:

- Calculate the *supply voltage* for your energy source. *Voltage* is a measure representing the product of the current and resistance flowing through all or part of a circuit. You may have a voltage estimate offhand for your battery, such as if you're using a coin cell battery (3V) or 9V battery. If not, turn your multimeter to a setting to calculate the supply voltage (probably 20V in the DC range) and check the voltage that comes from your power source. Note that newer batteries will oftentimes have a higher voltage than their package indicates and, likewise, older batteries will have less voltage, so it's always useful to calculate this even if you have a rough estimate.

- Calculate the estimated *voltage drop* across the LED. You also can check the supplier's information or online resources for estimates of standard voltages by LED color or model. If you're unsure, you can use your multimeter to measure the amount of voltage needed in order to illuminate your LED(s) properly.

- Input the *desired LED current,* which is the amount of current that the LED uses when properly powered. 20 mega-amperes (mA) will work for most regular LEDs, and Super Bright LEDs can go from 30 mA up to several amps. Check the supplier's information if you are unsure what to input. If you or your youths are concerned about safety, you might find it useful to draw a continuum of "harm," with an LED on one end, a wall lamp in the middle, power lines on the opposite end, and lightning beyond the power lines. While an LED's current is relatively harmless, the current when playing with a wall lamp poses significantly more harm, and power lines or lightning even more so. While the activities in this book pose little harm beyond causing a small shock, you still may want to encourage youths to stay in the safe pool of microelectronics so that they don't try to apply what is learned here to higher-current electronics that plug into the wall.

- Now that you have all this information, input it into a resistor calculator to get the value of the resistor(s) that you will need to purchase. There are many available on the web if you Google "resistor calculator"; for example, see www.hebeiltd .com.cn/?p=zz.led.resistor.calculator.

EXPANDING YOUR DIY ELECTRONICS TOOLKIT

As mentioned previously, the collection of hardware here is a purposefully constrained set of components (emphasizing LEDs, speakers, switches, and various energy sources). This list is meant to serve as an introduction to electronics.

As the group's expertise and curiosity about electronics begins to grow, we recommend branching out to explore additional hardware such as different types of sensors (like tilt, light, bend, and temperature sensors), small motors, potentiometers, capacitors, and speakers, as well as more sophisticated tools like soldering irons. Your extended electronics journey can take many different forms, depending on the interests and abilities of the youths:

- Keep discarded electronic toys, computers, and other household electronics for them to disassemble and investigate (without being connected to the energy source, of course).

- Purchase small quantities of new types of hardware for them to explore when they finish projects early.

- Explore some of the other electronics toolkits available on the market (like Lego Mindstorms or Snap Circuits), as well as other learning resources that are featured in the back of this book.

E-TEXTILES

Electronic textiles, also known as e-textiles or soft circuits, are electronic circuits that use conductive fabrics, thread, and other flexible materials in conjunction with sewable electronic components, including LEDs, speakers, sewable battery holders, switches, and so on. Historically, e-textiles have been a highly specialized area of design, occupied almost exclusively by professional engineers and designers. However, the market recently has seen an emergence of new e-textile construction kits, like the LilyPad Arduino, fabrickit, and Aniomagic kits, as well as a growing collection of DIY guides on e-textiles (see Lewis and Lin, 2008; Pakhchyan 2008; Eng, 2009).

The *Soft Circuits* volume focuses on the LilyPad Arduino toolkit, which allows for easy integration of simple circuits (LEDs, sewable battery holders, etc.) into simple sewing craft projects, but it also introduces some of the computational possibilities of e-textiles with tools like the LilyPad Simple Board. All LilyPad Arduino products are manufactured by SparkFun Electronics (find kits of the electronics needed for each design challenge at **www.sparkfun.com/Interconnections**) and a portion of the sales return to Leah Buechley, the creator of the LilyPad Arduino, to aid her in the continued development of and education through e-textiles.

The following materials provide the foundation for most e-textile projects: **(1) LilyPad LEDs**, unlike traditional LEDs, are mounted on easily sewable modules for fluid incorporation into fabric. They have labels that indicate the positive and negative ends. LilyPad LEDs are designed with a built-in resistor and can be purchased in an array of colors, including blue, pink, red, white, yellow, and green. **(2) 3V battery / coin cell battery** *(CR2032)* is a small, flat battery whose size (20 mm) and light weight makes it an ideal choice for discreet incorporation into circuits on wearables. Its front side is marked with a "+" and is positively charged and its back side is negatively charged. CR2032 batteries should power e-textile projects for weeks or months at a time. **Note:** To prevent these batteries from shorting out, do not allow them to touch each other or other conductive objects in storage. **(3) Sewable coin cell battery holders** are less expensive and have a neat pop-in, pop-out feature that makes changing 3V coin cell batteries easy. The feet of the holder have two small sew holes that allow it to be sewn into e-textiles or other garments. **(4) LilyPad coin cell battery holders** are similar to the sewable coin cell battery holder, but provide four large sew holes (two positive and two negative), instead of two. Only two out of the four holes need to be used to create the circuit; the other two can be sewn down to the fabric with nonconductive thread or for creating a separate circuit.

(5) The **LilyPad Button Board** sports a discrete momentary push-button switch (i.e., it closes the circuit when you push the button and opens it when you release the button) and two large sew holes that can be integrated easily into e-textile projects. **(6) LilyPad Slide Switches** can be used as a simple on/off switch in e-textile designs.

(7) The **LilyPad Arduino Simple Board** is a wearable, washable e-textile microcontroller that receives programs from the computer to control the behaviors of the electronic components in an e-textile. The LilyPad Simple Board has a built-in power supply socket for a rechargeable battery and an on/off switch; in addition, it has fewer petal connections than does the LilyPad Main Board. **(8)** The **LilyPad FTDI Basic Breakout Board** is a piece of e-textile-customized hardware that enables communication between a computer and the LilyPad Simple via a **(9) mini USB cable**—one side connects to the USB port and the other connects to your LilyPad pin.

(10) LilyPad LiPower is a sewable input unit, about the size of a quarter, that connects a rechargeable lithium polymer (LiPo) battery or another source of energy like a flexible solar panel to an e-textile circuit. Attach a rechargeable **(11) Single cell Lithium Polymer (LiPo) Ion Battery** (110 mA), flip the power switch, and you will have a 5V supply to power your project for approximately three hours.

(12) A LilyPad Buzzer is a small sound-emitting module that can produce a range of pitches. It can be embedded in your e-textiles projects and controlled by your LilyPad Arduino to create simple songs or sound effects that can be coordinated with your LEDs. It's even possible to create your own fabric or paper-based speaker with KOBAKANT's "fabric speaker" and related resources. The **(13) LilyPad LED Micro** is similar to LilyPad LEDs but without a built-in resistor.

Other LilyPad Arduino components are not required for the Design Challenges, but they may be interesting to explore or to have on hand for youths who finish their projects early. As you explore the SparkFun website and additional resources listed at the end of this book, you'll encounter an immense array of electronics that can be incorporated into your e-textile designs. For example, *LilyPad Micro LEDs* might be explored as a replacement for the LilyPad LEDs. LilyPad Micro LEDs still have sew holes, but they are smaller because they don't contain built-in resistors (which is why they cost less than their counterparts). However, LEDs with and without resistors function very differently and may cause unanticipated issues in your circuits—at the very least, play-test your circuits and avoid combining LEDs with and without resistors in the same circuit.

Another easy way to help youths get started with extended electronics explorations in e-textiles is to order the

ProtoSnap LilyPad Development Board, which includes a LilyPad Simple Board, LilyPad Button Switch, a LilyPad Slide Switch, five LilyPad White LEDs, a Lily-Pad red-green-blue (RGB) tricolor LED, a LilyPad Light Sensor, a LilyPad Temperature Sensor, a LilyPad Buzzer, and a LilyPad Vibe Board wired together on a single board (eliminating the need for alligator clips and the chance of mistaken connections). This makes it easy to explore the possibilities of the components before snapping the components apart and sewing them into a project. The prototype kits are also compatible with Modkit and come with a LilyPad FTDI Basic Breakout board, a LiPo battery, 60 inches of conductive thread, and a needle.

If the LilyPad Simple Boards are out of stock, they can be replaced with the LilyPad Arduino 328 Main Board. However, this is a more complex microcontroller (with a greater number of petal connections), and therefore you can expect some discrepancies between this LilyPad and the LilyPad Simple Board that we support. For example, the built-in LED is on a different petal than the two microcontrollers.

ORGANIZING YOUR SPACE

Physical design materials like those described in the previous sections require organized spaces for storage, as well as some attention to how you organize the room(s) with stations for youths to freely visit over the course of the project. In the following sections, we make some recommendations on ways to organize these materials to save time during the setup and cleanup stages of each of the Design Challenges. These suggestions are based on what we have found useful in our own work.

STORING MATERIALS

As you begin to order and receive materials, it's important to think immediately about how to store materials that are not in use between projects. If you plan to make *Soft Circuits* a regular part of your activities, we suggest dedicating at least one large cabinet or bookshelf to material storage, with several smaller but portable tackle or crafting boxes filled and ready to be distributed to the project tables (about one per group of three to eight youths). In addition, consider acquiring one or two expandable laundry bags to keep T-shirts and other consumable textile supplies, and plastic hardware and craft drawer cabinets to store and label tiny items for easy access. You also may find it useful to have a collection of expandable file folders so that each youth can have one to store in-progress projects, parts, and design notes.

Large Bookshelf/Locked Cabinet

We suggest using a large cabinet or open bookshelf to store folded scraps or bolts of fabric on a few of the shelves, and to stack boxes of electronic parts ordered from SparkFun or elsewhere on other shelves. Consider keeping specialty electronics in their boxes from the manufacturer to protect them until they are used. Fill the shelves with stackable nested storage bins to keep materials handy. **Note:** While a locked cabinet can help to ensure that the materials are stored safely when not in use, it also can prohibit youths from experimenting with and finding a use for materials that would not be used otherwise, which is something you might want to encourage. Finding a way to balance these two objectives is key to inviting youths to play with the materials in a sustainable way.

Hardware and Craft Cabinets

Hardware and craft cabinets are smaller cabinets with multiple small drawers or bins for sorting and storing materials. These cabinets can be stored in your larger cabinet or on a bookshelf and are not meant to be portable. Rather, they should be used for storing extra supplies or those that are less frequently used.

More expensive but portable hardware and craft cabinets are available on wheels and can be used to move between rooms as needed.

As your materials arrive in the mail, it's important to organize, clearly label, and store them so that they can be accessed easily. This is particularly important because many components may look alike (for example, LEDs can look similar but have different colors and unique levels of resistance), and some components may be used less frequently than others. This can make it difficult, particularly for novices, to recall which component is which over time. A clear sorting and labeling system for incoming materials will pay off over the course of the workshops.

Hardware and craft cabinets with multiple drawers in various sizes can be a simple way to prevent later problems and are relatively inexpensive (at around $30). The drawers then can be labeled so that it's clear to your participants about what goes where. We also suggest placing information packets from the manufacturer in the same drawer as the supplies. What may seem like irrelevant information may come in handy as the complexity of the projects grows over time. The biggest caveat is to avoid the urge to throw disparate supplies together in a single bin. Rather, create a storage system and encourage the youths to place materials back in their appropriate places at the end of the session.

Soft Circuits Group Toolboxes

Small portable toolboxes are extremely useful to have prepacked for small groups of youths. We suggest creating one toolbox for every three to eight youths. Toolboxes allow for easy setup and cleanup for your workshops, since small groups can access what they need quickly, daily cleanup can be made simpler when everyone works to place group supplies back in his or her own toolbox.

You can find an array of toolboxes online and at your local crafting, arts, home improvement, and hardware stores. We suggest looking for larger toolboxes with handles, lift-out trays, small compartments (to store supplies like needles and LEDs), and places to store or hang oft-used tools, like scissors.

Your *Soft Circuits* group toolboxes should be packed with your low-cost, highly used, and reusable items. For example, consider packing the following in each group toolbox:

- Multimeter
- Fabric scissors
- Four to five small embroidery scissors to cut thread
- Tape measure
- Pincushion
- Sewing needles
- Spool of conductive thread

- Multiple spools of colored (nonconductive) thread
- Small scraps of conductive Velcro and conductive fabric
- Spare LEDs
- Multiple sets of alligator clips
- Fabric glue (to seal knots)
- Fabric markers or fabric chalk
- Conductive tape (for quick repairs)

CREATING WORKSTATIONS

In addition to thinking through the general storage of materials, consider creating multiple stations in your space so that youths can access tools and materials efficiently as they create their projects. At each station, it's useful to cluster tools and materials that are typically used together to save time searching for materials.

Glue Gun Station

A glue gun is a useful tool for many of the activities in this volume. However, the tools and surfaces for the glue gun require some special safety attention and warrant having a special station set up in your space. At this station, you will want to consider covering the surfaces in some way to protect them from excess glue. Consider using scraps of cardboard, an old sheet, or another thick, heat-resistant material to protect the surface of the station. Include stands for the glue guns and a method to turn off and on (or unplug) the glue gun easily to avoid leaving glue guns on longer than needed. Depending on your need for glue guns in our Design Challenges, you should consider having one available for every 3 to 10 youths, if possible.

Cutting Station

Another useful station is a cutting station. Ideally, this station should include a large, self-healing cutting mat, fabric scissors, rotating cutting knife, measuring tape and/or ruler, and fabric. The large cutting mat can be used to measure and cut large amounts of material. Clearly label the scissors that are meant to cut fabric as opposed to paper, and keep them near this station. While this station is probably most likely to be used by the educator or group leader, it's helpful to have this station set up so that youths can have a central location to access fabric shears (which could be attached to the station by a long piece of yarn to help youths remember not to take them elsewhere or to use on paper).

Ironing Station

An iron and ironing board are useful for multiple projects but are especially helpful for creating a flat surface for sewing by pressing out creases in fabric. While this station will be used less often, it can be helpful to have irons or ironing boards placed away from general work areas to avoid accidental burns.

Technology Hub

Many of the activities in this volume require some access to an Internet-based computer. While ideally it's nice to have one computer or laptop per youth, most of the work will be conducted offline, crafting or using physical materials in some way. Therefore, you may want to experiment to see if your group can share a smaller number of computers in one central area. Youths will use the computers to share their work with online communities (like Instructables.com or others suggested at the Interconnections website), conduct research for their projects, and program their wearable computers (i.e., their LilyPad Arduino Simple Boards). Flexible access to this station is important to the success of many of the design projects.

In addition to computers, consider having one or more dedicated digital cameras with photo and video capabilities, as well as universal serial bus (USB) cord(s) or SD card slots to download material to the computer, at your technology hub. Encourage youths to document and share their work regularly within the local community and online to a much wider audience.

Using Modkit or Arduino software, the computers can be used to program and reprogram how wearable computers behave—as demonstrated in the Design Challenges featuring LilyPad Arduino Simple Boards. Programming environments like Modkit connect with the different boards via USB cables, so be sure to have materials like a LilyPad Arduino Simple, mini USB cables, and FTDI Basic Breakout Boards at the computers for groups to share.

Gallery Space

A gallery space to display and share projects in progress informally is useful to have readily available for larger, whole-group sharing and critique, as well as smaller informal share-outs during work sessions. Often, our educators would make use of the central projector and dry-erase boards for this purpose. However, this also could be a smaller station set up in the corner of a room.

A document projector can be useful to demonstrate sewing techniques or to share the details on particular projects or processes to larger groups that may be difficult to see otherwise. Our educators also would use document cameras or the cameras in their laptops frequently to project makeshift demonstrations and videos to the group (for how to tie knots, thread your needle, make a running stitch, etc.).

BRINGING YOUR CIRCUITS TO LIFE

Throughout the *Soft Circuits* Design Challenges, there are two tools: the LilyPad Arduino Simple Board and a visual programming language used to program the LilyPad Arduino, which, used with an online community, help youths to turn their clothing and other creations into rich, dynamic artifacts and share their projects with the world. Modkit and the Interconnections website both are available for free and were designed with educational groups in mind. Modkit offers a free web-based environment and also has a low-cost desktop application for educators tailored for school settings. Modkit's Desktop application is described within the relevant Design Challenges. Take time to explore these tools to learn more about them and to figure out if there are any issues with account creation or restricted firewall access on your machines.

MODKIT MICRO

Modkit Micro (modkit.com) and ArduBlock (learn.sparkfun.com/ArduBlock) are graphical programming environments that can be used with the LilyPad Arduino Simple, as well as other Arduino microcontrollers, via browser or desktop application options. Traditionally, programming languages for the LilyPad Arduino and other Arduino microcontrollers have been text-based (building upon the Wiring language). However, the text-based nature of the Arduino language makes it difficult for novices to program their devices successfully. Hoping to lower the barriers to programming, Modkit Micro's design was inspired by the visual programming environment Scratch (scratch.mit. edu/), which replaces text with easy-to-use blocks of code that can be snapped into place. Youths who have prior experience with Scratch (see also the *Script Changers: Digital Storytelling with Scratch* volume in this collection) will recognize similar blocks when they begin to use Modkit Micro.

Modkit Micro allows youths to program the LilyPad Simple to control the LEDs, Buzzers, and other LilyPad components in different ways. For example, using Modkit Micro, you can tell the LEDs to blink, to light in a particular pattern, or to turn on (or off) in the presence of light. Modkit Micro employs simple graphical blocks that can be dragged and dropped to make scripts (though Modkit lets you see the program in a text-based language if you want to compare the code to the graphic blocks). For more information on how to get started with Modkit Micro, consult the website. Additional information about how to use this software to program your LilyPad, as well as additional support materials, are found in the *Soft Circuits* Design Challenges 3 and 4.

As a bonus feature for those who purchased this book, Modkit has provided a special help area on their website (modkit.com/softcircuits). There, you can find instructions for the version of Modkit used here, additional guides, videos of others creating projects from this book using Modkit, and other features.

SHARING PROJECTS IN AN ONLINE COMMUNITY

Social networks like Instructables.com allow people to document and share projects that blend electronics, crafts, and textiles. Giving youths a few minutes to post their projects on such a shared community allows them to become part of the larger participatory culture and share their work beyond the local community. Images and videos are useful additions to any project post, so be sure to have a digital camera available (ideally with photo and video capture capabilities). There are several worksheets integrated throughout the book to help guide youths in generating ideas for the project posts.

SIMPLE CIRCUITS

Getting started in this volume requires a basic understanding of simple circuits, which are described here but also presented in greater depth throughout the Design Challenges in this volume. At its simplest, a circuit is a continuous loop through which electricity can travel. All circuits have a *power source*—in this volume, youths will use 9V batteries, 3V coin cell batteries, and rechargeable LiPo ion batteries. In addition, circuits may include *outputs* (such as lights or speakers) and *inputs* (such as switches or sensors). In designing a circuit, the goal is to guide the electricity out of the battery, through any components (like lights or switches), and then back to the battery.

One of the simplest circuits you can make consists only of a battery and a light, as shown here.

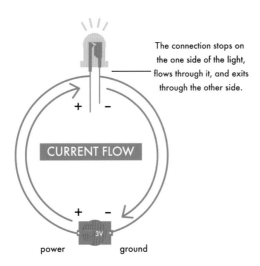

The connection stops on the one side of the light, flows through it, and exits through the other side.

Note Batteries and LEDs have a "positive" and a "negative" side. The positive side is also known as "+" or "power," and the negative side can also be called "−"or "ground."

In the figure shown here, the solid lines represent electrical connections between components made with some sort of wire,

alligator clips, or (in the case of an e-textile circuit) conductive thread. The arrows indicate the direction in which electricity is flowing through the circuit. You always should make connections from the positive end of one component to the positive end of another, and from negative to negative ends. If positive and negative connections ever touch or cross, this will result in a *short circuit.* To remind yourself and the youths of these rules, teach them the mantra, "positive to positive and negative to negative."

If your circuit looks like this:

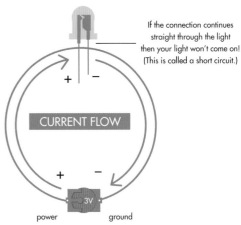

If the connection continues straight through the light then your light won't come on! (This is called a short circuit.)

then your light will not turn on. This is another example of a short circuit. It occurs because the wire between the positive and negative legs of the LED makes it easier for the electrical current to cross there, rather than moving through the LED itself. This is a common mistake when sewing a circuit in e-textiles.

E-TEXTILE CIRCUITS

Here is an example of this same circuit with LilyPad components and conductive thread.

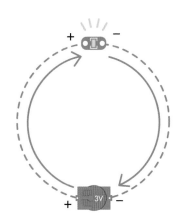

The LED is now a sewable LilyPad LED, and the wire is depicted in the figure as dotted lines where conductive thread would be sewn into the circuit.

Adding a Switch

In the simple e-textile circuit pictured above, you can turn the light on or off only by inserting and removing the battery from its holder. Adding a switch provides more control, and the battery can stay in its holder.

Here's how a switch works: a switch is simply any break in the circuit that can open and close.

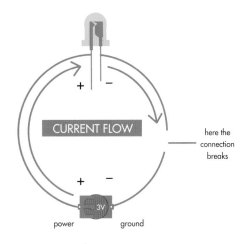

In this picture, the LED won't light up because there is a break in the circuit that prevents electricity from flowing all the way through the circuit and back to the battery. Adding a switch at that spot is similar to closing and opening the break in the circuit (and turning on the light) when you either push a button or slide a switch from "off" to "on."

If you were to sew a circuit with a button switch into fabric, it would look like this when you are not pressing the button:

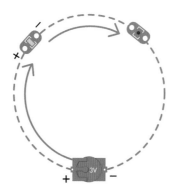

And it would look like this when the button is pressed:

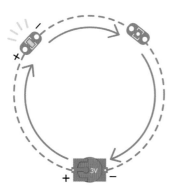

Note Switches don't have positive or negative sides, so it doesn't matter in which direction you place one within your circuit.

BEYOND THE BASICS

You can experiment with more complicated circuits by adding more lights and different kinds of switches. To add more lights, you'll need to arrange them "in parallel." For example, this could mean that the first light's positive end is connected to the second light's positive end. Likewise, the first light's negative end should be connected to the second light's negative end. Alternatively, all the lights could be in parallel to the circuit's energy source, as also depicted here. In this way, you can include several LEDs in your design. For more information on placing circuits in parallel, see later Design Challenges in this book.

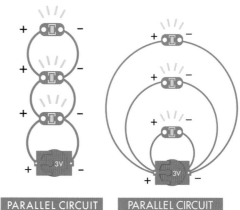

PARALLEL CIRCUIT   PARALLEL CIRCUIT

ESSENTIAL STITCH CRAFT

The types of e-textile Design Challenges found in both *Short Circuits* and *Soft Circuits* require basic hand-stitching skills. This section of the book contains various methods for threading needles (both traditional and self-threading), tying secure knots, and basic sewing stitches. We provide some diversity here in the techniques, as we've found that different tips resonate with different people. Once you find techniques that work for your group, feel free to ignore the rest. It's essential to take a few minutes to practice these basic techniques with youths to be sure that most, if not all, are able to sew independently. These sections can be shared with youths, but similar materials and information appear throughout the Design Challenges.

THREADING A NEEDLE

HOW TO DOUBLE-THREAD A TRADITIONAL NEEDLE

1. Cut a piece of thread about two to three feet in length.

2. Use one hand to pinch the thread very close to the end and put the short bristle of thread on the eye of the needle.

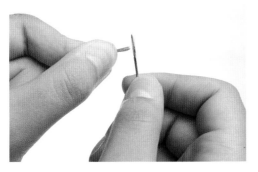

3. Pull the loose end through the eye of the needle until both ends of the thread meet and are equal in length.

4. If you have a problem threading the needle, beeswax could be used on the thread to help keep it from fraying, or try using a needle threader (see additional tips on using a needle threader later in this chapter).

5. If the thread is still fraying, trim off the frayed thread at a 45-degree angle and try again.

HOW TO DOUBLE-THREAD A CLOVER SELF-THREADING NEEDLE

Self-threading needles add an extra expense to a project but can save a lot of time, especially if you or any members of your group have poor eyesight, or if you are working with large groups. We recommend Clover self-threading needles, especially when working with conductive thread, as not all brands work well with that thread. When using self-threading needles, the thread pulls down over a bridge at the top of the needle (depicted visually here in three steps) and is not threaded through the eye of the needle.

1. Place your pincushion on a hard surface. Then put the self-threading needle in the pincushion pointing straight up to steady it.

2. Cut a piece of thread to about two to three feet in length.

3. Find the approximate center of the piece of thread.

4. Pinch the thread with your thumbs and forefingers in two places about an inch apart from one another (similarly to how you might floss your teeth).

5. Place the thread over the top notch of the needle (the "bridge" of the needle), as shown in the picture.

6. Pull down firmly on the thread, and it should snap down into the eye of the needle.

7. Move the thread back and forth within the eye to make sure all of the thread went through the passage (it should move freely back and forth). If not, remove the thread and try again. If it's stuck badly on the needle, you may need to cut your thread and begin again.

Important notes: Do not pull the thread any further down than the first eye! The second eye is not intended for use. Remember that self-threading needles are more delicate and should not be forced through the fabric or your e-textile components, as this could break the eye of the needle.

THREADING A NEEDLE WITH CONDUCTIVE THREAD

Some conductive thread tends to fray easily. Before pulling the thread through the eye of the needle, try pulling the thread taut and snip off the end at a 45-degree angle to give it a sharper point. Use a small amount of water, beeswax, or saliva to dampen the end of the thread, bringing the end of the thread to a point. Then take the needle in one hand, feed the thread slowly through the eye of the needle with the other hand, and pull the thread through.

USING A NEEDLE THREADER

You can use a needle threader to help pull the thread through a small needle eye. This can be used for conductive and non-conductive thread, but it is particularly useful for four-ply thread, which is the thickest of the conductive threads that we recommend.

1. Insert the wire of the threader completely through the eye of the needle.

2. Feed the thread through the wire loop.

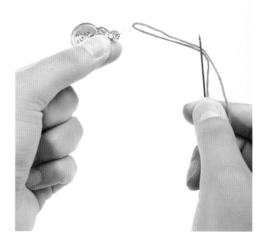

3. Then pull the needle threader back out the eye of the needle, bringing the conductive thread with it.

4. Even out the two ends of the thread so they are of equal length and prepare to tie your knot.

TYING KNOTS

Youths will need to learn how to tie knots at the start and end of their stitching lines. In e-textiles, you will need to tie knots more frequently than you would in a regular sewing or crafting project, so these techniques are particularly important to the group's productivity. We list several techniques here for tying knots, but you might want to use one technique and stick to it, as switching between techniques can add confusion for novices.

TYING BEGINNING KNOTS

Quilter's Trick

This tip comes from a quilting instructor and is consistent and very easy!

1. Once your needle is threaded, double up the thread by pulling the two ends of the thread together so that they are equal lengths to create the appearance of one thread.

2. Lay the needle and thread on the table in front of you to create a circle, with the ends of the thread facing the tip of the needle.

3. Pick up the threads and pull them toward the tip of your needle, overlapping the two just a bit.

4. Leaving a small tail at the ends of the threads, begin coiling the threads as a single unit around the needle (and toward the tip) two to three times (the more you wrap, the larger the knot will be).

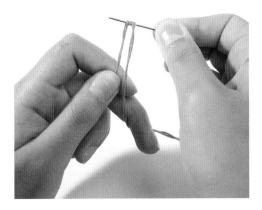

5. Pinch and hold the wrapped thread in place with one hand, then gently pull the coiled thread over the needle eye and continue down the length of the thread.

6. You have a knot!

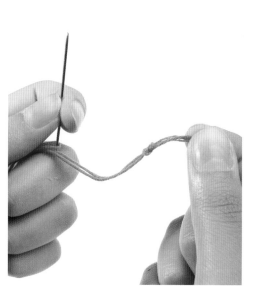

7. Trim the tail of the knot to leave about a 1/8- to 1/4-inch length of thread. Tails that are too long can cause problems with sewing and could cause shorts in conductive thread, while tails that are too short may cause your knot to come undone.

8. Remember to secure your knot with nail polish, fabric glue, or a low-temperature glue gun to keep it from unraveling (see later in this section).

Tying a Traditional Roll Knot

1. Once your needle is threaded, double up the thread by pulling the two ends of the thread together to be equal lengths to create the appearance of one thread.

2. Wrap the thread around your left index finger, crossing the threads in the middle of the index finger to make an X, with the tail of the thread facing your hand (this is where the knot will be).

3. Cover the X with your left thumb.

4. Then roll the thread between your thumb and forefinger until it rolls off the end of your finger.

5. Continue to roll the thread and use your middle finger to steady and tighten the knot while sliding it down to the end of the thread. Pull the thread tight with your right hand.

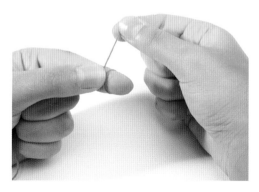

6. You have a knot!

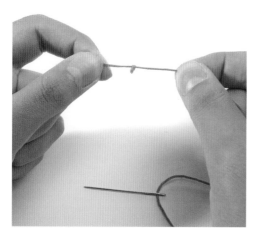

7. Trim the tail of the knot to leave about a 1/8- to 1/4-inch length of thread. Tails that are too long can cause problems with sewing and could cause shorts in conductive thread, while tails that are too short may cause your knot to come undone.

8. Remember to secure your knot with nail polish, fabric glue, or a low-temperature glue gun to keep it from unraveling (see later in this section).

Tying a Circle Knot

We have developed this technique (based on the traditional roll knot) during our workshops and have found it to be easier for younger participants.

1. Once your needle is threaded, lay your threaded needle on the table in front of you in a straight line. (Note that the images depicted here are of a single-threaded needle, not a double-threaded needle as we recommend. The same knotting technique can be used in both cases.)

2. Take the tail of the thread(s) and create a small circle.

3. Move the tail of the thread(s) through the inside of the circle. Although doing this once will work, if it's repeated two or three times to coil the thread around the circle, you'll create a bigger knot that is less likely to pull through your fabric.

4. Pull the needle and thread with one hand and pull the tail to close the circle with your other hand.

5. You have a knot!

6. Trim the tail of the knot to leave about a 1/8- to 1/4-inch length of thread. Tails that are too long can cause problems with sewing and could cause

shorts in conductive thread, while tails that are too short may cause your knot to come undone.

7. Remember to secure your knot with nail polish, fabric glue, or a low-temperature glue gun to keep it from unraveling (see later in this section).

ENDING KNOTS

For Double-Threaded Needles Only (Like Those Suggested Previously)

1. Stop sewing so you have a few inches of thread left before running out.

2. Cut the thread right below the eye of the needle (or if you have long threads, give yourself at least a couple inches of thread from the fabric to work with).

3. There are now two threads.

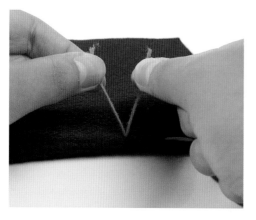

4. Make an X with the threads.

5. Bring one of the threads down and wrap it around the other thread, and pull the threads tight (similar to the first steps in tying your shoe).

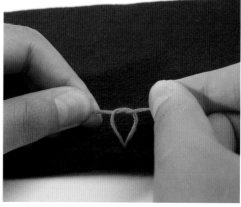

6. Repeat the last two steps.

7. Now you have a knot very close to the fabric!

8. Trim the tail of the knot to leave about a 1/8- to 1/4-inch length of thread. Tails that are too long can cause problems with sewing and could cause shorts in conductive thread, while tails that are too short may cause your knot to come undone.

9. Remember to secure your knot with nail polish, fabric glue, or a low-temperature glue gun to keep it from unraveling (see later in this section).

For Either Double- or Single-Threaded Needles

1. Take your needle and slip it under an existing stitch to form a loop.

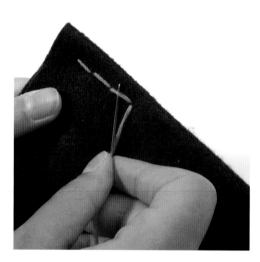

2. Guide your needle through the loop and tighten.

3. Repeat steps 1 and 2 two or three more times.

4. Now you have a knot very close to the fabric!

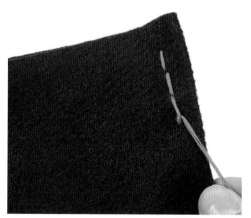

5. Trim the tail of the knot to leave about a 1/8- to 1/4-inch length of thread. Tails that are too long can cause problems with sewing and could cause shorts in conductive thread, while tails that are too short may cause your knot to come undone.

6. Remember to secure your knot with nail polish, fabric glue, or a low-temperature glue gun to keep it from unraveling (see later in this section).

SECURING KNOTS

Conductive thread knots are known to come undone. Here are a couple of suggestions to keep your knot tied and to help prevent your stitches from pulling out. You can use clear nail polish, fabric glue, or a low-temperature glue gun to do this.

Securing Beginning Knots: Glue or Polish

After you tie the *beginning knot* in your threaded needle (but before you start sewing), put a dab of clear nail polish or fabric glue on it.

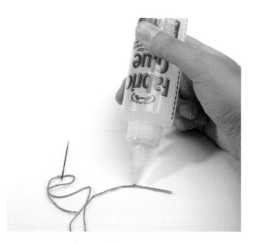

Blow it dry, and now it's ready to start stitching beneath your fabric. Remember to start your stitching on the opposite side of the fabric from your components to help prevent shorts!

Securing Ending Knots: Glue or Polish

For the ending knot, put just a dab of nail polish on the knot. Don't soak the thread or materials with nail polish, as it could damage it.

Securing Knots: Glue Gun

After the beginning knot is sewn in (on the backside of the fabric), put a dot of hot glue on it. Repeat the same on the end knot (on the backside of the fabric).

Note When using clear nail polish, limit the quantity. Youths mistakenly seem to believe that more is better, but it's not in this case. If saturation happens, the following bad outcomes will result:

- The material will become stiff and difficult to sew through.
- The conductive thread will harden, lowering its conductivity.
- If the electronics sew hole is coated with nail polish, the polish will act as an insulator on the metal, and a solid connection (thread to metal) won't be made.

STITCHES

Basic Running Stitch

The running stitch is an excellent stitch to use with novices and is particularly good to use when crafting soft circuits because it can be removed easily (as opposed to backstitching or other more decorative stitching techniques). To get started, perform the following steps:

1. Stick your needle through the fabric from back to front (this will hide the knot).

2. Pull the thread through until the knot is firm against the backside of your fabric.

3. Now, move your needle about 1/8 inch along the path that you'll be sewing and bring your needle through the fabric again, but from front to back.

4. You've just made your first stitch!

5. Repeat by bringing your needle from back to front, then front to back. Make sure to pull your thread taut each time you move your needle through the fabric to avoid unwanted lengths of thread, which can tangle or cause shorts when working with conductive thread.

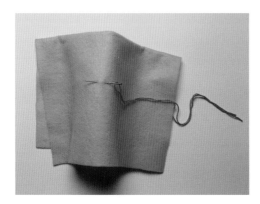

6. Keep stitches even and close to one another to prevent stitches from being snagged or touching another thread, either of which may cause a short when working with conductive thread.

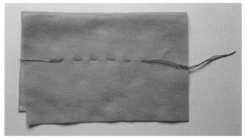

Other Stitches

There are a variety of other stitches that you can explore as your group gains more comfort with hand sewing, including the backstitch. However, we suggest that you refrain from introducing these techniques until the group becomes more familiar with hand sewing and e-textiles, as these techniques become more likely to tangle the thread and are more difficult to undo when you've made a mistake.

Stitching Tips

Youths may struggle at first with sewing, especially with conductive thread. No worries—if they're patient, they'll get used to the thread's behavior quickly. For instance, if the thread gets into a knot, they should not pull it tight, but patiently untangle it using a needle to pull the knot apart.

If stitching continues to be difficult for youths, try one or more of the following:

- Use fabric chalk to mark the dotted path that your needle should follow. It should brush off easily, but if not, wash your fabric with some water. Fabric markers (a more permanent mark) also can be used to sketch the path and even provide dots for even stitches between components.

- Keep stitches relatively close together. This will help the design to hold up better over time.

- For speed, slip your needle in and out of the fabric several times before pulling the thread through. Also try folding the fabric accordion-style to make it even easier to make multiple stitches at once. This is a more advanced technique, but it might be useful to introduce to your group early in the process.

- Use the "Running Stitch Practice" worksheet (found in Design Challenge 2 of this volume) to practice your stitching techniques by connecting the dots with nonconductive thread. Youths then can add their own dots and stitches to complete the diagram. As an extra challenge beads, buttons, and sequins can be incorporated into the design to help the youths think about using the thread to fasten physical objects to paper or fabric using nonconductive thread.

ESSENTIAL E-TEXTILES TIPS

The following list includes more advanced e-textiles tips than youths will need at first. We recommend that you return to this section once you have started working on your first project—most of this information will make little sense out of context. In addition, there are many more hints throughout each of the Design Challenges.

CUTTING CONDUCTIVE THREAD, CONDUCTIVE FABRIC, AND OTHER CONDUCTIVE MATERIALS

Always try to cut these materials in a spot that's away from your fabric or project, as small conductive "whiskers" will be released that could cause invisible problems in the circuit later.

CREATING SOLID CONNECTIONS

When you arrive at a component in your soft circuit, be sure to sew the thread through each sew hole *two to three times*, if possible, to ensure a solid connection between the petal and the conductive thread. A loose or dangling connection means that you've not completed the loop in your circuit. You should add these extra loops to the hardware only (rather than stitching through the fabric); extra stitches through the fabric will hold the hardware in place more securely, but if the stitches need to be removed during troubleshooting, they can cause more problems. If you find loose connections, consider using your glue gun to secure them better.

USING GLASS BEADS, PUFFY PAINT, AND OTHER MATERIALS TO INSULATE CONDUCTIVE THREAD

If your design requires you to cross the positive (Power) or negative (Ground) stitching lines, there are ways to avoid creating a short circuit:

1. Use rounded glass beads to insulate the conductive thread and raise the connection a safe distance above the other line. Avoid sharp-edged glass beads, particularly bugles, as they tend to fray the conductive thread. You also can use glass beads to help insulate the thread to prevent it from slowly tarnishing over time.

2. Other materials will insulate the thread as well, including puffy paint (remember to allow for drying time), hot glue, or other beads made from wood or plastic.

SHORT ON TIME TO SEW?

Instead of sewing the entire circuit, youths can use hot glue to run conductive thread between electric components if they don't have enough time to sew everything. If this method is chosen, it's important to sew the components in place first to get a solid connection. BONUS! The glue from the glue gun can help to insulate the thread as well. See also the additional stitching tips given previously to help speed up the hand-sewing process.

GETTING CREATIVE!

Think outside the box! One quick hint for youths is that stitched lines of conductive thread don't need to be straight to be functional. Once you've designed the layout for your circuit, you can connect your components by sewing interesting patterns or shapes. The Silly Bandz craze (involving rubber-band bracelets formed into shapes like hearts, stars, bones, etc.), taught us that there are lots of ways to create a loop other than a simple circle. Experiment with fun and curving shapes as you sew your conductive thread!

TROUBLESHOOTING TIPS

Each Design Challenge contains a list of specific debugging tips—things to look for if your circuits don't work. The following list is a general "quick list" checklist that you might want to bookmark for reference for all your simple circuit projects.

- *Check the battery power:* Take out the battery and straddle it with an LED, matching the positive leg to the positive side (printed side of a 3V battery)

and the negative leg to the negative side.

- *Check for polarity:* Make sure that the (+) sides of the LEDs are oriented toward the (+) end of the battery holder. Similarly, make sure that the (–) sides of the LEDs are connected to the (–) end of the battery holder.

- *Check for crossed lines:* Make sure that no two lines are touching in the design, as this will cause a short.

- *Check for solid connections*: Make sure that the conductive thread has been sewn around the component two or more times and the component is not dangling from the project.

- *Check the LEDs:* Make sure that none of the LEDs have been sewn through in a way that connects the positive to the negative end of the LED.

- *Check for frayed stitches:* Make sure that none of the stitching has been cut accidentally or has frayed. If you're unsure and have a multimeter, check the continuity of the lines. It will beep if there is a continuous connection between any two points in your circuit using the two probes. If it doesn't beep and you still have a problem, then look for a shorted or frayed conductive thread line.

- *Check for any loose strands of conductive thread:* Be sure to check the back of the project! Affix any dangling pieces (your glue gun is an easy way to tie things down) so that they are out of the way and not touching other conductive components.

- *Check your parallel circuits:* If you used more than one LED, are the LEDs sewn in parallel? (If not, the 3V battery will not have enough power to light more than one LED.)

- *Check your LED color choices:* Have you mixed the colors of your LEDs? Are only some LEDs (like the red LEDs) illuminating? If so, don't worry; your circuit is probably working, but your battery just doesn't have enough voltage to light all the LEDs in the current design. Consider removing some LEDs (such as those at the higher end of the light spectrum, like whites, blues, and greens) from your project.

ESSENTIAL DIY ELECTRONICS

In this section, we describe some essential techniques for your electronic equipment. These sections can be shared with youths, but similar materials and information appear as tips throughout the Design Challenges. In addition, this section contains how-tos for creating your own sewable electronics, which can be modded (modified) for use in various projects.

MULTIMETER BASICS

Your multimeter can be used to measure a variety of invisible properties of electronics, including *resistance, current*, and *voltage*. You also can use your multimeter to help debug the stitching in your project to find unintentional breaks in your circuit. Here are just a few benefits of the multimeter; but see the additional tips presented throughout the Design Challenges.

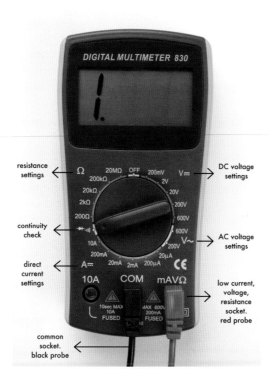

How to Measure Resistance in Materials (Using the Continuity Setting)

Are you wondering whether a material or object is conductive enough to use in your circuit? You can use your digital multimeter to check. Set the multimeter to Continuity mode (look for the image that looks like sound coming from a speaker if you're using the SparkFun Digital Multimeter recommended in this book). Now touch the probes together. The multimeter should emit a high-pitched tone. This shows that a very small amount of current is flowing successfully, with little or no resistance between probes. In testing a new material, touch the two probes to the surface. If current can flow between the negative and positive probes, you'll hear the multimeter emit a tone, indicating that the material has a low resistance and can be incorporated easily into your circuit. Note that the numbers on your meter show the degree of resistance in the material (some materials will have more than others). See also the "How Do I Use a Multimeter?" worksheet found in Design Challenge 1.

How to Test for Continuity in a Conductive Thread Line

At times, you might wonder whether the stitching has been cut or broken between two points in your circuit. You can use your digital multimeter to check. To get started, set the multimeter to Continuity mode. Place one probe at one end of a thread line and the other probe at the other end; you should hear a tone indicating that they are connected. If it does not emit a tone, then you can begin to trace the route by moving the probes along it to check if there are breaks, frays, or shorts in the thread line.

Measuring Voltage of a Battery

You also may be wondering whether your battery has enough power to light the LEDs or run the other components in your circuit. To find out, you'll need to measure its voltage. For example, to measure voltage on a LiPo battery, perform the following steps:

- Pull out your digital multimeter and make sure the black probe is plugged into the COM (common) jack and the red probe is plugged into mAVΩ.

- Set the multimeter to 20V in the DC range (DC is a straight line, while AC is the wavy line).

- Squeeze the probes with a little pressure against the positive and negative plastic terminals of the LiPo battery. The black probe is customarily connected to the ground or negative (–)

TOOLKIT | 81

side of the battery and the red probe to the positive or (+) side of the battery.

- The reading on the multimeter will tell you the remaining voltage on your battery.

Remember, if the battery loses too much of its voltage, it will be unable to light your LEDs or power your other components!

Measuring Current

Sometimes you may wish to know how much current is flowing through your circuit or through one of your circuit's components. To measure current, you must put your multimeter in *series* with your circuit, as follows:

- First, make sure the multimeter's black probe is plugged into the COM (common) jack and the red probe is plugged into mAVΩ.
- Set the multimeter to 20mA (or 200mA if you're expecting a stronger current).
- Disconnect your circuit at the point where you wish to measure the current (near the battery for measuring the current flowing through the whole circuit, and past a component if you have a circuit wired in parallel and you wish to measure the current flowing through that component). Close the newly made gap in the circuit with one probe from the multimeter on each side of the gap. (You may wish to use alligator clips to

connect the multimeter probes to your circuit to hold the probes in place.)

Note that measuring current through an e-textile circuit that has already been sewn down may be prohibitively difficult due to the necessity of disconnecting the circuit. Instead, consider measuring current on an incomplete sewn circuit.

TESTING YOUR COIN CELL (3V) BATTERIES AND LEDS

Testing Your 3V Battery

You can test your 3V coin cell battery quickly to see if it has been shorted by taking a two-pin LED (that you know to be working) and holding it directly on the 3V battery. Make sure that you place the longer of the two pins on the positive (printed) side of the battery and the shorter of the two on the negative side of the battery. If the LED illuminates, you have a working battery! It's important to note that it takes different levels of voltage to light different colors; for example, a red LED takes less voltage to light than does a blue LED. This is because the amount of voltage needed to light an LED depends on the light's wavelength. So be careful to test the battery with the appropriate LED(s) for your project.

Testing an LED with Your Coin Cell Battery

Similarly, there are several reasons that you may want to check your two-pin LEDs, including to check what color your LEDs are and to see if the LED is burned out (in case it was overloaded at some point). Grab a 3V coin cell battery that you know to be working and hold the LED's pins on either side of the battery to see whether your LED is working and what color it is. Make sure that you place the longer of the two pins against the positive (printed) side of the battery and the shorter pin against the negative side of the battery.

Note This is one of the simplest circuits you can make: a great activity to share with youths!

DIY SEWABLE ELECTRONICS

MAKING DIY SEWABLE LEDS

Creating your own sewable LEDs from standard two-pin LEDs is quite easy and cost effective. Here are a few simple steps to guide your process:

1. Bend the positive leg (i.e., the longer leg) out 90 degrees at a right angle.

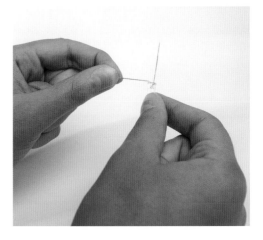

2. Curl the leg around needlenose pliers to form a spiral-like loop that you can sew through.

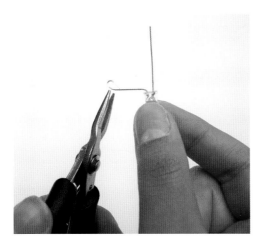

polarity with a flat spot on the negative leg side of the LED bulb.

3. Bend the second leg (i.e., the shorter negative leg) out 90 degrees in the other direction.

What If You Mix Up the Two Pins After They Are Bent?

Use your alligator clips to create a simple circuit, connecting your LED to your 3V battery in its holder. If it doesn't light, then try switching sides. Then use a permanent marker to mark the positive leg of the LED so you don't mix them up again.

Are These DIY Sewable LEDs Hand-Washable Too?

Yes, they are!

Are You Ready for More DIY Sewable Electronics?

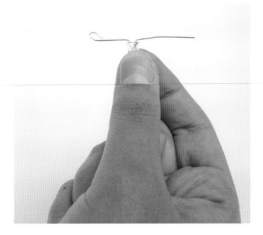

4. Consider bending this leg into either a triangle or square shape to distinguish it from the positive leg. Alternatively, you can use a permanent marker to mark the positive loop (as seen in the photo), and some LEDs indicate the

In the companion volume of this book collection, *Soft Circuits,* we provide two additional ideas for creating sewable electronics: a DIY switch for turning a circuit on and off, and a DIY battery holder. Look for these two optional e-fashion crafting ideas in Design Challenge 3 of *Soft Circuits*: ElectriciTee!

DESIGN CHALLENGE OVERVIEWS

CONTENTS

DESIGN CHALLENGE 1: INTRODUCTION TO THE ELECTRONIC CIRCUIT

Total time: 105 minutes

The goal of the first Design Challenge is to familiarize youths with several vital notions about systems. Youths will be introduced to the idea of electronic circuits as systems and learn to identify a system's components (e.g., load, energy sources, and wire), behaviors (e.g., conductor versus resistor), and intended goals [e.g., to power a light-emitting diode (LED)], as well as the fact that a system's overall function depends on its interconnections (i.e., the interactions among components and their behaviors). They also will experiment with creating a simple electronic circuit in order to light up an LED, and learn how balancing feedback loops can help them make the most of the limited resources in their circuits.

DESIGN CHALLENGE 2: E-TEXTILE CUFFS

Total time: 310 minutes

The goal of this Design Challenge is to explore how a system's structure determines specific component behaviors and larger system dynamics, or interconnections, in the context of e-textile tools and materials. Youths will experiment with different circuit structures and battery voltages to discover how circuits can be structured both in series and in parallel. They then will apply this understanding to the design and development of an electronic cuff or bracelet and are challenged to imagine, investigate, create, and write about their process.

DESIGN CHALLENGE 3: ELECTRICITEE

Total time: 345–435 minutes

In this Design Challenge, youths are introduced to the concept of nested systems—systems that have their own structure but also work together to form a new system. They will explore multiple systems (a unique T-shirt design, an electronic circuit, and a computer programming language), and examine how the goals and interconnections of one system affect others in the context of e-textiles. Activities incorporate a microcontroller and extend circuitry knowledge from previous Design Challenges, as well as introduce youths to the basics of fashion design and computer programming.

DESIGN CHALLENGE 4: SOLAR-POWERED BACKPACK

Total time: 490 minutes

Continuing prior explorations of limited (energy) resources in systems, youths learn about using alternative energy to create a backpack embedded with a flexible solar panel. Batteries with long lifespans often relegate conversations about energy being a limited resource to the sidelines; however, powering objects with alternative energy sources—such as water, wind, or solar—allows for a view into the systemic nature of energy, where it comes from, and how it can best be preserved. Youths explore the concepts of stocks and flows and dynamic equilibrium in play-based activities before creating and sharing their solar-powered backpacks (both in class and online).

DESIGN CHALLENGE 1 INTRODUCTION TO THE ELECTRONIC CIRCUIT

Total time: 105 minutes

OVERVIEW

The goal of this challenge is to familiarize youths with the notion that all systems are made up of components, that each component has a specific set of behaviors, and that the way that a system functions depends on the interconnections among its components. In this challenge, they will be introduced to the idea of electronic circuits as systems and will learn to identify the system's components (e.g., load, energy source, and wire), behaviors (e.g., conductor versus resistor), intended goals (e.g., to turn on a light-emitting diode [LED]), and an overall function that depends on the system's interconnections (i.e., the interactions among the components and their behaviors in the system). Youths will experiment to create a simple electronic circuit in order to light up an LED. In addition, youths will learn how balancing feedback loops can help them make the most of limited resources in their circuits. **Note:** This first challenge is duplicated in both books on circuitry: this book and *Short Circuits: Crafting e-Puppetry with DIY Electronics.*

PRODUCT

Construct and diagram a simple circuit.

TARGETED SYSTEMS THINKING CONCEPTS

An electronic circuit is one example of a system made up of a collection of components (each with unique behaviors) that work together to send power to an object. For a circuit to work, components must be set up in a particular way (structure), which determines their specific behaviors and interconnections with other components that make up the overall functioning of the system. Circuits are structured in particular ways to meet an explicit goal (for example, to light an LED). In doing so, circuits use the energy in a battery as a limited resource. Discerning the circuit's current state and using processes to move the circuit toward a desired goal state involve the process of balancing feedback loops.

PARTS

PART 1: LIGHT ME!

Youths will be challenged to illuminate an LED by tinkering with different arrangements of a battery, conductive fabric, and alligator clips. A discussion about the components, behaviors, goals, and interconnections within a circuit will help them see a circuit as an example of a system. A "human circuit role play" helps them model their understanding through embodied play, and a reflection activity follows.

Time: 50 minutes

PART 2: LEARNING ABOUT CONDUCTIVITY AND RESISTANCE

Youths will use multimeters on a variety of objects to learn how electric current passes through material. They will work together to guess which materials act as conductors and which act as insulators, learning about conductivity and resistance in the process. Finally, they will build circuits with little to no resistance to learn about limited energy resources, short circuits, and balancing feedback loops.

Time: 55 minutes

KEY DEFINITIONS

SYSTEMS THINKING

Identifying a system. Identifying a system and distinguishing it from other kinds of things that aren't systems. Specifically, a system is a collection of two or more *components* and processes that interconnect to *function* as a whole. Speed and comfort in a car for example are created by the interactions of the car's parts and thus are "greater than the sum" of all separate parts of the car. The way a system works is not the result of a single part but is produced by the *interaction* among the components and/or individual agents within it. A key way to differentiate things that are systems from things that aren't is to consider whether the overall way something works in the world will change if you remove one part of it.

Identify the way a system is functioning. The *function* of a system describes the overall behavior of the system—what it's doing or where it's going over time. A system's function might emerge naturally based on interconnections among components, or it might be the result of an intentional design (in which case, we also might refer to the function of a system as its *goal*). Regardless, the function of a system is the result of the dynamics that occur among components' interconnected behaviors.

Identifying components. Identifying the parts of a system that contribute to its functioning. Components have certain qualities and/or behaviors that determine how they interconnect with other components, as well as define their role in the system. Without being able to effectively identify the parts of a system, it's hard to understand how a system is actually functioning and how it might be changed.

Identifying behaviors. Identifying the specific actions, roles, or behaviors that a component of a system displays under various conditions. Being able to identify behaviors becomes important when we change systems, as often a component will look the same after the change, but its behavior will be different.

Identifying interconnections. Identifying the different ways that a system's parts, or *components,* interact with each other through their *behaviors,* and through those interactions, change the behaviors of other components.

Perceiving dynamics. Perceiving a system's dynamics involves looking at a higher level at how the system works. Dynamics in a system are often characterized by circles—patterns that "feed back" on another. These are called feedback loops. Understanding dynamics gives insights into the mechanisms and relationships that are at the core of a system and can be leveraged to create systemic changes.

Designing a system. Creating a system through engaging in an iterative design process, one that entails iterative cycles of feedback, troubleshooting, and testing. One of the most effective means of developing systems thinking is to regularly create and iterate on the design of systems, and doing so in a way that creates opportunities for students to think about generic systems models that apply across multiple domains and settings.

Distinguishing the goal of a system. The goal of the system is what a system that was intentionally designed is intended to do. Sometimes this might be the same as the functioning of the system ... other times the goal and the *function* are not aligned. A given system might have multiple goals or purposes that are at play simultaneously, and come into conflict. Being able to understand system purpose or goal gives a sense of the ideal state of a system from a particular perspective.

Balancing feedback loops. Relationships where two or more elements of a system keep each other in balance, with one (or more) elements leading to increase, and one (or more) elements leading to decrease. These processes keep a system at the desired state of equilibrium, the system goal. Usually, balancing feedback processes stabilize systems by limiting or preventing certain processes from happening. Having a sense of how balancing feedback loops operate can give a person a sense of what will make a system stable.

Limited resources. In any system, it is important to understand which resources are finite (i.e., will run out at a certain point). Keeping in mind which resources are limited helps people make decisions about how best to maximize resources.

CIRCUITRY

Conductor. A material through which electric current flows easily.

Conductivity. The degree to which a material conducts electricity.

Electronic circuit/circuit. The unbroken path(s) capable of carrying an electric current (i.e., a "loop").

Electric current. A flow of electric charge through a medium (e.g., wire, conductive fabric, or LED).

Current flow. The rate at which an electric charge passes through a point in the circuit.

Load. A device (like a lightbulb or motor) that requires electric current passing through it to give it power.

Resistance. A measure of how difficult it is to "push" current through a circuit. A *resistor* is a component in a circuit that limits, but doesn't stop, the flow of electric current.

Short circuit (or "short"). A low-resistance connection between the two sides of the battery, causing the energy of a battery to drain or terminate completely.

COMMON CORE STATE STANDARDS	NEXT GENERATION SCIENCE STANDARDS
• W.6–12.2 (anchor standard)	• 3-PS2–3
• W.6–8.3	• MS-PS2–3
• RST.6–8.4	• 4-PS3–2
• RST.6–8.7	• 3–5-ETS1–1
• RST.11–12.9	• 3–5-ETS1–2
• SL.6–12.4 (anchor standard)	• MS-ETS1–2

MATERIALS OVERVIEW

Find electronics at **www.sparkfun.com/Interconnections**. For each youth, you will need to create ahead of time a Circuit Kit that consists of a zip-closed bag filled with the following system components:

- A 3V or "coin cell" battery
- 2 alligator clips
- 1 piece of conductive fabric (to be cut in half)
- 1 LED light, either a two-pronged LED or a LilyPad Arduino[1] LED

For each group, you will need to create a Conductivity Kit, which is a container filled with the following:

- A variety of conductive and nonconductive materials, such as paper clips, conductive fabric, buttons, pencils, fabric, tinsel, coins, etc.

ADDITIONAL MATERIALS

- Digital projector
- Scissors
- Design journals (1 per youth)
- Multimeters (1 per group)
- Extra 3V batteries

- Sticky notes or 3" x 5" note cards with tape

- Graphite pencils

- Paper

- Distilled water

- Salt

- Conductive fabric

- Conductive thread

HANDOUTS

- "System of the Electronic Circuit"

- "An Electronic Circuit: An Example of a System"

- "How Do I Use a Multimeter?"

- "Tracing Current Flow"

OVERALL CHALLENGE PREPARATION

- Familiarize yourself with how a circuit works and is connected by referring to the "An Electronic Circuit: A System" worksheet, as well as additional resources on circuits and electricity in Appendix B.

- Familiarize yourself with how a battery works by using some of the additional resources in Appendix B.

- Familiarize yourself with the multimeter using the "How Do I Use a Multimeter?" handout.

- Create a sample connected LED circuit (see "Part 1: Light Me!").

- Prepare the sticky notes or 3" x 5" cards for the Human Circuit Role Play activity (see "Part 2: Learning about Conductivity").

- Prepare a Circuit Kit for each youth.

- Prepare a Conductivity Kit for each group.

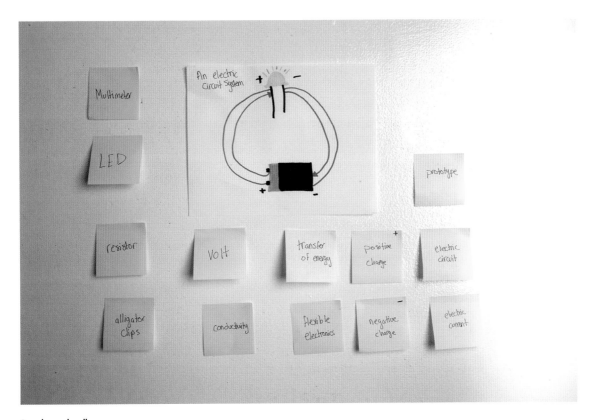

Sample word wall.

- Setting up a word wall can be helpful for integrating essential vocabulary into the activities in each challenge. Refer to the vocabulary often, and keep the word wall highly visible and clutter free. You can add new vocabulary in each unit to the terms already in use from previous challenges.

- Want to learn more about electronics? Check the list of great, novice-friendly resources featured in Appendix B.

PART 1: LIGHT ME!

Youths will be challenged to illuminate an LED by tinkering with different arrangements of a battery, conductive fabric, and alligator clips. A discussion about the components, behaviors, goals, and interconnections within a circuit will help them see circuits as an example of a system. A "human circuit role play" helps them to model their understanding through embodied play, followed by a reflection activity.

Time: 40–50 minutes

STUFF TO HAVE HANDY

- Circuit Kits (prepared in advance by the instructor; 1 per youth)
- Scissors
- Index cards and tape or sticky notes
- Pencils

HANDOUTS

- "An Electronic Circuit: A System"
- "System of the Electronic Circuit"

IMAGINE AND CREATE: LIGHT UP AN LED—10 MINUTES

Sending electricity to an object requires a power source and an uninterrupted circuit path, or *loop*, through conductive material. Usually, though, these requirements are invisible to youths in their everyday experiences with electric objects; for example, few young people know that electrical energy flows in two directions in a power cord, or why batteries have a positive (+) and negative (–) side.

This first activity makes the behaviors of components and interconnections in an electonic circuit more visible and gives youths an opportunity to test their assumptions about what is going on "behind the scenes" in any electricity-powered object.

1. Explain to youths that the first thing they are going to do is try to light an LED. Each youth (or each group) will receive a set of components that can help achieve this goal.

2. Before distributing the kits and allowing youths to experiment with the materials individually or in small groups, introduce each component in the Circuit Kit by holding it up for everyone to see. Build on youths' prior knowledge by asking if anyone is familiar with these components. Investigate their prior experience with circuitry concepts by asking if anyone has any guesses about what they might need to know to get the LED to illuminate.

	Alligator clip	An electrical connector (named for its resemblance to the jaws of an alligator) that gets attached to an electric cable to make a temporary connection to a battery or other component. Also called *alligator test leads*. SparkFun—PRT-11037
	3V battery (also called a *coin cell battery*)	An energy source in which chemical energy is converted into electricity. We recommend using the common CR2032 type battery for e-textile projects (20 mm), which should power e-textile projects for weeks at a time. SparkFun—PRT-00338

	Conductive fabric	A fabric woven with conductive metal strands. A variety of conductive fabrics are available that vary in their conductive materials (like silver or copper) and their degree of stretchiness. RIPSTOP: SparkFun—DEV-10056
	LED	An LED is a small device that lights up when an electric current passes through it. The positive end of the LED is the longer of the two legs. These LEDs also can be used in all e-textile projects by bending the legs in two circles with needle-nose pliers. LEDs are available in many colors. Sparkfun COM-09850

3. Hand out a Circuit Kit to each youth and challenge him or her to discover a way to light up the LED, working individually or collaboratively. The goal is for youths to discover that some configurations work, and others do not.

Note At first, avoid telling youths that their solutions need to take the shape of an uninterrupted circuit or loop, or that they'll need to incorporate all components into their design. Allow them to experiment with finding a solution themselves.

As the youths are working, keep in mind that some of them might know and understand the idea of batteries having "positive" and "negative" sides, although others might not know what that means. Likewise, some youths will understand that "positive goes with positive and negative goes with negative," but again, they might not understand why. These are ideas you can emphasize as they experiment with their circuits.

Depending on how open-ended you want the discovery process to be, you can give youths a hint about the LEDs and tell them that one side is positive and the other is negative (and tell them which is which). This could make the task more straightforward, but it also might keep them from testing other conjectures and ideas.

VOICES FROM THE FIELD

Have youth experiment with other ways to connect alligator clips. Many have a misconception that the clips need to be directly connected to the battery holder only, not thinking of the other conductive and insulating parts of the alligator clip. For instance, if the plastic sleeve is removed from the clip, another alligator clip can be easily attached, allowing another circuit to build off of the +/− lines' clips.

—DIANE GLOSSON, RESEARCH ASSISTANT AT INDIANA UNIVERSITY

---

4. After a few minutes, turn off the room lights to see if anyone has a glowing light. If some of the circuits don't function, ask the following guiding questions to allow youths to troubleshoot their circuits:

- Does the circuit make a *complete loop?*

- Are the *connections tight* between components?

- Is the *battery connected on both sides* to the LED?

- Have they connected *negative to negative* (e.g., battery to LED) and *positive to positive?*

IMPORTANT TIPS FOR THIS ACTIVITY

- If you are using two-pronged LEDs, keep in mind that the longer leg of the LED is the positive end (and, likewise, the shorter leg is the negative). Because youths might bend the legs of the LEDs in this exercise and later may have difficulty telling the positive and negative ends of the LED from one another, you may want to have them *mark the positive ends of the LED with a permanent marker* at the beginning of the exercise. Alternatively, you can look at the LED in this illustration. Most LEDs have one flat side to their base; the flat side is the negative side.

- If youths are having trouble incorporating the conductive fabric, you might give them a hint to use their scissors (i.e., the conductive fabric can be cut in half, with one piece used to connect to the positive side of the battery and the second piece used to connect to the negative side).

- It is also possible to create a working circuit *without* the conductive fabric.

- If some youths finish early or have prior knowledge of circuits, you can challenge them by giving them additional LEDs and more alligator clips to create more complex circuits in series or parallel configurations (see "Design Challenge 4: DIY Flashlights and Shadow Puppets" in this book or the "e-Textile Cuff" challenge in the *Soft Circuits: Crafting e-Fashion with DIY Electronics* for more detail).

- Youths may try to use the alligator clips to "clip" the 3V battery, but this would short out the 3V [connecting the (+) and (–) sides of the battery]. The same thing would happen if they decide to "wrap" the battery in conductive fabric. Have extra batteries on hand, and warn youths that *a warm or hot battery is a sign of a short!*

- If you're unsure of whether a 3V battery is still good, use a two-pronged (non-Lily-Pad) LED to test your battery by placing the negative leg of the LED on the (–) side of the battery and the positive leg of the LED on the (+) side to see if it lights up. If not, then the battery is shorted or is no longer working. In addition, this trick is useful to test whether the LED is blown, or what color it shows when illuminated.

Youth testing an LED.

SHARE: WHAT MAKES A WORKING CIRCUIT?—15 MINUTES

There are three goals to this discussion:

- First, it should serve to highlight some of the key vocabulary in becoming a systems thinker and how each applies to the system of an electronic circuit, including *components, behaviors, goals,* and *interconnections.*

- Second, we want to make sure that all youths understand that an *electronic circuit* is an unbroken path loop of interconnected components. *Electric current* can then *flow* through the circuit to power the *load* (in this case, the LED).

- Third, this is a good opportunity to start directing youths to think about circuits as a kind of *system.*

These goals can be accomplished simultaneously; in this first discussion, you can use some of the systems thinking vocabulary as you talk about how the circuit works. Specifically, you can talk about the circuit as a system, talk about the goal of the system (to light the LED), the components of the system, and identify what the behaviors of those components are and how they interconnect in order to conduct electricity (and light the LED) effectively.

1. Pass out the "An Electronic Circuit: A System" worksheet, introducing the concepts of flow and pointing out the loop or unbroken path in the electronic circuit, which makes the circuit capable of carrying an electric current. Also, point out the direction of the current flow and the positive and negative orientations of the battery and LED. *Some groups have adopted the mantra "positive to positive and negative to negative" to help youths remember the orientation of the components needed in a successful circuit.*

2. Introduce a system as something that can be described as having smaller parts, or *components,* that work together to achieve a goal. Present each component and show how all the components work together, Alternatively, if you think that some youths have a good grasp of these ideas based on their play and experimentation, you can have them present their circuit and explain what they have discovered.

3. The following questions could be used to facilitate the discussion:

- What are the components in this system that you created? *(Answer: Battery, conductive fabric, alligator clips, and LED.)*

- What are the behaviors of the different components in the system? *(Answer: The battery provides power, the conductive fabric and alligator clips carry electricity between the different components, and the LED produces light.)*

- What is the goal of this system? *(Answer: The goal of this circuit is to allow the energy from the battery to flow to the LED and give it power so that it lights up.)*

- What is happening to light the LED? *(Answer: Energy is flowing from the battery along the path of alligator clips and through the LED, which allows it to light up.)*

- This system works by routing electricity along a path. How does that energy move through the system? *(Answer: Batteries have one negative and positive side. When a circuit makes a closed loop, the battery's current flows through the conductive wires or thread to reach the load or LED, flowing through the device to give it power. The current flows toward the opposite side of the power source; i.e., the negative side of the battery.)*

- What are the interconnections in this system? *(Answer: The battery is connected to the alligator clips and conductive fabric through its behavior of providing electricity and their behavior of conducting or carrying electricity. The clips and LED are connected through the clips' behavior of conducting electricity and the LED's behavior of converting electricity into light.)*

- Can the components be connected in *any* way, or are there particular interconnections that are optimal? *(Answer: All components must be connected in a circular configuration so that the electric current has a path to flow along. If the parts are not connected and there is an opening in any part of the circuit, then the LED won't light up.)*

REFLECT: DOCUMENT YOUTHS THINKING—10 MINUTES

As a final activity, which can be used as an assessment, pass out the "System of the Electronic Circuit" worksheet. Ask youths to fill this out individually.

RESEARCH: WHAT'S GOING ON INSIDE THE CIRCUIT?—5 MINUTES

To further youths' understanding of how batteries and electronic circuits work, show one or more of the videos listed in Appendix B as an introduction to how electricity is generated within a battery and how current flows through a circuit.

One important difference between electronic circuits with lightbulbs (depicted in most of these videos) and those with LEDs is that like batteries, LEDs have positive and negative sides that must correspond with the direction of the electric current.

PLAY: HUMAN CIRCUIT ROLE PLAY — 10 MINUTES (OPTIONAL)

In this activity, groups of youths will model an electrical system, where each group member takes on the role of one component in a circuit. The goal of "acting out" the circuit is to embody the various pieces of the system and begin reasoning about its specific behaviors. This is also a collaborative activity for youths to make meaning collectively and talk through any misunderstandings that they have from the previous activity.

1. Divide the class into teams of 6–8 members who will create a human circuit. Have sticky notes (or 3" x 5" note cards) ready with each component of the circuit, including (1) the power (i.e., battery); (2) the load (i.e., LEDs or other components in the circuit that use electricity); and (3) the path or the connection between components or parts (i.e., the alligator clips, wires, conductive fabric, etc.). *Alternatively, you could have youths generate names of the components.*

2. Have participants label themselves as part of the system by placing the corresponding sticky notes or note cards on their shirts. *Optional: You might consider adding new components to the system that the youths are modeling, like a switch that interrupts the energy path (turning the circuit off and on) to prepare them for upcoming challenges.*

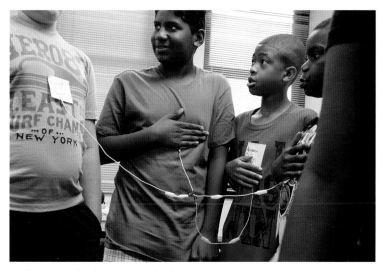

Youth acting out the "human circuit role play."

3. Have each youth verbalize the interpretation of his or her modeled component, clearly stating what it does in the circuit, and where that person thinks he or she should be within the circuit (e.g., next to other components). It is helpful to have a knowledgeable adult or peer to help each youth think through the new system components, the purpose of the circuit, and the end goal of a working circuit. Guide this verbalization with some focused questions, such as the following:

- What are the various components in the system? *(Answer: LEDs, battery, alligator clips, conductive fabric.)*

- What will the load (in this case, the LED) do when the circuit is complete? *(Answer: Light up.)*

- What is the structure of your circuit? *(Answer: An uninterrupted loop.)*

- What direction is electricity moving in? Is there any directionality of the components (i.e, are youths incorporating the positive and negative portions of the battery into their design and if so, how)? *(Answer: Yes, the current is moving from the positive end of the battery through the LED and returning to the negative side of the battery.)*

4. After the teams have created a complete circuit, they can present their circuits to the class. Each youth then can name his or her part and what it does.

VOICES FROM THE FIELD

Systems thinking took on a whole new meaning today, requiring me to step out of my comfort zone and teach a method of thinking that was still new to me. However, I was really surprised at how easy this concept was to apply. The students easily grasped the idea of seeing the electrical circuit as a system. They could discuss the components, the interconnections, the purpose, and the intended outcome of a circuit. They even constructed a human model of a circuit. Each student was able to explain the component they represented and describe the interrelationships in the system.

—LORI BELL, NATIONAL WRITING PROJECT

WHAT TO EXPECT

The "System of the Electronic Circuit" worksheet is primarily designed to ensure that youths grasp the fundamentals of both creating a working electronic circuit and understanding it as a system, which will be essential for the remaining Design Challenges in this book. If they don't understand key concepts, such as the conditions for and directionality of the current flow, they will face repeated frustration. This is also an opportunity to get them thinking about how systems differ from other kinds of cause-and-effect relationships.

The final question on the worksheet, "Explain how this circuit functions as a system," is intentionally broad, for the purpose of providing youths with an opportunity to apply their experience building the circuit to explaining what they understand conceptually about systems. We don't recommend scoring this final question for anything other than effort, as youths have few resources to answer it accurately at this point. Because it is an exploratory item, it might be worth having a whole-class discussion about this question once everyone has had a chance to complete the worksheet.

	Novice	Expert
Circuitry concepts	• Does not label parts of the electronic circuit diagram or does so inaccurately • Does not recognize the negative and positive sides of the LED and battery in the diagram • Does not connect the negative side of battery to the negative side of the LED (and likewise with the positive sides) • Does not use key vocabulary like *load, current,* and *circuit* • Does not incorporate conductive fabric or does so in a decorative/ nonfunctional way • Does not create a working circuit • Does not accurately indicate the direction of the current flow	• Labels all parts of the electronic circuit diagram accurately • Labels the negative and positive sides of the LED and battery in the diagram • Connects the negative side of the battery to the negative side of the LED (and likewise with positive sides) • Is able to use key vocabulary, like *load, current,* and *circuit* • Is able to incorporate conductive fabric into diagram in a functioning/ nondecorative fashion • Creates a working circuit (with only purposeful breaks or interruptions that would serve as switches) • Accurately indicates the direction of the current flow
Systems thinking concepts	• Unsure how to answer or does not give any answer • Describes a circuit simply as a collection of parts, with little attention given to how individual parts of the circuit contribute to the overall goal (i.e., lighting the LED) • Explanation does not acknowledge the relationship between the orientation of circuit parts [i.e., the (−) of the LED is not connected to the (−) of the battery] and the current flow in the circuit	• Can explain that a circuit is a system because it has multiple elements whose behaviors interconnect to make it work, and more specifically, that it is the way these elements interact with each other that causes the system to work (i.e., the LED to light up) • Can provide details about how a current flow is achieved through the proper orientation of circuit parts (i.e., the (−) of the LED is connected to the (−) of the battery)

DESIGN CHALLENGE 1, PART 1

AN ELECTRONIC CIRCUIT: A SYSTEM

This diagram depicts an electronic circuit and the direction of the current flow. In any working electronic circuit, it's important to have an unbroken path or loop, which makes the circuit capable of carrying an electric current to power the load (in this case, the LED). Notice the direction of the current flow and the positive and negative orientations of the battery and LED. It might be helpful to say out loud "positive to positive and negative to negative" to help you remember the orientation of the components needed in a working circuit.

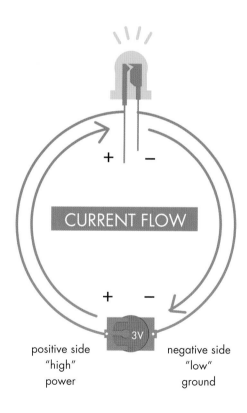

DESIGN CHALLENGE 1, PART 1

SYSTEM OF THE ELECTRONIC CIRCUIT

Components of the system: Draw the diagram of your electronic circuit in the space below. Be sure to label your diagram with all of the components.

Current flow: Indicate in your diagram where the positive side (+) and negative side (−) is in the battery and LED. Use arrows to indicate the direction that the current flows.

> **COMPONENTS TO LABEL**
>
> - 3V battery
> - LED
> - Conductive fabric
> - Alligator clips

Explain how this circuit functions as a system.

PART 2: LEARNING ABOUT CONDUCTIVITY AND RESISTANCE

Youths will use multimeters on a variety of objects to learn how electric current passes through material. They will work together to guess which materials act as conductors and which act as insulators, learning about conductivity and resistance in the process. Finally, they will build circuits with little to no resistance in order to learn about limited energy resources, short circuits, and balancing feedback loops.

Time: 55 minutes

STUFF TO HAVE HANDY

- Conductivity Kits (prepared in advance by the instructor; 1 per group)
- Multimeters (1 per group)
- Journals
- Graphite pencils
- Paper
- Distilled water
- Salt
- Conductive fabric
- Conductive thread
- *Optional:* Circuit Kits (prepared in advance by the instructor; 1 per youth)
- *Optional:* Scissors
- *Optional:* Extra 3V batteries

HANDOUTS

- "How Do I Use a Multimeter?"
- "Tracing Current Flow"

IMAGINE AND PLAY: CONDUCTORS VERSUS INSULATORS—15 MINUTES

In this series of activities, youths will learn more about how to determine which materials in their everyday environment are good conductors and which are good insulators.

1. Have youths visualize a very hot summer day in a playground. Tell them to imagine sitting down on the top of a shiny metal slide that's been exposed to the sun all afternoon. The slide is very hot and burns the underside of their legs, so they climb down the ladder and move to the plastic slide next to it. The plastic slide is hot, but it doesn't burn like the metal slide does.

   • Why did one slide get hotter than the other, and what does that say about the materials from which they're made? The answer is that metal is an example of a *conductor,* a material that lets heat and electricity pass through it.

   • Plastic, on the other hand, is a good *insulator,* a material that does not let heat and electricity go through it easily.

2. Ask youths if they have a sense of what kinds of materials might be conductive, and why. Do the same for the kinds of materials that might be insulating, and why. Document these initial conjectures on the board.

3. Show youths the multimeter and explain that it is a tool used for measuring multiple characteristics of electrics, especially voltage and current. Show how to use the (+) and (–) probes of the multimeter in Continuity mode (which shows the amount of electricity that can pass through a circuit) to discover which objects make better conductors and which make better insulators. Objects that make good conductors will cause the multimeter to beep, while the multimeter won't make a sound when it touches insulators.

	Multimeter	A handheld device with a negative and a positive probe, designed to measure electric current, voltage, and resistance, and to help determine whether a material or artifact is conductive or not conductive. SparkFun—TOL-09141
	Continuity mode	An electrical test used to determine the presence and location of a broken connection, as well as whether a particular material will be conductive. To set a multimeter to Continuity mode, turn the dial to the icon that looks like sound coming out of a speaker and place the black and red plugs on the probes in the holes as shown in the picture to the left.

Note We used the SparkFun digital multimeter in Continuity mode (not all multimeters have a Continuity mode, so look carefully at the device you are purchasing to make sure it has one). In addition, the Continuity mode might look different on your device.

4. Tell youths that the goal for the next 10 minutes is to predict whether a particular material is conductive, and then to test it. Suggest that they draw a graphic organizer in their journals with three columns labeled "Component," "Prediction," and "Outcome." Youths can use labels like "C" for conductivity materials and "NC" for nonconductive materials.

Sample Table

Component	Prediction	Outcome
Tinsel	*Conductive*	*Nonconductive*
Conductive Fabric	*Conductive*	*Conductive*
Paper Clip	*Nonconductive*	*Conductive*
Rubber Bouncy Ball	*Nonconductive*	*Nonconductive*

5. Distribute Conductivity Kits, multimeters, and "How Do I Use a Multimeter?" handouts to groups.

6. Tell youths to set the multimeter to Continuity mode and explain that they are listening for a beep. Ask youths to think about why some materials might be conductive while others aren't.

Note If you prefer, youths can work together in pairs to complete the activity.

IMPORTANT TIPS FOR THIS ACTIVITY

- Some common conductors are metals, like copper, aluminum, gold, and silver.

- Some common insulators are glass, air, plastic, rubber, and wood.

- Pencils are interesting to test because some parts (the lead) are conductive, and some parts (the wood) are not.

SHARE: WHAT MAKES A WORKING CIRCUIT?—10 MINUTES

Once youths are finished testing everything in their kits (and perhaps everything in the room!), you can bring the whole group back together for a quick debrief about what they found. If you kept a list of initial conjectures on the board, this is a good time to return to those conjectures to see how things panned out.

1. The following questions could be used to facilitate the discussion:

- Was anyone surprised or confused to discover that some fabrics are conductive (like the conductive fabrics in the kit), while others are not (like their own clothing)?

- Did anyone find that in some objects, a portion of it is conductive (like the metal on an alligator clip) while other parts aren't (like the plastic covering)?

2. Explain that multimeters measure the degree of *resistance* in a circuit, which is the measure of how much a material keeps electricity from passing through it. All materials contain some resistance.

3. If the idea of resistance is a little unclear, a water analogy can be helpful: resistance is like a garden hose filled with sand. When the hose is turned on, the sand slows down the flow of water in the hose. We can say that the hose with sand has more resistance to water flow than does a clear hose. Now, if we want to get more water out of the hose, we would need to turn up the water pressure at the faucet. The same is true with electricity—materials with low resistance (i.e., conductors) let electricity flow easily, while materials with higher resistance (i.e., insulators) require more energy to make the electricity flow.

4. This makes it sound like conductivity is always a good thing in circuits. However, that's not always the case. The next part of the discussion will highlight why you need some resistance in your circuit to balance the system.

IMAGINE AND PLAY: DEGREES OF RESISTANCE—10 MINUTES

What might not be readily apparent when youths simply test for conductivity is that every material has some degree of resistance, and that its resistance builds the farther that the current needs to travel (for example, a longer wire presents more resistance than a shorter wire). In this activity, youths will become familiar with measuring the degree of resistance.

1. Gather some materials in which youths can measure the degree of resistance readily, including one or more of the following:

   • A graphite pencil, to shade a large rectangular area on paper

   • Distilled water, to which you gradually add salt

   • A long strip of conductive fabric

   • A long piece of conductive thread

2. Explain to youths that the goal of the activity is to measure the maximum and minimum degree of resistance presented by one or more of these materials.

3. Have youths set the multimeter to Continuity mode and explain that they aren't just listening for a beep now—they also should be looking at the numbers shown on the meter.

4. For measuring materials like the graphite pencil on paper, the conductive fabric, or conductive thread, have youths start with the probes near one another (or touching) and then gradually move the two probes apart. They will find that the degree of resistance increases as the two probes move farther and farther apart.

5. For measuring materials like water with salt, youths should measure several times. For each measurement, place the probes in the same location, but stir in a bit more salt before each new measurement. Youths will find that salt decreases the resistance in the water (making it more conductive over time).

6. All in all, youths should discover that materials present a degree of resistance depending on the type of material and the length or area of the material. *In addition, they should realize that a material with high resistance is a poor conductor of electrical current.*

MOD THIS ACTIVITY: USE A HOMEMADE POTENTIOMETER

In fact, what youths learned about the difference in resistance across various materials in the activity just completed mirrors what happens in components called "potentiometers," which control the amount of resistance in a circuit (used to dim lights, for example). Have youths connect the homemade potentiometers that they just created to a simple circuit (i.e., a battery/battery holder, alligator clips, and LED) to control the brightness of the LED.

IMAGINE: TRACING FLOW, LIMITED RESISTANCE, AND BALANCING FEEDBACK LOOPS—10 MINUTES

One final important activity is for youths to think about the limited resource of energy and, in particular, how that energy source functions as a part of a system and needs to be in balance with other elements. The energy source—generated though the 3V battery in this case—is a crucial component of a system; indeed, without energy, the system of a circuit would not work (in the language of systems thinking, it couldn't achieve its goal).

1. What is the function of conductive and resistive materials in a circuit? Both are useful, but for different reasons. *(Answer: Conductive materials allow the circuit to flow freely, while resistive materials can be used to control the flow or stop it altogether.)*

2. Explain that batteries and other components like LEDs need to be part of a balanced circuit system. *Balancing feedback loops* are processes that are put in place to help move a system toward its goals or keep a system at a desired state of equilibrium. Usually, balancing feedback processes stabilize systems by limiting or preventing certain processes from happening. In electronic circuits, one way that we can balance the system is to think more deeply about conductivity and resistance (and we'll explore other ways in the remaining Design Challenges in this book).

3. Ask a couple of questions before you get started:

- When a circuit is built using materials that have too much resistance, what happens? (*Answer: The circuit fails to power the load or achieve the intended goal; e.g., to light the LED.*)

- When a circuit is built using materials that have too little resistance, what happens? (*Answer: If the circuit fails to meet any resistance, the current will be returned to the battery, causing it to short or die.*)

Add youths' conjectures to the board. You will be investigating these questions more deeply in the next exercise on short circuits.

4. Project the "Tracing Current Flow" handout or distribute it to youths in groups. Ask the following questions:

- What is different about Figure A and Figure B? Which of these represents a balanced system? What is going to happen to the LED and the 3V battery in both diagrams? Which circuit presents a greater degree of resistance? (*Answer: Three possible differences between the two figures are that the circuit in*

Figure B bypasses the LED, that the LED will not light up, and that the circuit poses too little resistance and the battery will short out (dispensing all of its energy at once and get hot). Figure A is the only system in balance, with a minimal amount of resistance posed by the LED so that the current isn't returned directly to the battery.)

- Are the path of the circuit and the lighting of the LED interconnected, and if so, why? (*Answer: Yes, they are related. In Figure B, the circuit bypasses the LED rather than flowing through it. This means that the energy from the battery is rapidly flowing through the circuit without meeting any resistance to limit the flow. And, equally important, no energy is flowing through the LED to power it.)*

- What do you think will happen in circuits A and B)? Is that problematic? Why or why not? (*Answer: The battery will be shorted in Figure B, and you'll need a new battery. In Figure A, the LED will turn on.)*

PLAY AND RESEARCH: LIMITED RESOURCES AND SHORT CIRCUITS—10 MINUTES

In this activity, youths will learn about what causes a short circuit, as well as certain signs or symptoms that can commonly occur when a short is draining the battery. At this point, you might want to search for videos or other resources to support this understanding. There are also activities you can try. For example, you may want youths to put together a circuit like the configuration in Figure B by hooking up an alligator clip to the positive and negative sides of the battery or just using a paper clip and connecting it to the positive and negative sides of the battery. What happens? What youths should experience is that the battery starts to get hot. They should discover then that if they try to use this battery to light their LED, the battery no longer has power: it has been shorted out. Warn youths that a "warm battery" is a sign of the battery being shorted. The goal is for them to understand first that the stored energy in the battery has run out. This is an experience that they are doubtless familiar with in their everyday experiences with batteries, but they may be less familiar with *why* and *how* a battery has drained.

Here's a short explanation of what is happening: Basically, a battery is made of a limited amount of chemicals that produce electricity. When an uninterrupted loop of conductive material is made in an electronic circuit, the current begins to flow. The presence of other components on the circuit (such as an LED) creates some resistance in the circuit and causes the chemical reactions to occur at a regular speed, thus prolonging the life of the battery. However, when the circuit has no or very little resistance, the energy from the battery is released more rapidly. It's useful to think about the battery as a limited resource, like water stored in a bathtub. Having some resistance in the circuit is like limiting the exit of water in the tub to a small trickle. Sticking with the water analogy, having little to no resistance is like having a wide open drain in the tub, which empties it almost immediately.

If a battery is shorted, it means that the positive and negative sides of the battery are connected through something with low resistance (like a wire), which causes a large amount of current to flow through the connection in a very short amount of time. This makes the battery discharge all of its energy, which is why the battery "dies." This large current through the battery also causes a rapid buildup of heat, which, for larger batteries, could even start a fire.

DESIGN CHALLENGE 1, PART 2

HOW DO I USE A MULTIMETER?

The multimeter tool is used to test and measure multiple characteristics of electronics (hence, *multi* and *meter*). Testing for continuity determines if an electrical path can be established between two points. This is handy when you want to check if your connections are secure in a circuit, or when you want to test various materials to see if a current can pass through them.

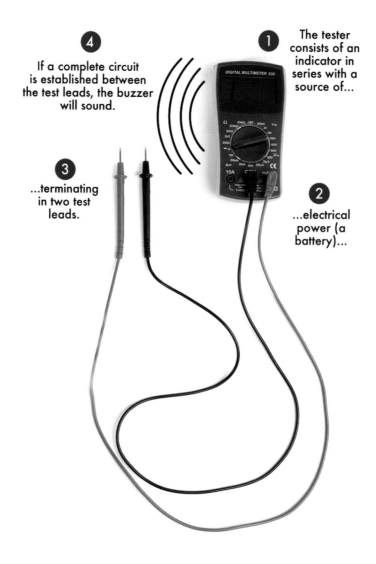

4 If a complete circuit is established between the test leads, the buzzer will sound.

1 The tester consists of an indicator in series with a source of...

3 ...terminating in two test leads.

2 ...electrical power (a battery)...

USING A MULTIMETER IN CONTINUITY MODE

Step 1: Turn Your Project Off

You can only test continuity when the device you're testing is not powered. Continuity works by poking a little voltage into the circuit and seeing how much current flows—the test is safe for your device, but if there is already voltage in the circuit, you'll get an incorrect reading, so always turn it off before you begin.

Step 2: Plug in Your Test Leads

Plug the black probe into COM and the red probe into mAVΩ.

Step 3: Configure Your Testing Mode

Turn the multimeter dial to the symbol depicted here with propagation waves around it (like sound coming from a speaker). (Note that this is not a universal symbol, and your multimeter may have a different symbol or settings.)

Step 4: Test Your Multimeter

Touch the tips of the probes together to ensure that your multimeter works. The display should change to a three-digit number (its displaying resistance), and it should emit a beep.
A beep means that power is flowing freely between the probes.
If there is no beep, resistance in the line is keeping the current from reaching the other side.

Step 5: Test a Component, Circuit, or Object for Continuity

Squeeze the probes with a little pressure against some objects—pencils, paper clips, glass, rubber bouncy balls, *anything!* Materials with low resistance (causing the multimeter to beep) are conductive.
Continuity is nondirectional, so it doesn't matter which probe you use on which end of the object that you're testing.

DESIGN CHALLENGE 1, PART 2

TRACING CURRENT FLOW

These two diagrams depict two similar but slightly different circuits. Use your finger to trace the path of each circuit. What is different about Figure A and Figure B? What is going to happen to the LED and the 3V battery in both diagrams? Which of these diagrams represents a balanced system?

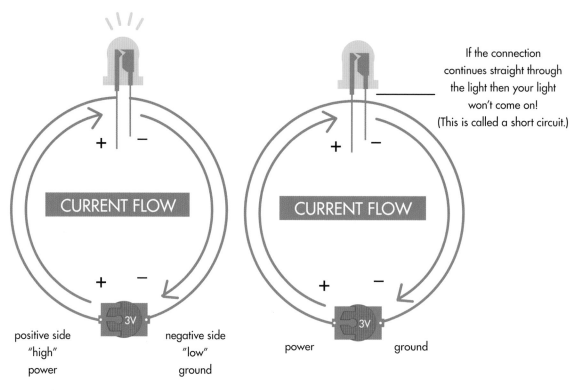

If the connection continues straight through the light then your light won't come on! (This is called a short circuit.)

Figure A: The connection stops on the one side of the light, flows through it, and exits at the other side.

Figure B

DESIGN CHALLENGE 2
E-TEXTILE CUFFS

Total time: 310 minutes

OVERVIEW

The goal of this Design Challenge is to explore how a system's *structure* determines specific component *behaviors* and the larger system dynamics, or *interconnections,* within the context of *e-textile* tools and materials. Youths will experiment with different circuit structures and battery voltages to discover how circuits can be structured, both in *series* and in *parallel.* They then will apply this understanding to the design and development of an electronic cuff or bracelet and are challenged to imagine, investigate, create, and write about their process.

PRODUCT

Youths will create a simple electronic cuff (e-cuff) from e-textile materials. The e-textile cuffs will involve multiple LilyPad light-emitting diodes (LEDs), necessitating that youths construct parallel circuits in their designs. The e-cuff then can be shared and posted to an online community. Consult our website at digitalis.nwp.org/gnl for suggestions but you may want to consider Instructables.com, DIY.org, or another venue for your sharing your work.

TARGETED SYSTEMS THINKING CONCEPTS

A system's structure is determined by the particular way that components are set up. The structure defines each component's specific behavior and its interconnections with other components. All components function together to accomplish a goal (in this case, to light multiple LEDs in a single circuit). The circuits that youths construct in this Design Challenge will contain multiple *leverage points* (i.e., points where you can intervene to change or create the conditions for balance in the system), including a switch to help preserve the system's limited resources in the battery.

PARTS

PART 1: EXPLORING SYSTEM STRUCTURES

The goal of this activity is to introduce youths to the idea that a system's structure is determined by the particular way that components are set up. In this activity, they will use identical components, but they will structure them in different ways to learn more about how the system's structure determines the components' specific behaviors and interconnections in the system. Youths will learn specifically about how to build circuits in series and in parallel to meet the goals of the system (i.e., to light all of their LEDs).

Time: 70 minutes

Note   Skip this part if your youths already have completed the corresponding part in "Design Challenge 4: DIY Flashlights and Shadow Puppets" in *Short Circuits: Crafting e-Puppets with DIY Electronics.*

PART 2: DESIGN TIME—MAKING E-TEXTILE CUFFS

In this activity, youths apply their knowledge about system structures to creating e-cuffs using e-textile materials.

Time: 150 minutes

PART 3: WRAP UP!

In the final part of this Design Challenge, youths will have an opportunity to share their projects with their local peer group. Finally, they will self-reflect on their e-textile cuff experience and connect to the core systems thinking concepts in this Design Challenge.

Time: 90 minutes

KEY DEFINITIONS

SYSTEMS THINKING

Identify the way a system is functioning. The *function* of a system describes the overall behavior of the system—what it is doing or where it's going over time. A system's function might emerge naturally based on interconnections among components, or it might be the result of an intentional design (in which case, we might also refer to the function of a system as its *goal*). Regardless, the function of a system is the result of the dynamics that occur among components' interconnected behaviors.

Identifying interconnections. Identifying the different ways that a system's parts, or *components*, interact with each other through their *behaviors*, and through those interactions, change the behaviors of other components.

Designing a system. Creating a system through engaging in an iterative design process, one that entails iterative cycles of feedback, troubleshooting, and testing. One of the most effective means of developing systems thinking is to regularly create and iterate on the design of systems, and doing so in a way that creates opportunities for students to think about generic systems models that apply across multiple domains and settings.

Distinguishing the goal of a system. The goal of the system is what a system that was intentionally designed is intended to do. Sometimes this might be the same as the functioning of the system … other times the goal and the function are not aligned. A given system might have multiple goals or purposes that are at play simultaneously, and come into conflict. Being able to understand system purpose or goal gives a sense of the ideal state of a system from a particular perspective.

Considering the role of system structure. Understanding how a system's *components* are set up in relation to one another gives insight into the *behavior* of a component. A system's structure affects the behaviors of those components and the overall *dynamics* and *functioning* of a system. When we try to understand and make changes in a system, it's important to know about its structure and not just the individual characteristics of the system's components. Often structures go unnoticed, but they have a big impact on what components in a system do.

Leverage points. Particular places within a system where a small shift in one thing can produce big changes in everything. Leverage points are difficult to find because they often lie far away from either the problem or the obvious solution. Not every place in a system is a leverage point—sometimes changing one thing in a system will produce only small effects that aren't felt throughout the system.

CIRCUITRY

Debugging. The iterative process of identifying and removing errors from hardware or software designs.

e-Textiles. Everyday textiles and clothes that have electronics embedded in them; also known as *electric textiles* or *smart textiles.*

Parallel circuit. When components are wired in parallel within a circuit, the electric current divides into two or more paths before recombining to complete the circuit. The current flows through three LEDs wired in parallel, and the electric current is split equally among the three of them. **Note:** The evenness of the split is contingent on the three LEDs being the same type and/or color.

Series circuit. When components are wired in series within a circuit, electric current flows sequentially through those components in a continuous loop. This means that as the current travels from the battery through each LED, it loses some of its original "electrical charge" or energy (also known as *voltage*—see next) such that the amount of voltage available for each subsequent LED decreases with each one that it passes through.

Switch. A component that controls the flow of electricity by opening and closing a circuit.

Voltage. *Voltage* is the force that causes electric current to flow through a circuit. Increasing the voltage in a circuit without changing the resistance involved increases the current that flows through the circuit.

Common Core State Standards	Next Generation Science Standards
• RI.7.3	• 3-PS2–3
• RI.7.4	• MS-PS2–3
• RST.6–8.3	• 4-PS3–2
• RST.6–8.9	• 4-PS3–4
• SL.7.2	• MS-PS3–2
• SL.7.5	• 3–5-ETS1–1
	• 3–5-ETS1–2
	• 3–5-ETS1–3
	• MS-ETS1–4

MATERIALS OVERVIEW

Find electronics at **www.sparkfun.com/Interconnections**. For each youth, you need to create a Systems Structure Kit that consists of a zip-closed plastic bag filled with the following system components:

- 9V battery
- 9V battery snap connector[1]
- 3V (or coin cell) battery[2]
- 3V LilyPad battery holder
- 6 LilyPad LEDs[3]

For each youth, you need to create an e-Textile Cuff Kit that consists of a zip-closed baggie filled with the following system components:

- 1 3V (coin cell) battery[2]
- 1 3V LilyPad battery holder
- 3–5 LilyPad LEDs[3]
- One of the following: set of metal snaps, metal magnetic snaps, or conductive Velcro (or provide a selection for youths to choose from to use as their cuff snap/switch)

ADDITIONAL MATERIALS

- Digital projector
- 9" x 2" pieces of felt in multiple colors (one or two pieces per youth)
- Plenty of alligator clips (at least seven to eight per youth)
- Conductive thread
- Regular thread
- Sewing needles and pincushions
- Clear nail polish, fabric glue, or low-temperature hot glue (to hold knots)
- Scissors
- Decorative materials like assorted buttons, fabric markers, glass beads, gems, or other materials
- Computer with active Internet connection (1 per youth)
- Digital camera(s) with photo and video capabilities, and universal serial bus (USB) cord(s) to download material to the computer

HANDOUTS

- "An Electronic Circuit: An Example of a System" (from Design Challenge 1)
- "Switch Diagram"
- "Multiple LEDs Diagram"
- "Series versus Parallel Circuits"
- "Running Stitch Practice" (preferably copied onto construction paper)
- "Sample e-Textile Cuff Circuit Diagram"
- "Posting Your e-Textile Cuff"
- "Self-Reflection on My e-Textile Cuff"

OVERALL CHALLENGE PREPARATION

- Setting up a word wall can be helpful for integrating essential vocabulary into the activities in each Design Challenge. Refer to the vocabulary often, and keep the word wall highly visible and clutter free. You can add new vocabulary in each unit to the terms already in use from previous Design Challenges.

- Prepare the Systems Structure Kits (1 per youth) as described previously.

- Prepare the e-Textile Cuff Kits (1 per youth) as described previously.

- Precut the pieces of felt into 9" x 2" strips (one or two pieces per youth). *Be sure to cut the felt an inch longer than a typical wrist measurement for the snap/switch.*

- Create a prototype of the e-textile cuff to serve as a model.

- Set up arts and crafts materials in one central location.

- Decide on the materials that you'll be using for the cuff snap/switch and test the materials (e.g., whether you will use metal snaps, metal magnetic snaps, or conductive Velcro). Metal snaps or magnetic snaps sometimes have an insulating coating that will prevent your circuit from making a solid connection. If you're unsure, use your multimeter in Continuity mode to test the materials. If there is a protective coating, you can use sandpaper or a fingernail file to scratch the surface and make a more solid connection, both with the conductive thread and with the two portions of the snap. This is a common problem encountered with this project, and the extent of it can vary by the size and brand of the snap.

PART 1: EXPLORING SYSTEM STRUCTURES

The goal of this first activity is to introduce youths to the idea that a system's structure is determined by the particular way that its components are set up. They will use identical components, but structure them in different ways to learn more about how a system's structure determines specific behaviors and interconnections in the system. They will learn specifically about how to build circuits both in series and in parallel to meet the goals of the system (e.g., to light all their LEDs).

Time: 70 minutes

STUFF TO HAVE HANDY

- System Structure Kits (prepared in advance by the instructor; 1 per youth)

- Permanent markers

- Plenty of alligator clips (at least seven to eight per youth)

HANDOUTS

- "Switch Diagram"

- "Multiple LEDs Diagram"

- "Series versus Parallel Circuits"

IMAGINE: DIAGRAMMING SYSTEM STRUCTURES—10 MINUTES

In this first activity, youths learn how to build a circuit that can support multiple LEDs to help them connect the concepts of structure, components, interconnections, and behavior.

1. Begin by sharing the big idea for the day: namely, that a system's structure is determined by the particular way that its components set it up. That setup determines the specific behaviors and interconnections in the system. Remind youths that so far, they've built projects where multiple LEDs have been used, but now they will discover more about the relationship between the battery's voltage and the number of LEDs that it can support.

2. Tell youths that they will be asked to build their own e-textile cuffs. For this project, they might want to incorporate more than one LED into their circuits and will need to learn how to balance the system's structure with the battery's voltage.

3. Ask the group what components they think that they'll need to make an e-cuff. (It's okay if they don't know, but this is a nice opportunity to see if they can transfer their circuitry knowledge from previous Design Challenges.) Things they can share might be felt, batteries, LEDs, a switch, and conductive thread.

4. Help youths to recognize that they will be building a circuit with a switch as well as multiple LEDs. As they add more LEDs to the system (thus changing the system's structure), the interconnections will have to change.

5. Use the following questions to activate youths' prior knowledge. As you ask the questions, have them record their hypotheses on plain sheets of paper:

- How do you think the additional LEDs will be incorporated into the circuit? Do you think you could put them together any way you like?

- What kinds of interconnections do you expect to create when you add components to the circuit?

- Where do you think the switch should go?

Note It probably will be helpful here to remind youths to label the positive and negative sides of the LEDs and battery, as well as point out where to incorporate a switch.

6. Invite youths to share their drawn circuits and ask them to explain their answers on the worksheet. *[Answers will vary. The goal is not for youths to necessarily get the "correct" answer here (they will be allowed to test their conjectures in the next section); the larger idea is about the system structures—the ways that a system's components are configured in relation to one another. The uniqueness of the structure will determine how those components behave, which will lead to specific ways that the overall system functions.]*

7. Pass out and discuss switch placement in the "Switch Diagrams" handout. Then explain that next, they are going to test their ideas to see what happens when systems are structured in different ways, with the aim of finding several different ways to illuminate multiple LEDs, as well as learn about some of the limitations of the components in the system.

VOICES FROM THE FIELD

Part of what I love about this activity is just watching how learners' ideas develop as they play and experiment with the materials. The kids had some experience already with circuits generally, but this is the first time they had to understand different circuit structures, and it's great that we didn't tell them up front about the difference between parallel and series circuits. I was able to see how they started with what they knew from the previous challenges, but then sort of had to stretch and expand their notions of how these materials operate when they're combined in new ways.

—RAFI SANTO, GRADUATE RESEARCH ASSISTANT AT INDIANA UNIVERSITY

PLAY: AN EXPERIMENT IN STRUCTURE—30 MINUTES

In this next part of the activity, youths will use the components found in their System Structure Kits to experiment with the system's structure and try to discover working solutions to lighting more than one LED with a single power source.

1. Distribute a System Structure Kit to each youth. Explain the goal: Try to light up as many of the LEDs as possible, using the materials in the kit. Encourage youths to collaborate and share ideas in the process of creation. Alternatively, they can work in groups of two or three if desired, or if materials are limited. Introduce components in the System Structure Kits as needed.

	Alligator clips	An electrical connector (named for its resemblance to the jaws of an alligator) attached to an electric cable for making a temporary connection to a battery or other component. Also called *alligator test leads*. SparkFun—PRT-11037
	9V battery	An energy source in which chemical energy is converted into electricity.

	9V battery snap connector	A snap connector is specifically designed to attach to a 9V battery. There are two wires (red is positive; black is negative) that can attach easily to the alligator clips or to other wires in your design. RS Electronics—HH-3449
	3V battery (also called "coin cell battery")	An energy source in which chemical energy is converted into electricity. We recommend using the common CR2032 type battery for e-textile projects (20 mm), which should power e-textile projects for weeks at a time. SparkFun—PRT-00338
	3V LilyPad battery holder	A 3V battery holder for the common CR2032 type battery. This component gives you four large sew holes (two positive and two negative) to allow it to be sewn into e-textiles or other garments. **Note:** Only two of the four holes need to be used to create the circuit (one positive and one negative). The other two can be used to sew the battery to the fabric or for creating a separate circuit. SparkFun—DEV-10730
	LilyPad LED	An LED is a small device that lights up when an electric current passes through it. It is frequently used as an indicator lamp in many everyday devices. LilyPad LEDs are designed with a built-in resistor and can be purchased in a wide array of colors, including blue, pink, red, white, yellow, and green. Note that the LED petals are labeled to indicate the positive and negative ends. LilyPad LEDs: SparkFun—e.g., DEV-10081

2. Hand out the "Multiple LEDs Diagram" worksheet. Instruct youths to discuss and sketch a couple of possible solutions to the problem. Warn them to leave extra room because after the experiment, they'll return to the worksheet and sketch what actually worked.

3. Instruct youths to put together the components to test their ideas, as well as experiment with new system structures (i.e., ways of putting the LEDs together). Have them record the outcomes of their systems when they are structured in different ways, noting the positive and negative sides of the battery and LEDs in their diagrams. Were they able to meet the goal of lighting multiple LEDs?

4. Point out that the 3V and 9V batteries don't just look different; they also have different *voltages*—the amount of force used to move an electric current through a conductor. Have youths look for at least one way to illuminate three LEDs using the 9V battery and at least one way to do so with the 3V battery. Things that they can experiment with might include:

- The number of LEDs that they use

- Which battery they use

- How the LEDs are connected to one another and to the battery.

5. There are a couple of things that you can expect to see (see "Possible Solutions"):

- The 9V battery will be able to support up to three LEDs in series (with one LED connected to the next one in a line).

- The 3V (coin cell) battery, however, will support only three LEDs if they are in parallel. Note that only one circuit in the diagram fails to light the LEDs.

POSSIBLE SOLUTIONS

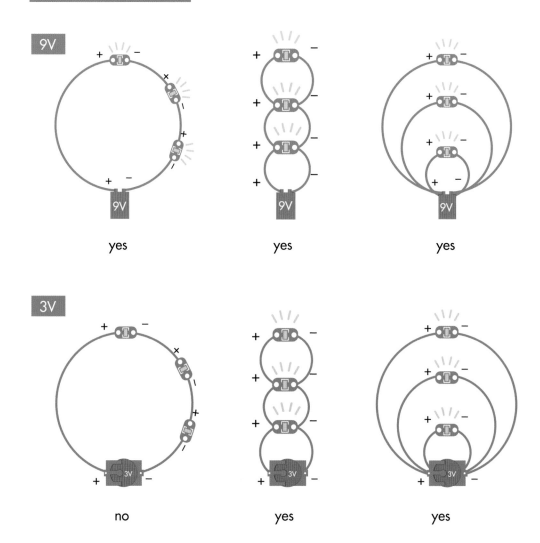

9V

yes   yes   yes

3V

no   yes   yes

6. Hopefully, some youths will "discover" both a series circuit structure and a parallel circuit structure in the process of experimenting. In case you do see any of the groups experimenting with changing the structure in these ways, note and name the kinds of structures for them as they emerge.

7. As youths experiment, make sure that one person in each group is documenting successful solutions on their "Multiple LEDs Diagram" worksheet so that they can share it with the larger group.

VOICES FROM THE FIELD

When I have the youth connect two LEDs in parallel form, I often tell them that the second LED can't have direct contact with the battery holder. This makes them reevaluate where they can successfully connect the +/- lines for the second LED. My hope is that they will then rebuild a few of their LEDs in parallel succession, linking one LED to another, which is more in line with the e-cuff parallel structure.
—Diane Glosson, Graduate Research Assistant, Indiana University

IMPORTANT TIPS FOR THIS ACTIVITY

- Although you don't necessarily need to announce this to the group (as they should be able to discover it in their play), it is important to always orient the LEDs in the circuit with respect to the battery, *not* with the other LEDs, regardless of whether the circuit is in parallel or series. In other words, the positive side of the battery needs to be connected to the positive leg of the LED and the negative to the negative.

- In a series circuit, often the first LED will light up, but not the others if there isn't enough voltage in the battery.

- When multiple alligator clips are trying to connect to the same component, it's helpful to clip one alligator clip to the component and the other(s) to the jaws of the first clip. Some alligator clips have an insulated plastic end, which can be slid back to expose the metal beneath if needed.

- Ensure that youths have a clear understanding of the orientation of the LEDs (especially for series circuits), as it makes a really clear difference in outcome for the system (i.e., whether the LEDs light up).

- Youths have used the LilyPad battery holder to replace half of a magnetic snap, so the holder itself is used in the snap.

- Remind youths that the batteries and the LilyPad LEDs have positive and negative ends.

- Note that different colors of light require different voltage levels. Warmer colors (like reds, oranges, and yellows) are lower in frequency and require less voltage. Cooler colors (like purples, blues, and greens), by contrast, are higher in frequency and require more voltage.

- In addition, don't mix LEDs with built-in resistors (e.g., LilyPad LEDs) and without built-in resistors (e.g., two-pronged LEDs) in a project. The current will flow to those LEDs that present the least amount of resistance in the circuit.

- Also, take a moment to introduce the 3V LilyPad Battery Holder; specifically, demonstrate how only two of the four holes on the unit need to be used in the circuit, while the other two holes can be used in the circuit (essentially creating two parallel circuits running off the same battery) or not.

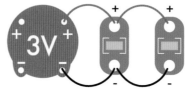

SHARE AND RESEARCH—SERIES VERSUS PARALLEL—15 MINUTES

In this portion of the activity, youths will share their solutions and learn more about series and parallel circuits.

1. After the groups have had about 30 minutes to experiment and hopefully have at least two or three different successful structures diagrammed, conduct a discussion about the successful solutions, including diagrams and circuits.

2. Move among the groups, naming and sorting circuits that are in series, parallel, or hybrid arrangements.

3. Ask youths what they notice (*Answer: All functioning series solutions should include a 9V battery only. All the parallel formations may include either a 3V or a 9V.*) Why is that? (*At this point, the answer could be informal, such as "parallel circuits need less voltage." The exact explanation of why this is so is not necessary and will come out of the later discussion.*)

4. This is a good time to introduce the "Series versus Parallel Circuits" handout and explain what is going on in both series and parallel circuit structures. See the box on the next page as you review the following:

   • When components are wired in series within a circuit, electric current flows sequentially through those components in a continuous loop. This means that as the current travels from the battery through each LED, it loses some of its original electrical charge or energy (also known as *voltage*), with the result that the amount of voltage available decreases with each LED it passes through.

   • When components are wired in parallel within a circuit, the electric current divides into two or more paths before recombining to complete the circuit. The current flows through three LEDs wired in parallel, and the electric current is split among the three of them equally. **Note:** the evenness of the split is contingent on the three LEDs being the same type.

   • The key difference between series and parallel circuits relates to current flow. In a series circuit, there is only one pathway for energy to travel, and as energy passes from the battery to each LED, less and less of the battery's energy will be available to each subsequent LED in the circuit. On the other hand, in a parallel circuit, energy is able to travel directly to every LED without passing through others, allowing each to receive some amount of energy from the battery.

SERIES CIRCUIT STRUCTURE	PARALLEL CIRCUIT STRUCTURE
When components are wired in series within a circuit, electric current flows sequentially through those components in a continuous loop. This means that as the current travels from the battery through each LED, it loses some of its original electrical charge or energy (also known as *voltage*) such that the amount of voltage available for each subsequent LED decreases with each one it passes through. Note that this structure will not work with the 3V battery for this reason.	When components are wired in parallel within a circuit (as opposed to one right after another), the electric current divides into two or more paths before recombining to complete the circuit. This allows the same amount of energy or voltage to reach each LED.

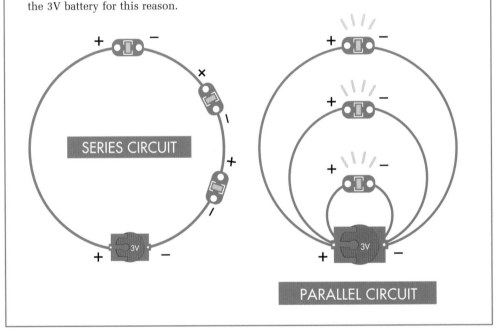

5. Ask youths to point out what they see as the major differences between the two circuit configurations. (*Answers may vary, but they might be something like "A series has one big loop" and "A parallel circuit has a several smaller loops."*)

6. Inform youths that:

   • In a *series* circuit, every component must function together to form a complete circuit.

   • In a *parallel* circuit, each component makes its own complete circuit (trace the lines on the diagram to help point this out).

7. Ask the following questions:

- For each type of circuit, what would happen if one LED were to burn out? (Answer: In the series circuit, it would break the circuit, while in a parallel circuit, any of the other two lights could be removed and the last one still would function.)

- Why would lights continue to function in one and not the other? (Answer: That's because the parallel circuit setup allows energy to flow to each LED separately.)

Note You may want to prebuild and demonstrate your own parallel circuit to model what would happen for youths. It is very important for youths to make the connection that the flow of energy is structured by the way that components are put together in the system. This will allow them to understand later why the series circuit that they will build does not light all the LEDs in the circuit.

8. Allow youths more time to tinker with the materials with these ideas in mind. Make sure that each youth creates both a parallel and a series circuit, as they may not have had an experience with both types.

9. Reiterate the importance of system structures—that is, the way that a system's components are configured plays a role in determining the behaviors of the components and the dynamic interactions or interconnections that they have with each other.

Interconnections are often contextualized with "if/then" statements, such as: "If a circuit uses a parallel structure, then it requires less voltage to light up all LEDs than it would if it was structured in series."

—RAFI SANTO, GRADUATE RESEARCH ASSISTANT, INDIANA UNIVERSITY

10. Prompt the group to try to think up other situations where a different configuration of identical components in a system could dramatically affect the ways that a system plays out.

- If they have trouble, have them consider the room that they're in, and ask what they could do to keep the same things in the room, but have them configured in such a way that the room would function in a totally different way. See if they can expand the idea to neighborhoods and the ways they're set up, or even cities.

REFLECT: LET'S TALK—15 MINUTES

Once everyone has created a functioning circuit in both parallel and series arrangements, conduct a large-group discussion. You can use the following questions to prompt the discussion (documenting their answers on the board):

- **What do we know about circuits as systems?**
  Answer: Circuits have components, like LEDs, batteries, switches, and alligator clips; circuits must be arranged in a closed loop to operate; if you incorporate multiple LEDs, you need to think about the system structure and the interconnections within the system between the battery and the LEDs; smaller batteries can't support multiple LEDs in a series, but larger batteries can; LEDs always have to be positioned with their positive and negative ends with respect to the battery.

- **Is the parallel LED circuit a system? Why or why not?**
  Answer: Yes, it is a system consisting of components with specific behaviors that interconnect to reach a goal (i.e., illuminating LEDs).

- **Is the series LED circuit a system? Why or why not?**
  Answer: Yes, it is also a system, consisting of components with specific behaviors that interconnect to reach a goal (e.g., illuminating LEDs).

- **If the 9V series and 9V parallel circuits are *both* systems, are they the same system and structured differently, or are they actually different systems? How are their differences related to how the system works?**
  Answer: While they are made of the same components, the fact that they are arranged in different ways means that as systems, they function differently, and so they could be thought of as different systems. The differences in the systems' structures produce different interconnections or interactions (i.e., whether the voltage is shared by the LEDs in series or distributed evenly across the LEDs in parallel).

- **What are the goals of this system? How do components in this system interconnect in order to reach those goals?**
  Answer: The goal of the system is to light up three LEDs; if the system is structured in series, then it needs a battery with enough voltage to power all components; if a system is structured in parallel, less voltage is required to power all LEDs.

WHAT TO EXPECT

The introduction of series and parallel circuits should help youths to understand that energy flows between components in a closed circuit and that energy in the system flows from the battery. *If that is not so, that is an indication that they are still working on their understanding of how a circuit functions.*

With respect to systems thinking concepts and vocabulary, the focus on system structure should hone youths' thinking on the interconnections among components. Specifically, asking them to think about *how* a new component is incorporated and how it changes the behavior of the system should help youths figure out how the behavior of one component affects the behavior of another component.

	Novice	Expert
Circuitry concepts	• Understands that in order for a circuit to be completed, it must be a closed loop, but is unable to create a system structure to support multiple LEDs • Finds difficulty grasping the concept that energy in a closed circuit flows between components, and is not comfortable playing with the electronic components • Is unable to diagram or prototype a working circuit • Doesn't appear to see interconnections between a battery's voltage and the number of LEDs that it can support • Doesn't understand that a series circuit requires more power from the battery to illuminate multiple LEDs than a parallel circuit requires • Connects the battery to the LED(s) without taking into account the direction that energy flows in the circuit	• Is comfortable playing with the electronic components in the process of exploring a wide number of solutions to create working circuits • Understands that there are at least two different structures that can be used in circuitry—series and parallel—and can diagram and prototype both • Understands that batteries have a particular voltage and that the amount of voltage determines how much power the battery has (and, in this case, how many LEDs it can support) • Understands that each LED in a series circuit structure drains resources (voltage) that is available for other LEDs in the system • Understands that multiple LEDs can be supported in a single circuit easily by using a parallel circuit structure (and therefore is a more efficient way to operate a circuit than using a more powerful battery) • Has a good sense of the directionality of flow and the relationship of the battery to the LED(s)
Systems thinking concepts	• Unable to identify and use basic systems thinking terminology to describe their circuit • Unable to describe how a system's parts interact with each other through their behaviors • Fails to see connections between system structure and system dynamics and interconnections • Is unable to identify potential leverage points, such as the voltage of the battery or the number of LEDs • Uncomfortable troubleshooting a nonworking circuit	• Can easily identify and use basic systems thinking terminology (*components*, *behaviors*, and *goals*) to describe their circuit • Can identify different ways that the system's parts interact with each other through their behaviors and begins to use terms like *systems dynamics* and *interconnections* • Understands that the way that a system is structured has effects on the behaviors of the components and the kinds of interconnections or interactions they have with one another; can contextualize this understanding in the discussions of their circuits, using phrases like "if a 3V battery is used, then the LEDs must be structured in parallel in order to light up" • Is able to identify a range of leverage points and explain how they work

DESIGN CHALLENGE 2, PART 1

SWITCH DIAGRAM

This diagram depicts an electric circuit with a switch in both the off and on positions. Consider if the circuit was controlling water instead of electric current: The switch would act as a valve or faucet to control the water flow out of the faucet.

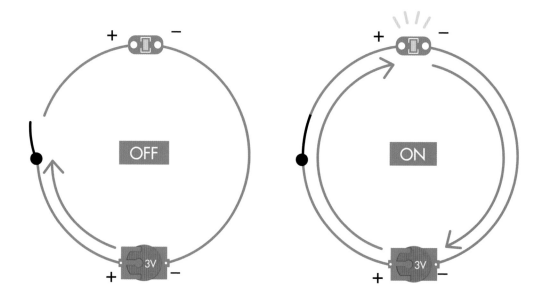

DESIGN CHALLENGE 2, PART 1

MULTIPLE LEDS DIAGRAM

Use this worksheet to diagram both your hypotheses and finding for your experiments to light multiple LEDs in a single circuit.

In the space below, share some of your ideas about how a system might be set up that will light at least 3 LEDs using (a) your 3V (coin cell) battery; (b) your 9V battery; or both.

After experimenting with the materials, diagram your successful solutions in this space. Do they look like the diagrams that you drew above? If not, how do they differ?

DESIGN CHALLENGE 2, PART 1

SERIES VERSUS PARALLEL CIRCUITS

When components are wired in series within a circuit, electric current flows sequentially through those components in a continuous loop. This means that as the current travels from the battery through each LED, it loses some of its original charge, or energy (also known as *voltage*), such that the amount of voltage available for each subsequent LED decreases with each one that it passes through.

When components are wired in parallel within a circuit, the electric current divides into two or more paths before recombining to complete the circuit. The current flows through three LEDs wired in parallel, and the electric current is split among the three of them equally. **Note:** The evenness of the split is contingent on the three LEDs being the same type. Otherwise, the current will flow more where it meets less resistance.

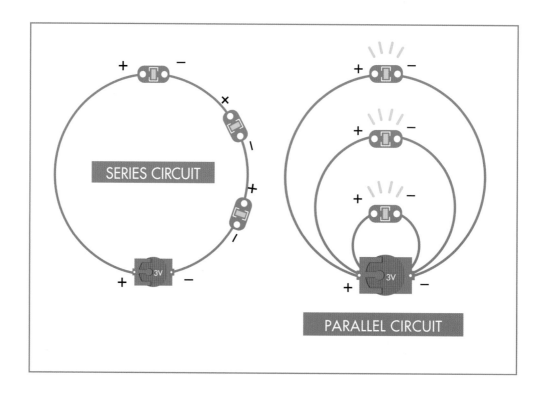

PART 2: DESIGN TIME—MAKING E-TEXTILE CUFFS

In this activity, youths apply their knowledge about system structures to creating e-cuffs using e-textile materials.

Time: 150 minutes

STUFF TO HAVE HANDY

- Prototype of an e-textile cuff, prepared in advance by the instructor
- e-Textile Cuff Kits (prepared in advance by the instructor; 1 per youth)
- 9" x 2" strips of felt in various colors (one or two pieces to layer per youth)
- Plenty of alligator clips
- Conductive thread
- Regular thread
- Sewing needles and pincushions
- Clear nail polish, fabric glue, or low-temperature hot glue (to hold knots)
- Scissors
- Decorative materials like assorted buttons, fabric markers, glass beads, gems, or other materials

HANDOUTS

- "Running Stitch Practice"
- "Sample e-Textile Cuff Circuit Diagram"
- *Optional:* "Tracing Current Flow Diagram" (from Design Challenge 1)

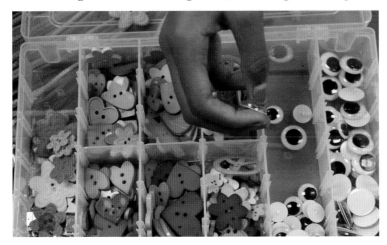

PLAY: PRACTICING RUNNING STITCHES—15 MINUTES

Youths should practice running stitches with nonconductive thread before starting the e-textile project.

1. Tell youths that they will be inserting their circuits into fabric toward the creation of an *e-textile,* any fabric object with electronics embedded in it. In this project, they will develop a cuff or bracelet into which they'll sew their circuits using conductive thread and other wearable components. Thus, some familiarity with sewing is required.

2. Before they get started, cover the basics of sewing as detailed in the "Essential Stitch Craft" section in the Toolkit of this book, which includes information on how to thread a needle, tie knots, and perform basic running stitches, as well as generally helpful craftwork guidance.

3. Youths can use the "Running Stitch Practice" worksheet to practice proper stitching techniques by connecting the dots with *nonconductive* thread and then adding their own dots and stitches to complete the diagram. As another option, you could also create stitching practice worksheets to replicate the bracelet layout diagrams.

Note For the "Running Stitch Practice" worksheet, construction paper is suggested because it is slightly better suited to sewing.

VOICES FROM THE FIELD

Youth often don't understand how to sew through the conductive holes while attaching the part to the fabric (some youth think if they simply stitch up and down through the material three times, the parts will be secured to the fabric somehow). An easy solution is to let each youth select two sequins for the eyes of their stitching sheet character. This allows them to practice stitching a sew hole *and* also reinforces the practice of starting a knot from the underside of the material.

—DIANE GLOSSON, GRADUATE RESEARCH ASSISTANT, INDIANA UNIVERSITY

RESEARCH AND PLAY: WORKING FROM E-TEXTILE CUFF DIAGRAMS—15 MINUTES

Youths use diagrams and group discussion to create an e-textile prototype.

1. Pass out copies of the "Sample e-Textile Cuff Circuit Diagram" worksheet.

2. Share your prototype e-cuff with LilyPad LEDs so that youths have a better sense of what they'll be creating. Ask some guided questions to help them understand the components of the design, such as the following:

- I can turn the light on and off by taking my cuff on and off—How do you think that works? (*Answer: It is done via a* switch, *a component that controls the flow of electricity by opening and closing a circuit. When the circuit is*

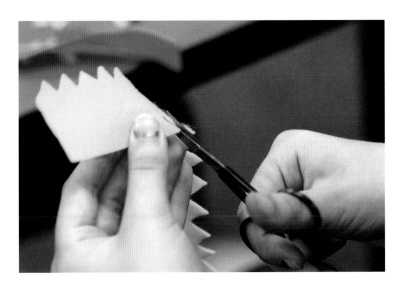

broken, the light is off; by placing the cuff on your wrist and connecting the snaps or two pieces of Velcro together, the circuit is reconnected, and the light turns on.)

- What qualities did the alligator clips have that made it possible to replace them with conductive thread? (*Answers: 1. The electric current can move through both alligator clips and conductive thread. 2. The connective thread can connect two things, one on each end, just like the alligator clip.*)

- How do you think conductive thread is different from regular sewing thread? (*Answer: Like the alligator clip, the thread is made of material that conducts electricity, usually thin strands of silver woven together.*)

3. Point out that the switch/clasp of the bracelet will take up the outer half-inch of each side of the bracelet, so youths need to make sure they keep about a 1-inch overlap *and* that they keep this area clear of decorative elements to avoid problems.

4. Take a few minutes to analyze the "Sample e-Textile Cuff Circuit Diagram" handout. Make sure that everyone clearly understands the diagram as well as the stitch lines before proceeding to address the following questions:

- Is this a series or parallel circuit? *(Answer: parallel.)*

- How do you know? (*Answer strategy: Have the youths look at the stitching lines and discuss. Point their attention to the ways the LEDs are connected via the stitches; each LED is separately connected to the battery, instead of having the current run through each LED before returning back to the battery.*)

- In what way are the LEDs connected to the battery? (*Answer: The negative side of the battery is connected to the negative ends of the LEDs. Conversely, the positive side of the battery is connected to one snap or piece of Velcro.*)

5. Pass out the e-Textile Cuff Kits and alligator clips. Have youths create the sample circuit depicted on the "Sample e-Textile Cuff Circuit Diagram" worksheet, making sure that they use the materials provided for the switch and that they affix the LEDs in parallel to the battery. Introduce the components as needed:

	Alligator clips	An electrical connector (named for its resemblance to the jaws of an alligator) attached to an electric cable for making a temporary connection to a battery or other component. Also called *alligator test leads*. SparkFun—PRT-11037
	3V battery (also called "coin cell battery")	An energy source in which chemical energy is converted into electricity. We recommend using the common CR2032 type battery for e-textile projects (20 mm), which should power e-textile projects for weeks at a time. SparkFun—PRT-00338
	3V LilyPad battery holder	A 3V battery holder for the common CR2032 type battery. This component gives you four large sew holes (two positive and two negative) to allow it to be sewn into e-textiles or other garments. **Note:** Only two of the four holes need to be used to create the circuit (one positive and one negative). The other two can be used to sew the battery to the fabric or for creating a separate circuit. SparkFun—DEV-10730

	Sewable metal snaps	Metal snaps with sew holes that can be sewn onto the bracelet easily. It is important to look for snaps that are conductive (i.e., not covered in a protective coating). Available at your local arts and crafts store.
	Sewable metal magnetic snaps	Metal snaps with sew holes that can be sewn onto the bracelet easily, magnetized for easy closure. It is important to look for snaps that are conductive (i.e., not covered in a protective coating). Available at your local arts and crafts store.
	Optional conductive Velcro	Similar to Velcro, but with a conductive silver coating. Conductive Velcro can be sewn in or glued, but no adhesive is supplied. Sparkfun COM-11831
	LilyPad LED	An LED is a small device that lights up when an electric current passes through it. It is frequently used as an indicator lamp in many everyday devices. LilyPad LEDs are designed with a built-in resistor and can be purchased in a wide array of colors, including blue, pink, red, white, yellow, and green. Note that the LED petals are labeled to indicate the positive and negative ends. LilyPad LEDs: SparkFun—e.g., DEV-10081

VOICES FROM THE FIELD

The students made iterations as necessary and even came up with several alternative methods to reroute the circuit. Marcello gave me a great description of how to fix his bracelet. Some students worked hard to fix conductivity problems. Xenia and Mariann were having a really hard time getting their switch to work. They identified the problem as the battery holder, and after making some changes to the system, they were able to get the switch to work.

—LORI BELL, GREAT BEAR WRITING PROJECT

CREATE: STITCHING CIRCUITS—110 MINUTES

Youths begin stitching their e-textile cuffs in this activity. Note that they often prefer to work incrementally between the decorative elements and the sewing of the circuit in their designs.

DECORATING THE CUFF

1. *Choose base colors:* Have youths choose one or two strips of felt for their cuffs. If they are using two pieces of felt, have them place the pieces on top of one another and consider how they want the two pieces to work together. (For example, making the top strip narrower to show the bottom as a border, or cutting eyelets into the top layer to reveal the color of the bottom layer.)

2. *Finalize the base color design:* Encourage youths to be creative in using scissors to make the two strips work together **Note:** Youths may choose to use only a single strip of felt, which is also fine.

3. *Add decorations:* Here is where youths explore the embellishments and decorative elements that you have gathered, developing a final design for the cuff. **Note:** Some items may be in high demand and short supply. You may want to devise some way of distributing the materials equitably among the group.

4. *Begin adding circuitry elements:* Make sure that every youth has an e-Textile Cuff Kit, and have each person lay out all the components on the decorated felt strip. Help the youths think through which components should be on the front of the cuff and which should be hidden on the back. Note that a variety of solutions for embedding the circuit successfully are possible.

THINGS TO CONSIDER BEFORE SEWING

- *Securing the knots:* Have youths prepare to sew with the conductive thread by threading their needle and knotting the thread. *(CRITICAL STEP!)* Whenever they knot the thread, it's important to use clear nail polish, fabric glue, or low-temperature hot glue to hold the knots.

  - *Before sewing:* Have them use the nail polish or glue on the knot before sewing to avoid getting it on the metal petals of the LilyPad parts (and insulating them).

  - *After sewing:* Encourage them to tie their end knots on the back side of the felt, and then use nail polish or glue to hold them in place.

  This will help prevent insulation of the metal petals of the LilyPad parts as well. *Remind youths that a little goes a long way when applying materials to secure the knots—no need to go overboard!*

- *Consider stitch sizes:* Ask youths what would happen if they made very large stitches or if they didn't loop through each component several times. *(Answer: The components would fall off or not make a solid connection with the thread.)* Point out that this is also true for the conductive fabric or tape, which requires a firm connection with the conductive thread. In addition, remind them that a circuit must be a complete loop in order to work.

- *Consider the dangers of short circuits:* Ask youths to consider that will happen if they don't cut the thread between components. *(Answer: They'll create a short in their circuit. See the "Tracing Current Flow Diagram" worksheet from Design Challenge 1, Part 2).*

SEWING THE ELECTRIC CIRCUIT

Consider starting this process as a whole-group activity, completing at least the first stitching line together as a way of modeling the activity.

1. *Sew the separate lines of the circuit:* Have them begin stitching to attach the components and create the circuit connections in their proposed designs. *(CRITICAL STEP!)* In the design shown in the "Sample e-Textile Cuff Circuit Diagram" worksheet, there are three *separate* lines that require stitching:

- Sew a line from the snap or Velcro closure on the left side to the (+) end of the battery holder. **Note:** You don't have to sew to both of the positive holes.

- Sew a separate line from the (−) side of the battery holder to the (−) sides of *all* the LEDs.

- Sew another separate line, this time from the (+) end of the LED to the metal snap or Velcro closure on the right side of the cuff.

2. *Make solid connections on components (CRITICAL STEP!):* During sewing, for each component in the circuit (LEDs, battery holders, or snaps/Velcro), *three stitches* must be taken to create solid connections with the conductive thread.

3. *Debug as you go:* Debugging—the act of identifying and removing errors from a design—is an essential skill for anyone working with electric circuitry design. Let youths know that almost every one of them will run into some type of problem that will require them to stop, correct, and recreate part of their e-cuffs. Assure them that this process, called *iteration,* is a good thing—in fact, it's one of the goals of this Design Challenge!

Note   Be sure to leave time for this type of learning. There is not a lot of required stitching for this project, but youths should be prepared to cut out their mistakes and try again as needed. The "Debugging Steps" section, later in this Design Challenge, lists some common problems and ways to solve them. However, try to avoid supplying the answers right away—errors in youths' designs often are fueled by misconceptions that can be best rectified through iterative testing and experimentation.

Congratulations—the e-textile cuffs are complete! Have youths test the circuit while wearing the e-cuffs on their wrists to see if they work.

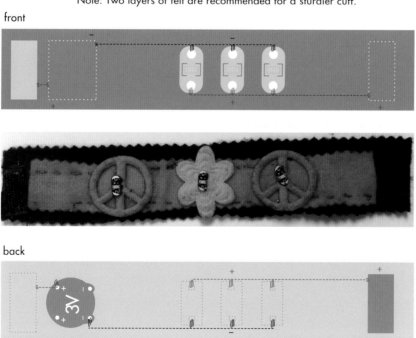

Sample e-textile cuff circuit diagram.

IMPORTANT TIPS FOR THIS ACTIVITY

- If you use snaps or magnetic snaps to close the e-cuffs, make sure that they don't have a protective/insulating coating that will prevent the circuit from making a complete loop. If you're unsure, use your multimeter in Continuity mode to test the materials. If there is a protective coating, you can use sandpaper or a nail file to scratch the surface and make a more solid connection. *This is a common problem encountered with this project.*

- The "Sample e-Textile Cuff Circuit Diagram" handout provides only one possible solution for how to create an e-textile cuff, but many other variations of this model can be successful. Encourage youths to experiment, but check in with them often during the design process to avoid time-consuming mistakes.

- Some youths may struggle at first with hand-sewing with the conductive thread, but they gain experience in the thread's behavior. For instance, when conductive thread catches or knots, don't pull it tight, but patiently untangle it, using a needle if necessary to pull the knot apart.

- If the positive and negative lines of thread ever need to cross (because of the design), glass beads can be slipped onto the thread of one line at the crossing point. This will insulate the conductive thread, preventing it from crossing another line.

- *Having trouble?* Refer to the this book's Toolkit and the debugging steps that follow for troubleshooting guidance and additional techniques for working with conductive thread.

- *Washing instructions:* First, remove the battery and then hand-wash the cuff in mild detergent. Allow it to drip dry. *All LilyPad components are washable, including the battery holder and LEDs.*

VOICES FROM THE FIELD

We've noticed that youth sometimes have trouble seeing how the e-cuff is a complete circuit and a closed loop since they sew it in a straight line. It works well to take some time to trace current flow through the cuff together, so that youth will see that the cuff does make a complete loop when the switch is closed.

—SOPHIA BENDER, GRADUATE RESEARCH ASSISTANT, INDIANA UNIVERSITY

DEBUGGING STEPS

- Make sure that no lines are crossed in the design because this will cause a short.

- Make sure that the (+) sides of the LEDs are oriented toward the (+) end of the battery holder. *Positive to positive!*

- Make sure that the (−) sides of the LEDs are connected to the (−) end of the battery holder. *Negative to negative!*

- Make sure that each component has a solid connection (i.e., the conductive thread has been sewn around the component two or more times) and is not dangling from the cuff.

- Make sure that the thread doesn't connect both ends of any LED. (Remember, positive to positive and negative to negative *only!*)

- Make sure that none of the stitching has been cut accidentally or frayed. If there are any questions about whether the stitching is still good, use the multimeter in Continuity mode (don't forget to remove the battery before doing so!).

- Make sure that the LEDs are sewn in parallel from the battery holder, not in series.

- Check the back of the cuff to make sure that there are no long tails on the knots or any threads that make unnecessary loops. Use the hot-glue gun to affix any dangling pieces so that they are out of the way and not touching other conductive components.

EXAMPLE PROJECTS

Flower Power cuff

Feathers and Bows cuff

Starry Night cuff

SHARE: GALLERY DISPLAY—10 MINUTES

It's time to get some bragging rights!

1. Have youths place their cuffs on a central table as a gallery display, and ask volunteers to come to the front to share their designs. Use guiding questions to help them explain their work, such as:

- Why did you design your e-cuff in the way that you did?

- How did you construct your e-cuff?

- What was the easiest part of the creation? What was hardest?

- Describe your circuit: How does each component fit together to work as a system?

- What problems did you encounter, if any? How did you solve the issue?

- If you were going to create another e-cuff, what might you do differently? Why?

2. Encourage and model "warm" feedback (positive comments) from the audience, and then add "cool" feedback with ideas for how to improve their work next time. (See the "Introduction" to this book for more feedback suggestions.)

DESIGN CHALLENGE 2, PART 2

RUNNING STITCH PRACTICE

Practice sewing a running stitch by connecting the dots in this picture with *nonconductive thread.* Then add your own dots and stitches to complete the diagram.

RUNNING STITCHES GO OVER & UNDER THE FABRIC

1 Double thread the needle and knot it at the end.
Push the needle through the underside of the paper and by the #1 •
Connect the dotted line by sewing in and out of the dots, making sure to stay on the line.

2 Continue to connect the dots.

3 Use the thread to make a line.

4 Use your running stitch to complete the picture by sewing the penguin a collar, ending at Point 1.

DESIGN CHALLENGE 2, PART 2

SAMPLE E-TEXTILE CUFF CIRCUIT DIAGRAM

This diagram depicts a sample e-textile circuit layout with a clasp (either snaps or conductive Velcro) that operates like a switch for the cuff. When the cuff is affixed to the wrist, the circuit closes and lights the LEDs.

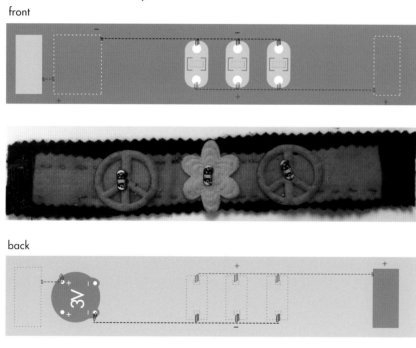

9"x 2" felt (cut to fit wrist + overlap)
Note: Two layers of felt are recommended for a sturdier cuff.

front

back

1. Choose one or two pieces of felt for your cuff. Customize them by cutting out shapes in the fabric, making a cool border, or designing it with fabric markers.

2. Lay out the components in your e-Textile Cuff Kit (LilyPad LEDs, 3V battery and holder, and switch materials) on your design. Which components should be on the front of the cuff, and which should be hidden on the back?

3. Get ready to sew! Thread a needle with conductive thread and knot the ends of the thread together. Use nail polish or fabric glue on the knot before sewing.

4. Create end knots on the opposite side of the LilyPad parts and then secure clear nail polish, fabric glue, or low-temperature hot glue to hold the knots.

5. Sew down each component and stitch the connections between them. Stitch through each component *three times* to create solid connections with the conductive thread. You also need to knot and cut the thread when you get to the end of one of the stitching lines (avoiding long tails).

6. When your components and connections are sewn, test the circuit on your wrist to see if it works! Consult the *Stitching Tips Guide* if your LEDs don't light up or if you run into trouble along the way.

PART 3: WRAP UP!

In the final part of this Design Challenge, youths will have an opportunity to share their projects with their local peer group. Finally, youths will reflect on their e-textile cuff experience and connect to the core systems thinking concepts in this Design Challenge.

Time: 90 minutes

STUFF TO HAVE HANDY

- Computer with active Internet connection (1 per youth)
- Digital camera(s) with photo and video capabilities and USB cord(s) to download material to the computer
- Youths' finished e-textile cuffs

HANDOUTS

- "Posting Your e-Textile Cuff"
- "Self-Reflection on My e-Textile Cuff"

PUBLISH: POSTING TO THE WEB—60 MINUTES

Today's youths are becoming both consumers and avid producers of media online. The goal of this part of the activity is to give them time to post their e-textile cuffs to an online community like the ones discussed in the Product section of this Design Challenge. There are several public websites that are ideal for posting e-textile projects like those found in this book. Giving them a few minutes to do this allows youths to post their work and become part of the larger participatory culture.

1. If you haven't already done so, create log-in usernames and passwords (or allow time for youths to create their own logins), and test the firewalls in your computer lab to make sure you can access the website.

2. Allow youths time to visit the chosen website and briefly explore the projects posted there, leaving comments or "liking" projects as they go (*login required*). It might be useful for them to make notes as they explore about what makes a good post (for example, a great picture, interesting text accompanying the post, an attention-grabbing title, etc.).

3. After they've taken time to view other users' offerings, distribute the "Posting Your e-Textile Cuff" worksheet. Ask youths to complete the worksheet before they post their projects on the website. Remind them to refer to their notes about what makes a good post as they work on their own writing.

GIVE YOUR PROJECT A NAME

What will you call your e-textile cuff? Give it a unique and inspiring name! The name is also the title of your post.

WRITE A PROJECT DESCRIPTION

- What inspired you?

- Describe the materials you used to create your e-textile cuff, including all the circuit components.

- Describe how your e-textile cuff works and any other details that you think are important for others to know about.

PHOTO SHOOT PLANNING

What should the photo(s) look like online? Sketch or write a description of what they should look like. (Example: "Photo 1 should be the e-textile cuff with the LEDs turned on; photo 2 should be the entire e-textile cuff laid out flat.") Should there be a video of someone modeling your fashion for the site? If so, what should show in the video?

1. Have small groups of youths take turns taking pictures and/or videos of their finished projects. Scanning some of the planning materials also would make interesting additions to the posts as well. Remind youths to refer to their notes about what they thought makes a good post as they work on their own pictures and videos.

2. Once they have drafted their ideas for their post, have youths log in to the website to post their projects.

3. Encourage youths to:

- Give their project a unique name/title.

- Tag the project with "Soft Circuits," "e-Textile Cuff," or another unique tag for your group.

- Write a compelling project description.

- Link to other web materials (like videos that need to be posted on YouTube before youths create their online submissions).

IMPORTANT TIPS FOR THIS ACTIVITY

- In order to post videos in a shared online community, they need to be hosted on a site like YouTube or Vimeo, and a link needs to be copied to the chosen site.

- What makes a good post? Suggest to youths that they photograph their work up close, with few distractions in the background of the image. Encourage them to write a clever title and catchy text that is both informative but to the point, and to think of their audience when describing their project, how it works, and what they used to put it together.

- In a few days, check to see if there are any comments on any of your group's posts and/or encourage them to comment on each other's work too—reading and responding are important aspects of joining an online community!

REFLECT AND SHARE: LET'S TALK!—30 MINUTES

As a final activity, which can be used as an assessment, distribute the "Self-Reflection on My e-Textile Cuff" worksheet. Ask youths to fill these out individually and to take some time to think about what they now know and understand about circuits and systems as a consequence of designing and crafting an e-textile cuff.

- What was the system structure of the circuit you used in your e-cuff? Describe how the components in this particular structure interconnect to make the cuff work.

- What role does conductive thread play in helping the circuit to meet its goal?

- Balancing feedback loops prevents certain processes from happening. What leverage points do you have in your e-cuff, and what do they have to do with balancing feedback loops?

- What are other leverage points that you could put in your e-cuff? What would each addition do to the behaviors of your existing components?

After the worksheets are completed and projects are posted, bring the youths together to share their thoughts. This is an opportunity for them to move away from the specifics of their cuff designs and start thinking more generally about circuits and the extent to which they are instances of systems. You might start the discussion by reviewing the questions on the self-reflection worksheet, or you can use the following questions:

- Encourage youths to explain how they constructed their e-textile cuffs, including the following points:

- The location of the circuitry components

- How the switch was created

- The design choices that they made to embellish the cuff

- How each component fits together to work as a system

- Encourage the use of the essential vocabulary that was introduced in Part 1:

  - What was the goal of the e-textile cuff?

  - How do the components of the e-textile cuff work together in order to accomplish that goal? What components make up the system?

  - What are the components' respective behaviors?

  - How do the components of the circuits interconnect?

  - How does the behavior of one component affect the behavior of another component?

WHAT TO EXPECT

This reflection will allow youths an opportunity to express their conceptual understanding of a circuit as a system of interrelated parts that are structured in particular ways. The descriptions that follow give a range of possible feedback from youths in response to the first three questions, as the answers offer an excellent opportunity to evaluate their understanding of both circuitry and systems thinking concepts.

	Novice	Expert
Circuitry concepts	• Can identify the basic elements of an electronic circuit—LEDs, switch, battery, wire—but struggles to label important interconnections between components, or does so incorrectly (such as the orientation of the LEDs and battery, the switch, and the flow of current in the circuit) • Struggles to understand how energy flows through a circuit • Struggles to explain why or how a circuit has to be completed • Cannot identify the structure of the circuit (e.g., parallel or series)	• Identifies all basic components of an electrical circuit, and can describe accurately the core interconnections between all components in the circuit (e.g., if a 3V battery is used, then you need to use a parallel structure to light more than one LED) • Readily identifies the structure of the circuit (e.g., parallel or series) • Understands that in order for a circuit to be completed, it must be a closed loop, and can create a circuit/circuit diagram incorporating more than one LED in a circuit in a system (in series or in parallel)

	Novice	Expert
	• Understands that in order for a circuit to be completed, it must be a closed loop; however, has difficulty incorporating more than one LED in a circuit in a system (in series or in parallel) • Understands that a switch closes and opens an otherwise complete circuit, but struggles to understand that there is a continuous flow of energy from the battery in a complete circuit and that a switch serves to interrupt and reestablish that flow to conserve the battery's energy • Inappropriately associates conductive thread with insulating the electric charge as opposed to carrying or enabling it to flow through the circuit	• Can explain how a switch should be incorporated into a circuit in order to function • Shows clear understanding of the dual role of the conductive thread: that it serves to close the circuit, and that energy travels through the conductive thread to enables a continuous flow of energy between the battery and LED(s) • Can explain how the transfer of energy in a circuit is achieved through the use of conductive thread to close and complete the circuit via delivering electric charge between circuit parts (i.e., LED and battery), and therefore demonstrates understanding of how components interconnect in order to achieve circuit's goal (i.e., lighting the LEDs)
Systems thinking concepts	• Describes the circuit simply as a collection of components with specific behaviors with little attention given to how individual components interact to achieve the overall goal (i.e., lighting the LED) • Fails to see connections between system structure and system dynamics and interconnections • Is unable to identify potential leverage points, such as the voltage of the battery, the system's structure, or the switch • Primarily discusses aspects of a circuit causally (e.g., the LED works because it's connected to the battery), and therefore is unable to offer an explanation detailing how the thread functions to carry energy • Is unable to describe that systems can be structured in different ways (i.e., this doesn't make them a different system)	• Gives an explanation that conveys an understanding that a circuit is a system of multiple components, each with unique behaviors, and that it is the interconnections or interactions between these components (e.g., that the switch needs to be in the On position for the LEDs to turn on) that enables the system to reach its goal (i.e., the LEDs light up) • Understands that the way that a system is structured affects the behaviors of the components and the kinds of interconnections or interactions they have with one another; can contextualize this understanding in the discussions of their circuits, using phrases like "if a 3V battery is used, then the LEDs must be structured in parallel in order to light up" • Can explain how adding the component of a switch changes the behavior of other components and, to a lesser extent, the overall goal of the system (i.e., the conservation of energy)

DESIGN CHALLENGE 2, PART 3

POSTING YOUR E-TEXTILE CUFF

Use this worksheet to help plan what you will say about your e-textile cuff.

GIVE YOUR PROJECT A NAME:

- What will you call your e-textile cuff? Give it a unique and inspiring name!

WRITE A PROJECT DESCRIPTION:

- What inspired you?

- Describe the materials you used to create your e-textile cuff, including all the circuit components.

- Describe how your e-textile cuff works.

PHOTO SHOOT PLANNING:

What should the photo(s) look like? Sketch them or write down a description of what they should look like in the space below. (Example: "Photo 1 should be the e-textile cuff with the LEDs turned on; photo 2 should be the entire e-textile cuff laid out flat.") Should there be a video of someone modeling the e-textile cuff? If so, what should show in the video?

DESIGN CHALLENGE 2, PART 3

SELF-REFLECTION ON MY E-TEXTILE CUFF

Let's take a moment to think about what we've created through this activity.

1. What was the system structure of the circuit that you used in your e-cuff? Describe how the components in this particular structure interconnect to make your cuff work.

2. Balancing feedback loops prevents certain processes from happening. What leverage points do you have in your e-cuff, and what do they have to do with balancing feedback loops?

3. What are other leverage points that you could put in your e-cuff? What would each addition do to the behaviors of your existing components?

DESIGN CHALLENGE 3
ELECTRICITEE

Total time: 345–435 minutes

OVERVIEW

In this Design Challenge, youths are introduced to the concept of *nested systems*—systems that have their own structure but also work together to form a new system. They will explore multiple systems (a unique T-shirt design, an electronic circuit, and a computer *programming* language), and examine how the *goals* and *interconnections* of one system affect others within the context of *e-textiles*. Activities incorporate a *microcontroller* that extends youths' circuitry knowledge from previous Design Challenges and also introduce them to the basics of fashion design and computer programming. Ultimately, youths post their projects to an online community.

PRODUCT

Youths will design and make an electronics-enhanced T-shirt that incorporates a programmable LilyPad Simple microcontroller and light-emitting diodes (LEDs). The ElectriciTee then can be shared and posted to an online community. Consult our website at digitalis.nwp.org/gnl for suggestions, but you may want to consider Instructables.com, DIY.org, or another venue for sharing your work.

TARGETED SYSTEMS THINKING CONCEPTS

Almost all systems are nested within larger systems. The system function of an e-textile affects the way that its constituent subsystems—physical textiles, electronic circuits, and computer programming—each behave, and changes to any of these subsystems manifest in the way that the e-textile functions. Like previous analyses of circuitry systems, physical textiles and computer programs each contain unique components, behaviors, and structures, which interconnect to create an overall system function that accomplishes the goal of each discreet system.

PARTS

PART 1: GETTING STARTED WITH THE LILYPAD AND MODKIT MICRO

This activity introduces youths to two new tools: the ProtoSnap-LilyPad Development Simple board (or the ProtoSnap Simple for short); and the novice-friendly, visual programming environment Modkit Micro (or ArduBlock). The ProtoSnap Simple contains a LilyPad Simple, a wearable microcontroller that can be integrated easily into clothing or other textile artifacts and can be programmed using Modkit Micro software. The board also contains four white LilyPad LEDs and a LilyPad buzzer. Modkit Micro can tell the LilyPad how to control light from the LEDs, sound from the buzzer, and other elements through graphical programming.

Time: 35 minutes

PART 2: EXPLORING NESTED SYSTEMS

This activity is designed to look at two interconnected systems, one digital (Modkit) and one physical (the ProtoSnap Simple and the other physical components). The goal of this activity is to help youths think about the ways that different systems work together to create a new system. In this case, there are two separate systems (the LilyPad kit and Modkit software), which are nested within a larger, interconnected system.

Time: 60 minutes

PART 3: T-SHIRT PLANNING AND PREP TIME

Here, youths plan their designs and nest their LilyPad Simples within another system: the T-shirt! First, they will create the designs for their shirts, transforming them from boring to beautiful with a variety of decorative techniques. Then they will create a circuit diagram to plan for the circuitry additions coming in Part 4.

Time: 40–130 minutes

PART 4: MAKE IT YOUR OWN WITH MICROCONTROLLERS

It's time to begin programming and snapping apart the ProtoSnap Simple board to embed its circuitry into youths' T-shirt designs. During this phase of the challenge, youths not only will add electronics, they also will practice debugging skills.

Time: 120 minutes

PART 5: SHARE AND PUBLISH!

The goal of this part is to have youths share and reflect on their ElectriciTees. Sharing is an important part of learning, as is a mindful, guided reflection on the learning process. The activity ends with youths connecting their design decisions to the core systems thinking concepts addressed here.

Time: 90 minutes

KEY DEFINITIONS

SYSTEMS THINKING

Identifying a system. Identifying a system and distinguishing it from other kinds of things that aren't systems. Specifically, a system is a collection of two or more *components* and processes that *interconnect* to *function* as a whole. Speed and comfort in a car for example are created by the interactions of the car's parts and thus are "greater than the sum" of all separate parts of the car. The way a system works is not the result of a single part but is produced by the *interaction* among the components and/or individual agents within it. A key way to differentiate things that are systems from things that aren't is to consider whether the overall way something works in the world will change if you remove one part of it.

Identify the way a system is functioning. The function of a system describes the overall behavior of the system—what it is doing or where it's going over time. A system's function might emerge naturally based on interconnections among components, or it might be the result of an intentional design (in which case, we might also refer to the function of a system as its goal). Regardless, the function of a system is the result of the dynamics that occur among components' interconnected behaviors.

Identifying components. Identifying the parts of a system that contribute to its functioning. *Components* have certain qualities and/or *behaviors* that determine how they *interconnect* with other components, as well as define their role in the system. Without being able to effectively identify the parts of a system, it's hard to understand how a system is actually *functioning* and how it might be changed.

Identifying behaviors. Identifying the specific actions, roles, or behaviors that a component of a system displays under various conditions. Being able to identify behaviors becomes important when we change systems, as often a component will look the same after the change, but its behavior will be different.

Identifying interconnections. Identifying the different ways that a system's parts, or *components*, interact with each other through their *behaviors*, and through those interactions, change the behaviors of other components.

Designing a system. Creating a system through engaging in an iterative design process, one that entails iterative cycles of feedback, troubleshooting, and testing. One of the most effective means of developing systems thinking is to regularly create and iterate on the design of systems, and doing so in a way that creates opportunities for youths to think about generic systems models that apply across multiple domains and settings.

Distinguishing the goal of a system. The goal of the system is what a system that was intentionally designed is intended to do. Sometimes this might be the same as the functioning of the system ... other times the goal and the *function* are not aligned. A given system might have multiple goals or purposes that are at play simultaneously, and come into conflict. Being able to understand system purpose or goal gives a sense of the ideal state of a system from a particular perspective.

Considering the role of system structure. Understanding that the ways that a system's *components* are set up in relation to one another affect the behaviors of those components and the overall dynamics and function of a system. When we try to understand and make changes in a system, it's more important to know about its structure than to just know the individual characteristics of the system's components. Often structures go unnoticed, but they have a big impact on what components in a system do.

Nested systems. Systems that are a smaller part of other systems. Almost all systems are nested within larger systems. With nested systems, a larger system will affect the way that a subsystem behaves, and the subsystem will affect the way that the larger system behaves. The nature of systems as nested within one another means that it's usually possible to zoom in or out of systems in order to see systems that are either around them (if those systems are bigger) or within them (if those systems are smaller).

MODKIT/LILYPAD

Blocks. Puzzle-piece shapes that are stacked to create programs in Modkit. Blocks connect to each other like a jigsaw puzzle, preventing common programming syntax errors. In Modkit, there are six categories of blocks: Setup, Output, Input, Operators, Control, and Variables.

Code. Language that describes the instructions or program used in software; in this challenge, code is created in Modkit, through simplified blocks, to tell the LilyPad Simple how to behave.

Microcontroller. A small computer on a circuit board, containing a processor core and memory, which can be programmed for various types of hardware like LEDs, speakers, and other devices like temperature and light sensors. The microcontroller used in this Design Challenge is the LilyPad Simple.

Petal. A silver shape that lines the outside of the LilyPad Simple and other LilyPad components. Each petal can be programmed independently within Modkit to send signals to a particular input or output device, like an LED. (Also called *pins* in Modkit.)

Programming. The act or process of writing sequences of instructions that are designed to be executed by a computer.

Script. An automated series of instructions carried out in a specific order. In this Design Challenge, scripts will be created in Modkit Micro and carried out by the LilyPad Simple.

COMMON CORE STATE STANDARDS	NEXT GENERATION SCIENCE STANDARDS
• RI.7.5	• 3-PS2–3
• RI.8.5	• MS-PS2–3
• RI.8.7	• 4-PS3–2
• W.8.7	• 4-PS3–4
• RST.6–8.3	• MS-PS3–2
• SL.6–12.4 (anchor standard)	• 3–5-ETS1–1
• WHST.6–8.6	• 3–5-ETS1–2
	• 3–5-ETS1–3
	• MS-ETS1–2
	• MS-ETS1–4

MATERIALS OVERVIEW

Find electronics at **www.sparkfun.com/Interconnections**. Each youth will need the following to create an ElectriciTee:

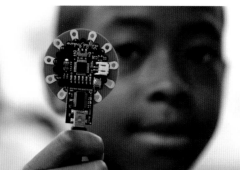

- T-shirt or other sewable textile item
- ProtoSnap - LilyPad Development Simple board
- Two or more LilyPad LEDs (four white LEDs are included in the ProtoSnap Simple kit)
- LilyPad Buzzer (included in the ProtoSnap Simple kit)
- LiPo batteries (lithium polymer ion battery: 110 mAh is recommended, to provide about a 3-hour charge; included in the ProtoSnap Simple kit)
- Mini universal serial bus (USB) cables
- LilyPad FTDI Basic Breakout board (included in the ProtoSnap Simple kit)
- Four or more alligator clips
- *Optional:* Embroidery hoop (a 10-inch diameter is recommended)
- *Optional:* Additional LilyPad LEDs

ADDITIONAL MATERIALS

- Digital projector
- Colored pencils, markers, and/or crayons
- Paper
- Fabric scissors
- Needlenose pliers
- Clear nail polish, fabric glue, or low-temperature hot glue (to secure knots)
- Conductive thread
- Regular thread
- Sewing needles and pincushions
- Extra alligator clips
- Fabric markers

- Computer with Modkit Micro (or ArduBlock) software available (1 per youth)

- Digital camera(s) with video capabilities, as well as USB cord(s) to download material to the computer

- *Optional:* Craft foam sheets for creating coasters during prototyping

- *Optional:* A scanner (to scan drawings and diagrams)

- *Optional:* Multimeters (to test for continuity in conductive stitching lines)

- *Optional:* Conductive tape (for quick but temporary repairs)

- *Optional:* Double-sided tape (to secure LilyPad parts temporarily while sewing)

- *Optional:* Needlenose pliers (to pull needle through fabric if it gets stuck)

- *Optional:* Glass beads (to decorate as well as insulate thread when needed)

- *Optional:* Blank 8.5" x 11" sticker sheets (for creating homemade stickers of LilyPad parts), found in paper supply stores and online

HANDOUTS

- Set(s) of "My First Blink" Modkit Micro Cards (preferably printed in color and laminated)

- Set(s) of "Nested Systems" Modkit Micro Cards (preferably printed in color and laminated)

- Set(s) of "Buzzzzer" Modkit Micro Cards (preferably printed in color and laminated)

- "Nested Systems Challenge"

- "ElectriciTee Diagram"

- "Posting Your ElectriciTee"

- "Self-Reflection on My ElectriciTee"

OVERALL CHALLENGE PREPARATION

- Setting up a word wall can be helpful for integrating essential vocabulary into the activities in each Design Challenge. Refer to the vocabulary often, and keep the word wall highly visible and clutter free. You can add new vocabulary in each unit to the terms already in use from previous Design Challenges.

- Create enough copies of the Modkit Micro Cards for each small group to have a set and review them before beginning the activities.

- Set up Modkit Micro (**modkit.com**) or ArduBlock (**learn.sparkfun.com/ArduBlock**) on all computers and test with a ProtoSnap Simple board. **Note:** As a bonus feature for those who purchased this book, Modkit has provided a special help area on its website (**modkit.com/softcircuits**), where you can find instructions for the version of Modkit used here, additional guides, videos of others creating projects from this book using Modkit, and other features.

- Create a working ElectriciTee prototype to serve as a model.

- Arrange for each youth to have a T-shirt.

  - You can find T-shirts at your local thrift store, or ask youths to bring in an old shirt of their own (with permission, of course!).

  - Rather than plain shirts, consider T-shirts printed with a range of designs; preprinted shirts often can give youths ideas for embellishments and original designs.

  - If you are gathering the shirts, you may want to ask youths to give you their preferred T-shirt sizes.

  - Because each T-shirt will be different, be sure to pick up a few extras in every size to ensure that youths have some choices in their selections.

- Review the "Mod Your T-Shirt" section in Part 3 for ideas on whether and how to encourage youths to design their T-shirts.

- *Optional:* To aid in the diagram creation in Part 3 (and in the T-shirt creation process), consider printing stickers of the LilyPad parts using 8.5" x 11" blank sticker paper—one set for each youth. Print images of the components in actual size, and then have youths cut them out and affix them to their diagrams. **Note:** SparkFun.com also has a PDF of the LilyPad parts that is ready to print.

Battery preparation: *Caution!* With repeated bending and use, wires can break at their connection points without some sort of protection. To minimize wear and tear, put a protective coating of hot glue around the points on your LiPo battery where the wires meet the battery and where the wires meet the plug connector. Encourage youths to be careful pulling these out of the LilyPad connection—they should use needlenose pliers to pull on the *connector,* not the wires.

NOTES TO THE INSTRUCTOR

By now, youths are aware that a circuit is a system. In this Design Challenge, the system becomes more complex with the addition of the computational components of the LilyPad Simple, which are controlled by the Modkit programming environment. We refer to the physical system of the LilyPad Simple and the digital system of Modkit as *nested systems* because, although each can be understood separately as a system, when combined, they also work together to make a new, more complex system.

- *Physical system:* The LilyPad Simple acts as a kind of *switch* in the larger system, but it is more complex than the switches that have been used up to this point. Rather than simply turning lights on and off, adding computational components to your circuit allows the lights to turn on and off in particular ways.

- *Digital system:* Modkit and ArduBlock are software programs that allow youths to create a system of code that can prescribe *a series of actions*. The Modkit system consists of components (i.e., blocks of code), each of which has its own behaviors that, when interconnected, affect the behaviors of other components.

The goal is for youths to explore the ways that these two systems are interconnected and the ways that their interconnections affect the overall system's behavior.

PART 1: GETTING STARTED WITH THE LILYPAD AND MODKIT MICRO

This activity introduces youths to two new tools: the LilyPad Simple and the novice-friendly, visual programming environment Modkit Micro. The LilyPad Simple is a wearable microcontroller that can be integrated easily into clothing or other textile artifacts and can be programmed using Modkit Micro software. Modkit Micro can tell the LilyPad how to control light, sound, or other elements through graphical programming.

Time: 35 minutes

STUFF TO HAVE HANDY

- Computer with Modkit Micro software available (1 per youth is recommended; if this is not possible, youths can work in teams of two or three)

- Protosnap - LilyPad Development Simple board (1 per youth)

- Mini USB cable (1 per youth)

- LilyPad FTDI Basic Breakout board (1 per youth; included in the ProtoSnap Simple kit)

HANDOUTS

- Set(s) of "My First Blink" Modkit Micro Cards

OVERVIEW

In this exercise, you will introduce the ProtoSnap – LilyPad Development Simple board and the Modkit Micro visual programming environment, which can be used to program (i.e., control) the LilyPad microcontroller within the ProtoSnap Simple. An in-depth overview of using the LilyPad Simple with Modkit Micro can be found at the following website: **modkit.com/softcircuits**. Here, we briefly describe what the LilyPad and Modkit Micro will allow youths to do, and explain how that differs from the circuits that they have been working with to this point.

WHAT IS THE LILYPAD ARDUINO SIMPLE BOARD?

Communities of e-textile designers, both novices and experts, are widely using devices called *LilyPad Arduinos*—wearable computers that can be sewn into clothing or other textiles and are hand-washable. LilyPad kits contain a set of sewable electronic components, including a programmable microcontroller and an assortment of sensors and actuators that enables designers to embed electronic hardware into textiles. The hole on each petal (or pin) of a LilyPad Arduino is large enough for a sewing needle to pass through, which allows users to sew LilyPad modules together with conductive thread.

In this activity, we recommend a simplified LilyPad Arduino board kit called the *ProtoSnap - LilyPad Development Simple board* (ProtoSnap Simple for short). It contains a programmable microcontroller called the LilyPad Simple, which has fewer petals and larger sewing holes than does the regular LilyPad Arduino. The ProtoSnap Simple kit also comes with four white LilyPad LEDs, a LilyPad buzzer, an FTDI Basic Breakout board for connecting to a USB cord, a LiPo battery, needles, and conductive thread. Each kit comes with a demo program already

uploaded, and all the LilyPad components are already connected to their respective petals (however, once the board is snapped apart, the components must be sewn to those same petals with conductive thread). This demo program flashes each LED in sequence and then plays a note on the buzzer. The buzzer also makes a sound when the pad in the upper-right corner of the board, marked A3, is touched. This pad is not programmable as is, however, so we will not focus on it during this activity. To get started, users must define the behaviors that they want their components to exhibit by employing the Modkit Micro programming environment (another choice is a text-based programming environment, Arduino, with AduBlocks, which works very similarly). These programs will enable them to manage the sensor and output modules (like LEDs) employed in their designs via the LilyPad Simple.

WHAT IS MODKIT MICRO?

Modkit Micro (modkit.com) is a graphical programming software that can be used with the LilyPad Simple and other Arduino microcontrollers. Modkit Micro's design was inspired by Scratch (scratch.mit.edu), which was developed by the Lifelong Kindergarten Group at the MIT Media Lab. Youths with prior experience using Scratch (see also the *Script Changers: Digital Storytelling with Scratch* volume in this collection) will recognize similar blocks when they begin to use Modkit Micro.

Modkit Micro allows youths to program the LilyPad Simple to control the LEDs, buzzers, and other LilyPad components in different ways. For example, using Modkit Micro, you can tell LEDs to blink, to light in a particular pattern, or to turn on (or off) in the presence of light. Rather than using a text-based computer programming language like Arduino, Modkit Micro employs simple graphical blocks that can be dragged and

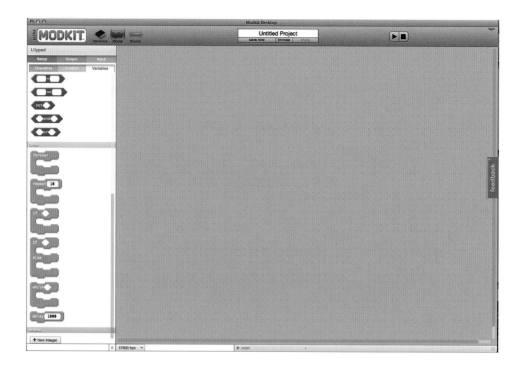

dropped to make scripts. **Note:** Modkit does allow users to see the program in a text-based language if you want to compare the code to the graphic blocks, but that isn't necessary for our purposes.

RESEARCH AND PLAY: AN ORIENTATION TO THE LILYPAD AND MODKIT MICRO—15 MINUTES

The goal of this activity is for youths to become familiar with the coding interface: how blocks fit together, how hardware can be configured, and so on.

1. In the computer lab, with Modkit Micro accessible on all computers, pass out a ProtoSnap Simple board, a LilyPad FTDI Basic Breakout board, and a mini-USB cable to each youth. Take a few moments to introduce each component:

	Protosnap - LilyPad Development Simple board	A wearable, washable e-textile technology whose large connecting pads can be easily sewn into clothing or other textiles. It contains a programmable LilyPad Simple Board with a built-in power supply socket for a LiPo battery and on/off switch, four white LilyPad LEDs, and a LilyPad buzzer. SparkFun—DEV-11201 *Note that the LilyPad Simple, LilyPad LEDs, and a LilyPad buzzer also can be bought separately from SparkFun.*
	LilyPad FTDI Basic Breakout board	E-textile-customized hardware that enables communication between a computer and the LilyPad—one side connects to the USB port and the other connects to your LilyPad pins. SparkFun—DEV-10275 *Note that this board is included in the ProtoSnap – LilyPad Development Simple kit, but they also can be purchased separately from SparkFun.*
	LiPo battery	This battery is small, light, and rechargeable and can be plugged directly into the LilyPad Arduino components. We suggest the 110-mAh LiPo battery, which gives about 3 hours of charge. SparkFun—PRT-00731 *Note that one is included in the ProtoSnap Simple kit, but they also can be purchased separately from SparkFun.*
	Mini USB cables	Mini USB cables connect many cellular phones and personal digital assistants (PDAs) to the USB port on a computer. This cable connects the computer to the FTDI Basic Breakout board. It has USB Type-A male to Type-B-Mini 5-pin male connectors. SparkFun—CAB-00598 *Note that this is not included in the ProtoSnap – LilyPad Development Simple kit.*

2. Spend extra time reviewing the ProtoSnap Simple board. Point out each part of the board, including the LilyPad Simple, the four LEDs, and the buzzer. Show that each of the petals on the LilyPad is labeled with a specific number, and that the numbers 5, 6, 9, 10, and 11 are repeated because those petals are connected to the LEDs and buzzer. Note where to plug the battery and FTDI Basic Breakout board into the LilyPad Simple's pins. Have them notice also that there is a built-in LED on the LilyPad's petal 13, an off/on slide switch, and a push-button switch on the board.

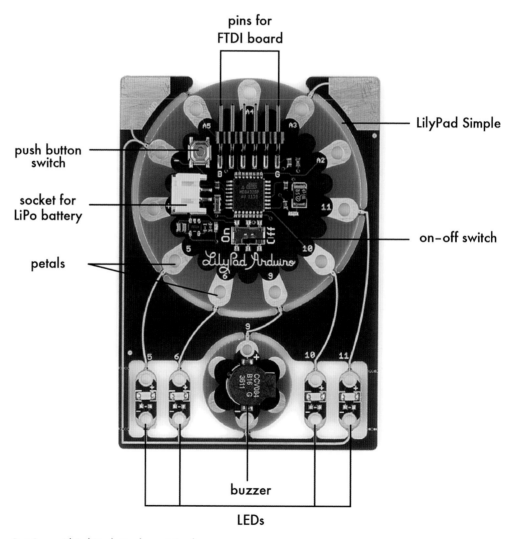

ProtoSnap – LilyPad Simple Development Board.

3. As needed, help youths set up and connect their LilyPad Simples to their computers.

4. While youths work with their own LilyPads at the computers, expect and encourage on-topic discussions, sharing of information, and peer-to-peer engagement.

5. Once the Modkit Micro Editor is running, ask them to click on the "Hardware" tab at the top of the screen, which will open the Modkit interface that they will explore in the next step.

Hardware and Blocks tabs in Modkit.

6. Explain that *hardware* is a general term for the wiring and other physical components that can be connected to the LilyPad microcontroller. Point out the hardware accessible to them with the LilyPad Simple by reviewing the Modkit interface. Allow time for youths to play with the drag-and-drop feature of Modkit, adding and removing the components that can be incorporated into their designs, including, among other options, the LED, LilyPad push-button switch, and LilyPad buzzer. Point out that within the LilyPad Hardware area, they can select which petals will be used for the components that they select. Note that more than one component can be dragged onto the screen, including multiple LEDs that youths will use for this Design Challenge.

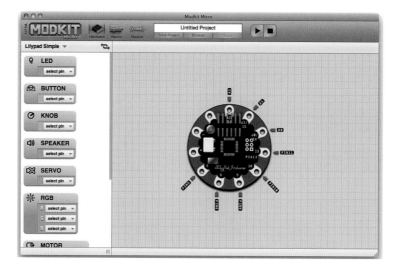

7. Once youths have become comfortable with the drag-and-drop components, have them drag one LED into the hardware area, assigning it to pin 13. This corresponds to the built-in LED on the LilyPad.

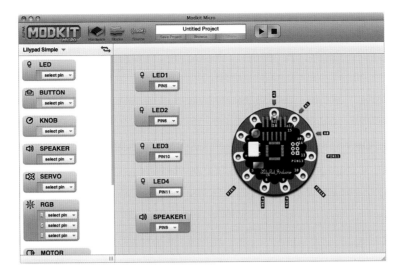

8. Have them explore the "Blocks" tab, noting the six categories of blocks in the programming palette. Blocks are the puzzle-piece shapes that are used to create code in Modkit. The blocks connect to each other like a jigsaw puzzle. There are six categories of blocks: Setup, Output, Input, Operators, Control, and Variables. Have youths drag and drop blocks into the scripts area and play with them. Don't expect them to create usable stacks of code at this point. The current goal is to explore the interface.

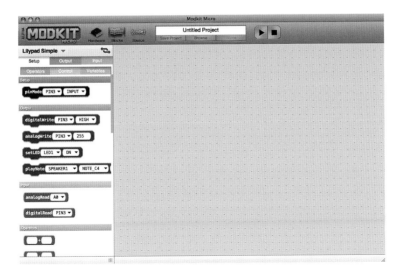

9. As youths explore the "Blocks" interface, introduce various stacks of code as needed. Note that some blocks won't appear until the hardware is dragged and dropped onto the stage. Here are a few blocks that they will be using during this activity:

forever	Forever loop	Yellow indicates "Control" blocks. This Control block, called the *forever loop,* enables an action to repeat without stopping. Blocks that are dragged and nested within the forever loop will be executed from top to bottom and then from top to bottom again, looping "forever"... or until the program is actively stopped, at least.
setLED LED1 ▼ ON ▼	setLED block	Blue indicates "Output" blocks. For example, the setLED block allows the LilyPad Simple to communicate with LEDs. This particular command allows the user to program the LED to be "on" or "off." Clicking on the drop-down arrows in the white ovals allows the user to choose from a discrete set of options (e.g., the range of pins available, whether the LED is set to "on" or "off," etc.). In this sample block, LED1 will be set to "on."
delay 1000	Delay block	Another Control block, delay, creates a pause in your code for a specifiable number of milliseconds (1,000 milliseconds = 1 second). If you insert a delay block between two Output blocks and enter "2000" into the blank field, your pin/petal will pause for 2 seconds before receiving the next message in the code. Delay commands are necessary for the changes in the LED setting to be seen by the human eye (if it is shorter than 100 milliseconds, an action will come and go too fast to be seen). So delays must be inserted between commands to ensure that they are executed slowly enough.

10. Have youths experiment with dragging and dropping the "Hardware" and "Blocks" onto the respective scripts areas and allow them to play with how they fit together and can be configured. For example, how many different blocks can they link together? **Note:** Don't worry about creating usable stacks of code at this point. The goal here is to explore the interface without uploading any code to the LilyPad Simple.

11. While youths are exploring, ask guiding questions like the following:

- What do you notice about the blocks and interface?

- What can you do with the blocks?

- How do you delete the blocks once they're in the scripts area?

- What else is happening while you are playing around and exploring this interface?

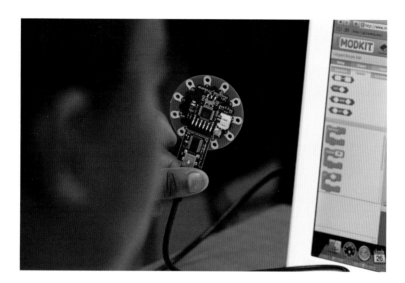

IMPORTANT TIPS FOR THIS ACTIVITY

- Be sure to plug the FTDI Basic Breakout Board into the LilyPad Simple with the SparkFun name facing down. It will damage the LilyPad if it is positioned the other way.

- To delete one or more blocks from the scripts or hardware area, simply drag and drop the blocks over to the palette on the left.

PLAY: MY FIRST BLINK—PRACTICE UPLOADING CODE TO THE LILYPAD—10 MINUTES

The second part of this activity involves helping youths connect the code blocks in Modkit Micro with an action in the LilyPad Simple. Rather than having them design a stack of code for themselves, begin by providing a stack of code that they then can interpret and analyze. Before you begin, make sure that the LilyPad Simples are connected to Modkit via the computers, as they were in the previous activity.

1. Have youths clear the scripts area in Modkit (in the "Blocks" interface) to prepare for this activity. Distribute the "My First Blink" Modkit Micro Cards, and have youths use them to create the script shown here. If the hardware is not already configured as pictured above, have them drag an LED onto the hardware stage and assign it to pin 13.

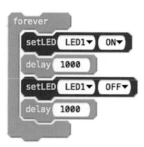

2. After they have built this stack of code (the program), youths can click the "Play Program" button to upload the program to the LilyPad Simple. The "Play Program" button looks like the triangle shown here.

VOICES FROM THE FIELD

I think the Modkit work helps make the LilyPad coding understandable. Once the coding and circuit design work, I think the sewing and making become rewarding acts of publication.

—CHAD SANSING, NATIONAL WRITING PROJECT

IMPORTANT TIP FOR THIS ACTIVITY

This program will cause the built-in LED located on pin 13 to blink on and off. However, this LED also flashes to indicate that a program has finished loading onto the LilyPad. When youths start to write other programs and connect additional LEDs to the LilyPad Simple, the built-in LED will blink when their program is finished loading, whether they have programmed behaviors for that LED or not.

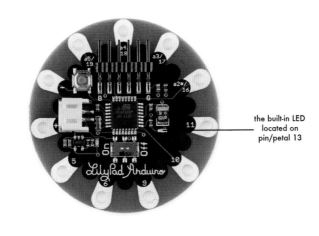

the built-in LED located on pin/petal 13

PLAY: MOD THE CODE!—10 MINUTES

Once youths are able to get their LilyPad Simples to perform the action of blinking, the whole group can discuss how Modkit directs the actions of the LilyPad Simple. Then they will be ready to experiment with creating their own code.

1. Review the code created for "My First Blink." Ask youths to *mod* (modify or make a small change to) the code and then upload the new program to the LilyPad Simple using the "Play Program" button. **Note:** When they do this, it will erase the previous code, as the LilyPad Simple can store only one program or stack of blocks at a time.

2. As youths work, ask the group questions like the following:

- What happens when any one of the blocks is removed from the system?

- Explain the function of the blocks that you are playing with.

- What happens when you change the value of the delay? Experiment with different values to see how the delay gets shorter or longer based on your input.

  - Can you get the light to change after 3 seconds rather than after just 1?

  - Can you get the light to stay on for 5 seconds and then off for 1?

  - How fast can you get the light to blink while still *seeing* it blink?

IMPORTANT TIPS FOR THIS ACTIVITY

- Modkit Micro will allow you to create more than one stack of code. However, the LilyPad Simple can run only one stack at a time. If you create more than one stack, Modkit Micro will upload the code for the last stack that you edited or clicked on with your mouse.

- A delay function appears twice in the code. You can control the length of the delay by changing the number in the parentheses. This number indicates the number of milliseconds (1,000 milliseconds = 1 second) to wait before executing the next line of code.

- New ProtoSnap Simples come with a default program that flashes each LED in sequence and then plays a note on the buzzer, but if you use one that has been used before, expect that the last code that was uploaded still will be stored in the board's memory.

- Note that blocks are all nested within a yellow (Control) forever loop. Other Control blocks can be used (like repeat), but forever is an easy way for youths to know whether their programs are functional, as it will run the code continuously. Encourage them to use forever loops for their first stacks before they experiment with other types of Control blocks.

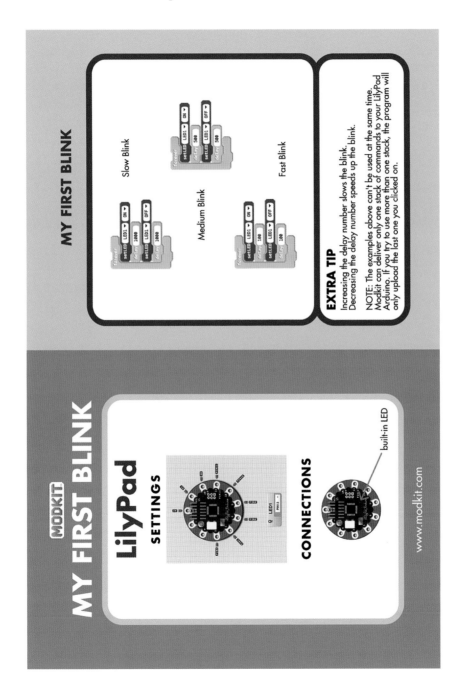

DESIGN CHALLENGE 3, PART 1

PART 2: EXPLORING NESTED SYSTEMS

This exercise is intended to look at two interconnected systems: one digital (Modkit) and the other physical (the ProtoSnap Simple and the other physical components). The goal of this activity is to help youths think about the ways that different systems work together to create a new system. In this case, we have two separate systems (the Proto-Snap kit and Modkit software), which are nested within a larger, interconnected system.

Time: 60 minutes

STUFF TO HAVE HANDY

- Computer with active Internet connection and Modkit Micro software available (1 per youth)
- ProtoSnap - LilyPad Development Simple board
- Mini USB cable (1 per youth)
- LilyPad FTDI Basic Breakout board (1 per youth)
- Alligator clips (4 or more per youth)
- *Optional:* Craft foam sheets for creating coasters during prototyping
- *Optional:* Extra LilyPad LEDs in multiple colors

HANDOUTS

- "Nested Systems Challenge"
- Set(s) of "Nested Systems" Modkit Micro Cards
- Set(s) of "Buzzzzer" Modkit Micro Cards

PLAY: EXPLORING NESTED SYSTEMS—45 MINUTES

This next series of mini-challenges is intended to help youths see that there are at least two nested systems in the ProtoSnap Simple designs: (1) the stacks of code and (2) the physical hardware and connections. Changes in either of these two systems will affect the behavior of the overall system. Each "mini-challenge" requires that youths have Modkit running and the LilyPad Simple connected to their computers. **Note:** A time limit could be given for each mini-challenge. After five to seven minutes, have volunteers share successful solutions with the entire group.

MINI-CHALLENGE 1: PROGRAMMING YOUR LEDS

The goal of this mini-challenge is for youths to see how changes in one nested system (the Modkit program) can affect a seemingly separate nested system (the ProtoSnap Simple and other hardware components).

1. Lead youths to practice the steps on the "Nested System" Modkit Micro Card to configure their ProtoSnap Simples, as follows:

    a. Click on "Hardware" at the top of the screen. Drag and drop the two LEDs into the hardware area, and then set the individual petals/pins of the LilyPad Simple using the settings indicated on the "Nested System" Modkit Micro Card (see the image here).

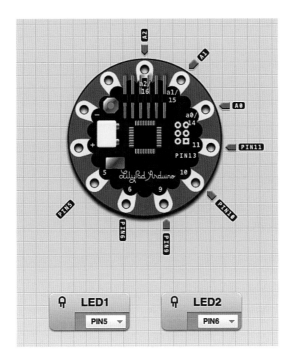

    b. Have youths create the stack of code in Modkit shown on the "Nested System" Modkit Micro Card and upload it to their LilyPad Simple by clicking the "Play Program" button.

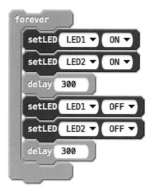

2. After they have created the connections above, and *without changing or removing any of the hardware components*, encourage them to find a way to change the behaviors of the LEDs.

3. Have them record their findings in the "Nested Systems Challenge" worksheet. *(Hint: They must use Modkit to reprogram the LEDs.)*

4. Ask youths to experiment by altering only the Modkit code to find a way to make the LEDs blink on and off at the same time. **Note:** One potential solution could look like this:

Possible solution for coordinated blink experiment.

This series of activities aims to highlight that while Modkit and the ProtoSnap Simple kit can be considered two separate systems, they are at times interconnected—*nested*—within one another.

IMPORTANT TIP FOR THIS ACTIVITY

The setLED block will be visible only when the LEDs have been pulled to the Hardware screen in Modkit.

MINI-CHALLENGE 2: LIGHTS, ACTION, SOUND!

Up until this point, we have only been working with one type of output device: LEDs. In this next mini-challenge, we'll move from controlling lights to controlling sound by using the LilyPad Buzzer on the ProtoSnap Simple board. For this exercise, youths will need to keep their LilyPad Simple connected to a computer running Modkit. In addition, they will need a copy of the "Buzzzzer" Modkit Micro Card.

1. Introduce the LilyPad Buzzer module.

	LilyPad Buzzer	A small, sound-emitting module that turns electrical signals into rapid on/off movements, producing sound waves. The faster the oscillation between on/off positions, the higher the pitch it produces. A buzzer is included in the ProtoSnap Simple board, but it also can be purchased individually from SparkFun. SparkFun—DEV-08463

2. Have youths use the "Buzzzzer" Modkit Micro Card to configure the settings and connections as shown here:

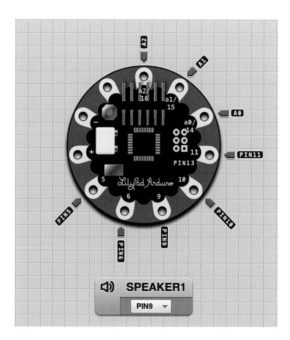

Note If you're working without the ProtoSnap kit, refer to the image on the "Buzzzer" Modkit Micro Card for how to hook your buzzer to the LilyPad.

3. Once the buzzer is configured and communicating with the computer, have them compose an original tune by piecing together a stream of pitches and rests using the blue playNote block as follows:

- On the playNote blocks, there are three pull-down menus. The first is the speaker that you want to play the note (SPEAKER1 in this sample program); the second is the note (or rest) that you want the speaker to play; and the last is the duration of the note or rest.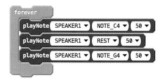

- Modkit accepts note names from A-G, followed by a number (1–6) that tells the computer which octave the note sounds. (*Hint: the lower the number, the lower the octave.*)

- Encourage youths to experiment with how many notes they string together, as well as varying the delay time between notes using the duration drop-down arrow or by adding rests.

IMPORTANT TIPS FOR THIS ACTIVITY

- The playNote block will be visible only when the buzzer has been pulled to the Hardware screen in Modkit.

- Youths also could incorporate LEDs into their designs. For example, can they make the LED blink to the beat of their songs?

- For more inspiration in combining lights, sounds, and programming, check out the Instructable and other resources for the "Soundie" at http://instructables.com/id/musical-conductivity-detecting-light-up-hoodie.[1]

MINI-CHALLENGE 3: SNAPPING APART AND RECONNECTING!

The goal of this mini-challenge is for youths to understand how changes in the interconnections of the LilyPad Simple and other hardware components can affect the behaviors of the overall system.

1. Now it's time to snap apart the ProtoSnap Simple board! Snap apart all components by carefully bending and twisting at the perforations. (If youths have trouble with snapping or find that the perforations are leaving sharp edges on their components, let an adult cut the components out of the board or cut off the sharp edges with large scissors.)

2. Ensure that "Hardware" is configured in Modkit in the same way that it was for Mini-challenge 1, and as depicted on the "Nested Systems" Modkit Micro Card.

3. Next, create the physical connections depicted here using the LilyPad Simple, LEDs and alligator clips. Note that all four wires must be used (see picture).

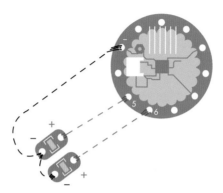

Have youths create the stack of code from their "Nested Systems" Modkit Micro Card to create the "Opposite Blink" depicted on the card (see Mini-challenge 1).

4. Challenge youths to find a way to keep the code the same but produce a coordinating blink (i.e., both LEDs blink at the same time). Have them record their findings in the "Nested Systems Challenge" worksheet.

5. After they have documented some early experiments, see if they can find a way to get their LEDs to blink on and off at the same time by altering only the physical components (i.e., the alligator clips and LED placement). One potential solution could look like this:

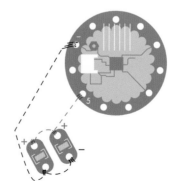

6. Debrief the mini-challenge with guided questions like the following:

- What can be done to configure different "light behaviors" without changing the code or uploading a new program?

- What are some ways to alter the system?

- How do the lights behave if you alter how the hardware is connected to the LilyPad?

- How do you create LEDs in series and parallel to the LilyPad? Are the LEDs depicted on the "Nested Systems" Modkit Micro Card in series or in parallel to the power source? *(Answer: they are in parallel.)*

IMPORTANT TIPS FOR THIS ACTIVITY

- Youths should figure out at least two different ways to hook up their LEDs to the LilyPad Simple with different results.

- Placing the LEDs in a parallel configuration is key to finding a solution to this exercise. It might be useful to review the information about series and parallel circuits introduced in Design Challenge 2 before or during this activity.

- Placing the two LEDs in parallel to one of the petals/pins on the LilyPad Simple will look like the following (this configuration will utilize all four wires as well):

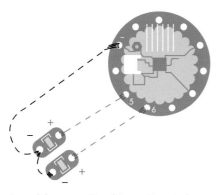

Original diagram on Nested Circuits Micro Card

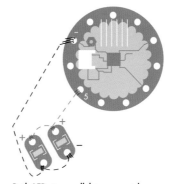

Both LEDs in parallel to one petal

IMPORTANT TIPS FOR THIS ACTIVITY

- The setLED block will be visible only when the LEDs have been pulled to the Hardware screen in ModKit.

- When connecting two or more alligator clips to a single petal on the LilyPad Simple or one of the LEDs, you can connect the first alligator clip to the petal itself. Then you can attach the remaining alligator clips to the first clip instead of the petal. They will attach more securely to one another than to the same small pin on the LilyPad Simple. If there is a plastic shield around the alligator clip, gently push it back off the clip to expose the metal. Be gentle, though, as the alligator clip can come off the wire easily. If this happens, it can be soldered back on for continued use if there is a soldering iron available.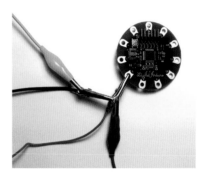

- In addition, if the alligator clips slip off the LilyPad pieces, create a "coaster" using craft foam sheets. Trace the component on the foam sheet, cut out, and then place under the component when using the alligator clips for a more secure connection.

SHARE: LET'S TALK!—15 MINUTES

After youths have completed the mini-challenges, bring everyone together to debrief about what they've found. The following topics can be useful for discussion:

1. What is a "nested system"? (*Answer: a nested system is a system that contains two or more smaller systems; when these systems interconnect, they affect each other's behavior.*)

2. In this activity, which systems are nested? (*Answer: Modkit, a digital system, and the LilyPad kit, a physical system.*)

3. What are the components, behaviors, interconnections, and goals of each system? How do they interconnect with each other? (*Answer: The goal of Modkit is to create usable code that can be uploaded to the LilyPad Simple controller. Modkit consists of several components, including programming blocks and hardware representations. Each block has its own behaviors; i.e., a setLED LED2 ON block can generate code to turn LED 2 on. For example, one interconnection in Modkit is that when an LED is dropped to the "Hardware" screen, "settLED" appears in the "Blocks" view.*)

Note The ProtoSnap Simple kit is a system whose components include the LilyPad Simple, LEDs, FTDI Basic Breakout board, buzzer, and the mini-USB cable. The goal of the system is to illuminate an LED or play notes on the buzzer. The behaviors and interconnections between these components are addressed in previous Design Challenges.

One of the interesting characteristics of nested systems is that distinguishing the subsystem to which some components belong can be tricky. Components that enable interconnections between the two systems, such as the mini-USB cable and FTDI Basic Breakout board, are arguably components part of either the LilyPad or the Modkit nested systems.

4. If you make a change to the LilyPad Simple, what happens in Modkit? If you make a change in Modkit, what happens to the LilyPad Simple? (*Answers vary: Youths can share the results of their experiments with Design Challenge 1 and 2.*)

WHAT TO EXPECT

These assessment activities are designed to get youths to see multiple levels of a system, as well as how separate systems can interconnect with each other. In addition, they have added *computation* to their circuits, making the simple circuits from the previous Design Challenges more complex.

	Novice	Expert
Circuitry concepts	• Is unable to launch Modkit Micro without assistance • Is unable to upload a program to the LilyPad Simple using the Modkit programming environment • Is unable to hook up the LEDs or other peripheral devices to the LilyPad Simple to test programs using the alligator clips • Understands that the LilyPad Simple is a programmable microcontroller but has difficulty explaining and naming the various parts of the device (i.e., the petal numbers, the plug for the FTDI Basic Breakout board, etc.) and what they're used for • Has difficulty remembering and using the essential vocabulary for this Design Challenge (e.g., *code, scripts, blocks, hardware,* etc.) • Is able to assemble simple scripts on the Modkit Micro Cards, but is unable to modify the scripts successfully and with purpose • Has difficulty understanding how to connect lights both in parallel and in series to the LilyPad Simple	• Is able to launch Modkit Micro without assistance • Is able to upload a program to the LilyPad Simple using the Modkit programming environment • Is able to hook up the LEDs or other peripheral devices to the LilyPad Simple to test programs using the alligator clips • Understands that the LilyPad Simple is a programmable microcontroller and can explain and name the various parts of the device (i.e., the petal numbers, the plug for the FTDI Basic Breakout board, etc.) and what they're used for • Has a command of the essential vocabulary for this Design Challenge (e.g., *code, scripts, blocks, hardware,* etc.) • Has a command of the Modkit Micro programming language and can modify or edit simple scripts successfully and with purpose • Understands how to connect lights both in parallel and in series to the LilyPad Simple
Systems thinking concepts	• *(Complete novice)* Continues to struggle to describe either LilyPad or Modkit as a system • *(Gaining expertise)* Can explain that LilyPad and Modkit are systems, but struggles to think about the two systems as being "nested" • Has difficulty understanding that the reconfiguration of components in a system does not create an entirely different system, but rather different outcomes for the same system	• Can convey an understanding that both LilyPad and Modkit are systems that function based on interconnections among the behaviors of their elements • Can explain how the two systems are nested; that is, how making a change in one system affects the behavior of another system • Understands that the way that the components are structured has effects on the way a system operates, leading to different outcomes for the same system

DESIGN CHALLENGE 3, PART 2

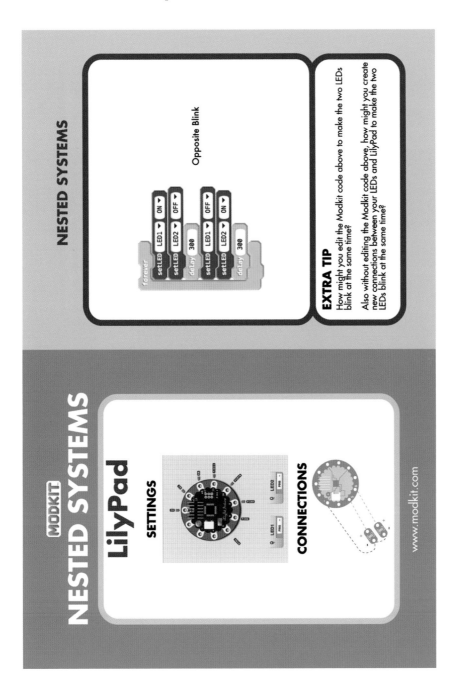

DESIGN CHALLENGE 3, PART 2

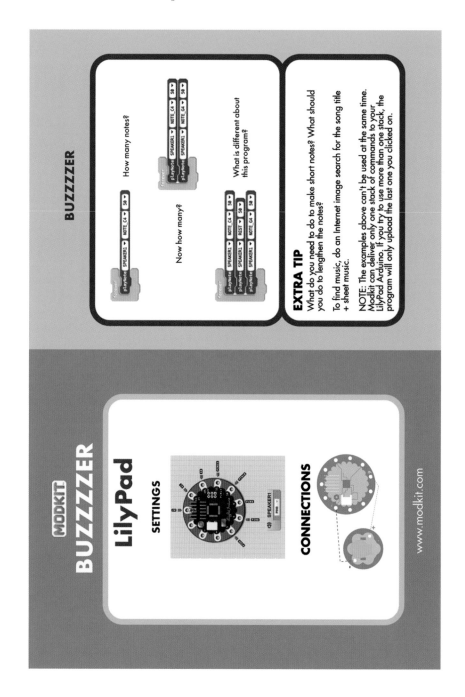

BUZZZZER

How many notes?

Now how many?

What is different about this program?

EXTRA TIP

What do you need to do to make short notes? What should you do to lengthen the notes?

To find music, do an Internet image search for the song title + sheet music.

NOTE: The examples above can't be used at the same time. Modkit can deliver only one stack of commands to your LilyPad Arduino. If you try to use more than one stack, the program will only upload the last one you clicked on.

MODKIT

BUZZZZER

LilyPad

SETTINGS

SPEAKER1

CONNECTIONS

www.modkit.com

DESIGN CHALLENGE 3, PART 2

NESTED SYSTEMS CHALLENGE

MINI-CHALLENGE 1

Without changing or removing any of the hardware components, can the behavior of the system be altered?

- What is the first thing that you changed?

- What happened?

- What is the second thing that you changed?

- What happened?

MINI-CHALLENGE 3

Choose a stack of code from your Nested Systems Modkit Card. What behavior does it produce in your system? Without changing the code, how can you change the LilyPad system so that it behaves in a different way?

- What is the first thing you changed?

- What happened?

- What is the second thing you changed?

- What happened?

PART 3: T-SHIRT PLANNING AND PREP TIME

Here youths plan out the designs for and nest the components of their ProtoSnap Simple boards within another system: the T-shirt! First, they will plan and create the designs for their shirt, transforming it from boring to beautiful with a variety of design techniques. Then they will create a circuit diagram to plan for the circuitry additions coming in Part 4.

Time: 40–130 minutes

STUFF TO HAVE HANDY

- T-shirts

- *Optional:* Additional T-shirt design materials (see suggested supplies for various project ideas later in this activity)

- Colored pencils, markers, and/or crayons

- Paper

HANDOUTS

- "ElectriciTee Diagram"

IMAGINE: CHOOSING YOUR T-SHIRT — 10 MINUTES

In this activity, youths will choose their T-shirts and get ready to either mod them or think through their circuit diagram ideas before they get ready to incorporate their LilyPad into their designs in Part 4 of this Design Challenge.

1. You should have gathered a collection of T-shirts for this activity. Distribute the shirts so that everyone has his or her own to work with:

    - If youths brought their own shirts in from home, you are ready to move on to the "Create" step, next.

    - If you gathered a collection of printed T-shirts from a local thrift shop or other source, devise a "fair" way for youths to choose from the selections, such as the following possibilities:

        - Create systems thinking or circuitry "trivia question" cards (use the Systems Thinking Concept Cards from Appendix D or look through some of the discussion questions in this and earlier Design Challenges for

inspiration). Draw a card and ask the question; the youth who answers the question first gets to pick out a T-shirt.

- Place youths' names in a bowl and draw them out one at a time.

2. When the shirts are distributed, allow about five minutes for youths to examine the shirts that they will use in their design. Each youth should think about the following questions:

- Look at the design that is printed on your shirt. How might you make it better?

  - By adding a border around the image, using paint to change the image itself?

  - By adding decorative elements like buttons, decals, sequins, or ribbons?

  - By changing the shirt itself, by altering the sleeves, by modifying the hem or the side seams? How about by adding fringe?

- You might choose to allow youths to trade shirts with one another at this point, or simply move on to the "Imagine: Creating Diagrams with the LilyPad Simple" step if they are satisfied with their choices.

MOD YOUR T-SHIRT—90 MINUTES (*OPTIONAL*)

Beyond the preexisting designs printed on the thrift-store T-shirts, there are many ways for youths to personalize the designs on their shirts. Here are some additional ideas for this part of the activity:

1. Consider inviting a local artist or art teacher to help youths create a unique T-shirt for this activity.

2. Want to work with something besides T-shirts? Youths can embed their LilyPad circuits in a simple tote or handbag or any other article of clothing. **Note:** Handmade totes can be assembled from scraps of cloth and simply sewn together, or they can be bought inexpensively at local arts and crafts stores.

3. If time and resources permit, consider the following methods for youths to customize the design of their T-shirts. Make available the materials needed for them to put together their T-shirt designs, and assist when necessary.

MOD YOUR T-SHIRT IDEAS

Additional Inspiration	Suggested Supplies
Draw your own T-shirt designs using fabric markers, puffy paint, or other materials.	• Light-colored T-shirts • Fabric markers • Puffy paint • *Optional:* stencils
Have youths use *scraps of fabric* to cut out unique shapes and affix them to their T-shirts using fabric glue or adhesive backing.	• Any color T-shirt • Fabric scraps of varying textures/colors/sizes • Nonconductive thread and needles • Fabric glue or iron-on adhesive backing • Iron and ironing board • Fabric scissors
Have youths *download and edit images* from the Internet *or create unique text* to create an original *collage* for their T-shirt. Then print the image on iron-on transfer paper using your inkjet printer to affix to their T-shirt.	• Light-colored T-shirts • Computer with internet connection • Image editing software (e.g., Adobe Photoshop or Aviary.com) • Iron-on transfer paper • Color printer (to print iron-on transfers) • Iron and ironing board • Paper scissors
Have youths *take a digital photograph* for their T-shirt. Then print the image on iron-on transfer paper using your inkjet printer to affix to their T-shirt.	• Light colored T-shirts • Computer with internet connection • Digital camera and USB cord to download images • Image editing software like Adobe Photoshop or Aviary.com • Iron-on transfer paper (compatible with your printer) • Color printer (to print iron-on transfers) • Iron and ironing board • Paper scissors

Additional Inspiration	Suggested Supplies
Have youths *affix assorted buttons, gems, beads, or other appliqués* to their T-shirt using a low-temperature glue gun or hand-sewing the pieces on the garment. **Note:** Warn youths that they won't be able to sew easily into where the glue gun has been, which they should consider when making their designs.	• Any color of T-shirt • Assorted buttons, gems, beads, or other appliqués • Nonconductive thread and needles • Fabric glue or iron-on adhesive backing • Iron and ironing board
Embellish the form with *ribs, side-ties*, or *lace panels*.	• Any color T-shirt • Nonconductive thread and needles • Fabric scissors • *Optional:* lace
Infuse a healthy dose of the 1960s into youths' shirts using *tie-dye*.	• Dyes (for light shirts) or bleach (for dark shirts) • Large bowl or bucket • Rubber gloves • Rubber bands • Plastic sport bottles (to dispense dye) • Clothes hangers and a place to hang the shirts

Consult books like *99 Ways to Cut, Sew, Trim, and Tie Your T-Shirt into Something Special* by Faith Blakeney, Justina Blakeney, Anka Livakovic, and Ellen Schultz to find unique ways to transform your T-shirt into a unique design with basic materials.

VOICES FROM THE FIELD

It's amazing the kinds of ideas youth will come up with to enhance the designs of their shirts! What to do with the LilyPad seems to be an issue that confronts many of them. Some are all right with displaying it on the front of the shirt, but others have devised ingenious ways to hide it in a pocket or to incorporate it directly into the shirt's design. For instance, one youth put his LilyPad in the center of his design, with LEDs around it like the rays of the sun, while his buzzer played the "Sun Song" from a popular video game.

—SOPHIA BENDER, GRADUATE RESEARCH ASSISTANT, INDIANA UNIVERSITY

IMAGINE: CREATING DIAGRAMS WITH THE LILYPAD SIMPLE—30 MINUTES

Let the creativity flow! After youths have designed the textiles of the T-shirts, it's time to think about inserting LilyPad Simple circuitry within those designs. In this part of the Design Challenge, they will produce a circuit diagram for their T-shirts and think through the interconnections of their nested systems.

1. Distribute the "ElectriciTee Diagram" worksheet, as well as colored pencils, crayons, or markers, and invite youths to sketch their T-shirt designs. They should begin with any alterations to the shape of the shirts and add the images, alterations, and embellishments that were completed in the previous exercises.

2. Have them think about how the T-shirts, LilyPad components, and behaviors can work together in a *synergistic* way. For example:

   - If there is a fish on the shirt, the designer might consider creating a hook from a bent paperclip, which could act as a switch to complete the circuit.

   - A shirt with an outline of a youth's home state could include LEDs in all of the cities where he or she has lived.

   - A basketball shirt could show the path that the ball would take to go through the hoop.

3. Then they should use a darker color to outline the circuitry components on the worksheet, including:

   - LilyPad Simple board, with plans for an activity programmed from Modkit

   - LiPo Battery and, if desired, a pocket sewn to the shirt to store the battery[2]

   - Two or more LilyPad LEDs of any color

   - Stitching lines, indicating where the conductive thread lines will be sewn. The lines from the LEDs should run to the same petals they were attached to on the ProtoSnap Simple board (i.e., petals 5, 6, 10, and 11). [3]

   - *Optional*: The buzzer explored in Part 2 of this Design Challenge, with a sewing line connecting it to petal 9.

4. Be sure to have a process of peer and/or adult approval for the designs in order to help Part 4 of this Design Challenge go more smoothly. In the approval process, you'll be looking for problems like the following:

   - Stitching lines that cross.

   - System design errors, such as not having all LEDs oriented with the (+) side toward a numbered petal and the (–) side oriented toward the ground or (–) petal on the LilyPad.

- A common mistake is simply to use the (+) petal on the LilyPad rather than a numbered petal in their designs. Remind youths that the numbers are like the (+) petal (although they offer more options for the design because they can be programmed within Modkit to perform different functions).

5. If youths finish early, have them get started programming their LilyPad Simple in Modkit and determining the exact behaviors of the components in their system (see Part 4 of this Design Challenge).

VOICES FROM THE FIELD

Diagramming the circuit for sewing was important in getting the children started in sewing correctly. It also challenged them to think of ways to fit the aesthetics of their design: for example, would the conductive thread fit into their design, or if they preferred it to be hidden.

—VERILY TAN, GRADUATE RESEARCH ASSISTANT, INDIANA UNIVERSITY

IMPORTANT TIPS FOR THIS ACTIVITY

- Be sure to have youths include the circuit connections in the drawing (i.e., connections sewn with conductive thread to LilyPad petals, placement of LEDs, and/or other components, etc.).

- Have youths keep the components close to one another in their designs (unless they have quite a bit of sewing experience). This limits the amount of time needed for sewing.

- Look at the drawings to make sure that the lines don't cross, which would cause a short in the project. Unlike the alligator clips, the conductive thread is not insulated. If two lines need to cross in the design, glass beads can be used as an insulator for one of the lines at this intersection.

- If the (–) petal on the LilyPad Simple is blocked or in an inconvenient place from an aesthetic standpoint, you can convert any petal to your (–) petal by using Modkit. Here's how:

  1. Drag the "Digital Write" command block into your scripts area and insert it as one of your first blocks in your script.

  2. Choose the petal number that you want to set to (–) (for example, "pin 10") and change the value to LOW. [In electronics, "LOW" means (–) or ground, and "HIGH" means (+) or power.]

DESIGN CHALLENGE 3, PART 3

ELECTRICITEE DIAGRAM

Use this worksheet to help plan how you will embed your LilyPad circuit into your ElectriciTee.

Components of the system: Draw your proposed T-shirt design in the space below. Be sure to label your diagram with all of the components that you will be using in your LilyPad Simple circuitry. Consider marking the direction of current flow in your diagrams [it will operate in similar ways to the simple circuits you conducted in previous Design Challenges, running from (+) to (−) through all components.]

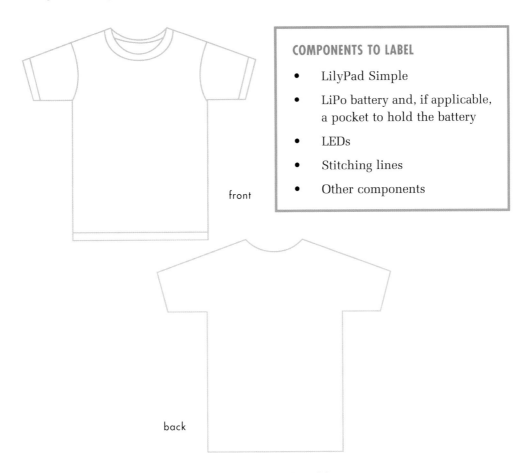

front

COMPONENTS TO LABEL

- LilyPad Simple

- LiPo battery and, if applicable, a pocket to hold the battery

- LEDs

- Stitching lines

- Other components

back

Name and explain some of the *interconnections* in this system on the back of this paper.

PART 4: MAKE IT YOUR OWN WITH MICROCONTROLLERS

It's time to begin programming and embedding the LilyPad Simple circuitry into youths' T-shirt designs. During this part of the Design Challenge, youths will not only add electronics, they also will practice debugging skills.

Time: 120 minutes

STUFF TO HAVE HANDY (FOR EACH YOUTH)

- The circuit diagrams created in Part 3
- Computer with Modkit software available (1 computer per youth is recommended; see the "Management Note" that follows)
- T-shirt or other sewable, textile item
- Two or more LilyPad LEDs (white and/or color)
- LilyPad Simple board (can be the same one snapped out of the ProtoSnap Simple board)
- LiPo battery
- Mini USB cable
- LilyPad FTDI Basic Breakout board
- Alligator clips (four or more)
- *Optional:* Embroidery hoop (10-inch diameter recommended)
- *Optional*: LilyPad Buzzer

ADDITIONAL MATERIALS (FOR THE GROUP)

- Fabric scissors
- Clear nail polish, fabric glue, or low-temperature hot glue gun (to secure knots)
- Conductive thread
- Regular thread
- Sewing needles and pincushions
- Fabric markers

- *Optional:* Multimeters (to test for continuity in conductive stitching lines)

- *Optional:* Conductive tape (for quick but temporary repairs)

- *Optional:* Pliers (to pull needle through fabric if stuck)

- *Optional:* Glass beads (to decorate as well as insulate thread when needed)

HANDOUTS

- Set(s) of Modkit Micro Cards, including "My First Blink," "Two LEDs," and "Nested Systems"

- Optional: Set(s) of "Buzzzzer" Modkit Micro Cards

MANAGEMENT NOTE

In this part of the Design Challenge, one computer per youth is ideal. If that is not possible, have youths take turns using the available computers. To manage this, you might want to set up two workstations:

Station 1: Computers for the "Programming Your LilyPad Simple" activity
Station 2: Tables with supplies for the "Stitching the LilyPad Circuitry" activity

While some youths are working on the computers, the others can be stitching the circuit. Rotate them away from Station 2 to the computers as they become available.

ITERATE AND CREATE: PROGRAMMING YOUR LILYPAD SIMPLE—30 MINUTES

This series of steps provide some loose guidance for structuring the programming of the LilyPad using Modkit Micro in the ElectriciTee designs. **Note:** If you have a limited number of computers, consider this Station 1, as suggested in the "Management Note." Ensure that youths in both stations are monitored and given any assistance that they need to complete the two tasks.

1. Pass out the supplies that youths will be using in their ElectriciTees, including the LilyPad Simple, LiPo battery, LEDs, and/or buzzer, as well as the FTDI Basic Break-out board, alligator clips, and mini-USB cables. Make sure each person takes along to the computer the "ElectriciTee Diagram" worksheet.

2. Have them launch and log in to Modkit Micro (if necessary). Then have them drag four LEDs and one speaker into the hardware area, assigning them to the pins that they previously were connected to on the ProtoSnap Simple board (unless they

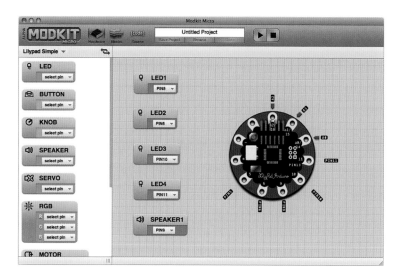

plan to change their petal assignments for aesthetic reasons or to prevent threads from crossing). The LEDs should be assigned to pins 5, 6, 10, and 11, and the speaker to pin 9, as pictured here:

3. Ask each youth to make the physical connections needed for his or her ElectriciTee design with the alligator clips, LilyPad, LEDs, and any additional components. Unless they plan to change their petal assignments, the positive sides of any LEDs that they plan to use should be attached via alligator clips to petals 5, 6, 10, and/ or 11, and the positive side of the buzzer should be attached to petal 9. The negative sides of all components should be attached to the (−) pin on the LilyPad Simple. Additional components can be attached to the remaining pins.

4. Based on youths' designs from Part 3, and perhaps building on some of the code that they wrote in Parts 1 and 2 of this Design Challenge, have youths create and save a stack of code for their LilyPad Simple ElectriciTee projects.

5. Using alligator clips, youths should test their programs and be sure that the LEDs and/or other components display the desired behaviors. If not, have them work to debug their projects. Allow them to have some time to debug, and avoid pointing them to the solution directly. If they continue to struggle, you might want to give them some direction, as follows:

- Talk me through what you're trying to do and what you've tried so far.

- Are all of your blocks nested in a forever loop? (Remember that the forever block causes the actions nested within it to repeat endlessly.)

- Do you have just one stack of blocks or multiple stacks? (Remember that LilyPad Simples can handle only one stack at a time.)

- Have you checked the way that your LEDs are hooked up to the LilyPad? Do the (–) ends connect to the ground or the (–) petal/pin of the LilyPad Simple?

- Have you checked the petal/pin numbers or LED numbers to make sure that they match what you intend?

6. Once youths are satisfied with the programs that they have created in Modkit, make sure that they upload the program to the LilyPad Simple.

7. Before leaving the computer, youths must save the program in Modkit so they can edit or debug it later if there are problems.

8. To avoid confusion with other projects, it's useful to remind youths to create a file name with their name or initials, as well as the title of the project that the program will be used for (for example: Sarah G ElectriciTee).

ITERATE AND CREATE: STITCHING THE LILYPAD CIRCUITRY—90 MINUTES

This series of steps provides some loose guidance for stitching the circuitry of the LilyPad circuit diagram onto the T-shirt. **Note:** If you have a limited number of computers, consider this Station 2, as suggested in the "Management Note" given previously. Ensure that youths in both stations are monitored and given any assistance that they need to complete the two tasks.

1. Have youths use their ElectriciTee Diagrams, created in Part 3 of this Design Challenge, to guide their designs—although obviously they can continue to iterate on (modify) these earlier ideas.

2. Make sure that they have the supplies that they will be using in their ElectriciTee circuits, including the T-shirt, LilyPad Simple, LiPo battery, LEDs, and/or buzzer, as well as have access to fabric scissors, conductive and nonconductive thread, sewing needles, and clear nail polish, fabric glue, and/or low-temperature hot glue to secure knots.

3. Remind them *not* to plug in their batteries until their projects are finished. **Note:** If a project isn't working, first check the battery's charge and make sure that it has a solid connection with the LilyPad.

4. *Optional*: Have youths place embroidery hoops on their T-shirts over the area where they intend to place their LilyPad and other components. Be sure you catch only one side of the T-shirt in the loop. (A common mistake is for youths to sew through both sides of their T-shirt as they are working!) The embroidery hoop also helps to create a flat surface for sewing.

5. Have youths lay out all their components on their T-shirts where they intend to affix them. **Note:** It may be useful for youths to use double-sided tape to affix their components to the T-shirt temporarily while sewing to prevent the pieces from moving around.

6. For youths who are novices at hand-stitching, it is important to restrict them to the area inside a circle for their LilyPad and LED connections. This is easily done with the embroidery hoop (ask them to keep all components within the circle), and it limits the amount of time needed for sewing and provides a natural scaffold.

7. Create a check-in point and have youths show you their designs and talk through their plans before they get started. Remind them to make sure their stitching lines do *not* cross—otherwise, there will be a short in the project. Unlike the alligator clips, the conductive thread is not insulated. **Note:** If two lines need to cross because of a youth's design, you can opt to do either of the following (listed in order of preference):

    •   String glass beads on one of the lines in this intersection to act as an insulator and keep the two threads from touching.

- Reroute the wires to prevent them from crossing each other. (See the "Important tips for this activity" section in Part 3 for instructions on how to make another [–] petal on the LilyPad besides the default.)

8. At this point in the activity, you also may need or want to re-review common crafting techniques that were covered in Design Challenges 2 and 5, such as threading a needle, tying knots, and sewing running stitches. You can make copies of this handout available to youths for self-service troubleshooting.

9. If youths need additional guidance about where to run their stitches or how to keep their stitches nice and even, have them use fabric markers (or another suitable substitute) to create dots between the components and then connect the dots with conductive thread.

10. *CRITICAL STEP:* Have the youths form a plan to sew down the components progressively and stitch the connections in their proposed designs. For example, in the design illustrated here, there are three *separate* lines that require stitching (listed in the order that you need to tackle them):

    - From Petal 6 to the positive end of LED1

    - From the negative side of LED1 to the negative side of LED2 *and then* continue to the negative petal of the LilyPad without cutting the thread

    - From Petal 5 to the positive end of LED2

11. *CRITICAL STEP:* Whenever youths reach a sew hole in a component, they need to stitch through the component *three times,* tie a knot, and then cut the thread. (The only exception to this rule is the sewing of the second line mentioned previously, which goes from the negative side of LED1 to the negative side of LED2 and then continues to the negative petal of the LilyPad, which can be done without cutting the thread.) This same technique can be used for LEDs in parallel to one another off one of the petals of the LilyPad (i.e., the positive ends of LEDs and negative ends of LEDs can be sewn together so long as they are going to the same place).

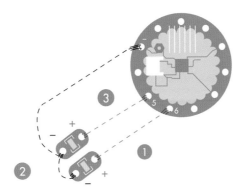

12. Ask youths what would happen if they made very large stitches or if they didn't loop through the component several times at the end. (*Answer: The components would fall off or not make a solid connection with the thread.*) This is also true for the conductive fabric or tape, which needs to have a firm connection with the conductive thread. Remember that the circuit must be a complete loop in order to work!

13. Ask youths what will happen if they don't cut the thread between components. (*Answer: they'll create a short in their circuit. See the "Tracing Current Flow Diagram worksheet from Design Challenge 1, Part 2.)*

14. Use a very small dab of clear nail polish or glue on the beginning and end knots to secure the knot, or it will come untied eventually. **Note:** Be careful not to get any of this adhesive on the metal ends of the components, or it could create an insulating barrier.

Test the ElectriciTee to see if it works. If it does, congratulations—you've created your e-textile!

OPTIONAL SUPPLEMENTAL ACTIVITIES FOR THE ELECTRICITEE

You might want to consider two bonus craft ideas for adding more creativity to and saving money with e-textiles. Show youths how they can create their own hand-sewn battery holders and switches using fabric instead of hardware, with the activities found at the end of this challenge (after the "Self-Refection on My ElectriciTee" handout).

IMPORTANT TIPS FOR THIS ACTIVITY

- The LiPo batteries can be charged at any time in the project by plugging them into the LilyPad Simple and then using the FTDI Basic Breakout board and mini-USB cable to connect to your computer. The LiPo is charging while the orange light on your LilyPad is illuminated. Once the orange light turns off, the LiPo is fully charged, and you should unplug the LiPo; otherwise, it may overheat. Alternatively, there are separate chargers available to charge the LiPo batteries that you can experiment with using.

- When debugging projects, the multimeter's continuity test settings can be useful if you're unsure of whether there is a break or a short in one or more of the lines (i.e., if you're unsure if the current is flowing through the LED, you can place one end of the multimeter on either side of the LED and test for continuity). Be sure to remove the battery before doing so.

- Having trouble? Refer to the "Stitching Tips" section of the Toolkit in this book for troubleshooting guidance and additional techniques for working with conductive thread.

- The buzzer is the only LilyPad component that is *not* washable, so have youths sew this onto something they don't intend to wash.

VOICES FROM THE FIELD

One really clever idea I saw at a workshop recently is to sew the buzzer onto a small piece of fabric along with two snaps, then sew from the positive side of the buzzer to one snap, and from the negative side of the buzzer to the other snap. Then, on the shirt, the other sides of the snaps will be connected to the positive and negative lines that you want to lead to your buzzer. This allows your buzzer to be removable for washing!

SOPHIA BENDER, GRADUATE RESEARCH ASSISTANT, INDIANA UNIVERSITY

DEBUGGING STEPS

- Check to make sure that the battery is fully charged and has a firm connection with the LilyPad.

- Check to make sure that no two lines of conductive thread are crossed in the design, as this will cause a short.

- Make sure that the (+) sides of the LEDs are oriented toward the LilyPad petals.

- Make sure that the (−) sides of the LEDs are connected to the (−) petal on the LilyPad.

- Check to make sure that each component has a solid connection (i.e., the conductive thread has been sewn around the component two or more times) and is not dangling from the T-shirt.

- Check to make sure that none of the LEDs have been sewn through (i.e., make sure that the stitching stops at each sew hole and is knotted and cut).

- Check to make sure that none of the stitching has been cut accidentally or has frayed. If there are any questions about whether the stitching is still good in portions, use the multimeter in Continuity mode.

- Make sure that the LEDs are sewn in parallel from one of the petals and not in series.

- Check the back of the T-shirt to make sure there are no long tails on the knots or any threads that make unnecessary loops. Affix any dangling pieces so that they are out of the way.

EXAMPLE PROJECTS

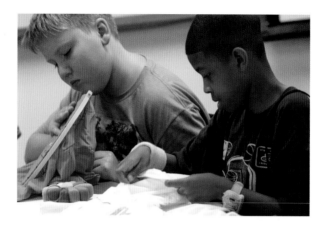

PART 5: SHARE AND PUBLISH!

The goal of this part is to have youths share and reflect on their ElectriciTees. Sharing, both with local peers and in an online community, is an important part of learning, as is a mindful, guided reflection on the learning process. The activity ends with youths connecting their design decisions to the core systems thinking concepts addressed here.

Time: 90 minutes

STUFF TO HAVE HANDY

- Computer with active Internet connection (1 per youth)

- Digital camera(s) with video capabilities and USB cord(s) to download material to the computer

- Youths' finished ElectriciTees

- *Optional:* Youths' original plans or diagrams for their ElectriciTees

- *Optional:* A scanner or camera (to capture drawings and diagrams)

WORKSHEETS

- "Posting Your ElectriciTee"

- "Self-Reflection on My ElectriciTee"

PUBLISH: POSTING TO THE WEB—60 MINUTES

Today's youths are becoming both consumers and avid producers of media online. The goal of this part of the activity is to give them time to post their ElectriciTees to an online e-textiles communitywhich allows people to document and share projects that blend electronics and textiles. Giving them a few minutes to do this allows youths to post their work and become part of the larger participatory culture. They will be adding to their online portfolio of work from Design Challenges 2 and 5, if those activities have been completed already.

1. If you haven't already done so, consult the the website's user guide to create log-in usernames and passwords (or allow time for youths to create their own logins), and test the firewalls in your computer lab to make sure that you can access the website.

2. Allow youths time to visit the online community and briefly explore the projects posted there, leaving comments or "liking" projects as they go. It might be useful for them to make notes as they explore about what makes a good post (for example, a great picture, interesting text accompanying the post, an attention-grabbing title, etc.).

3. After they've taken time to view other users' offerings, distribute the "Posting Your ElectriciTee" worksheet. Ask youths to complete the worksheet before they post their projects on the website. Remind them to refer to their notes about what makes a good post as they work on their own writing.

GIVE YOUR PROJECT A NAME

What will you call your ElectriciTee? Give it a unique and inspiring name! The name also will be the title of your post.

WRITE A PROJECT DESCRIPTION

- What inspired you?

- Describe the materials that you used to create your ElectriciTee, including all the circuit components.

- Describe how your ElectriciTee works and any other details that you think are important for others to know.

PHOTO SHOOT PLANNING

What should the photo(s) look like when posted to the web? Sketch them or write down a description of what they should look like. (Example: "Photo 1 should be the Electrici-Tee with the LEDs turned on; Photo 2 should be someone wearing my ElectriciTee.") Should there be a video of you modeling the design? If so, what should show in the video? **Note:** Be aware of safety issues online; you might want to have students pose wearing their T-shirts with their faces averted or croppedout for any Internet postings.

1. Have small groups of youths take turns taking pictures and/or videos of their finished projects. Scanning or photographing some of the planning materials would make interesting additions to the posts as well. Remind youths to refer to their notes about what makes a good post as they work on their own pictures and videos.

2. Once they have drafted their ideas for their post, have them log in to the chosen website to post their projects. It might be useful to have all the youths in your

group use a single login to post projects, so that you have the ability to edit projects or content if needed.

3. Encourage youths to do the following:

- Give their project a unique name/title.

- Tag the project with "Soft Circuits," "ElectriciTees," or another unique name for your group.

- Write a compelling project description.

- Link to other web materials (like their videos, which would need to be posted on YouTube before creating their submissions).

4. Another way that youths can share their programmable e-textile projects is to upload the Modkit code that they used to program their LilyPads. You can copy and paste the code from their projects by logging into Modkit Micro, opening their saved program for their ElectriciTee, and switching to Code view by pressing the {code} button at the top of the interface. This will reveal the text-based code, which can be copied and pasted elsewhere.

IMPORTANT TIPS FOR THIS ACTIVITY

- In order to post videos online, they need to be hosted on a site like YouTube or Vimeo, and a link will need to be copied to the chosen online community.

- What makes a good post? Suggest to youths that they photograph their work up close, with few distractions in the background of the image. Encourage them to write a clever title and catchy text that is both informative but to the point, and to think of their audience when describing their project, how it works, and what they used to put it together.

- In a few days, check to see if there are any comments on any of your group's posts and encourage them to comment on each other's work too—reading and responding are important aspects of joining an online community!

- If youths are taking the LilyPad Simple home, each one will need an FTDI Basic Breakout board and mini-USB cable to both charge the battery and reprogram the LilyPad, if needed.

- To wash the garment, a youth would need to remove the battery, hand-wash the garment in mild detergent, and allow it to drip dry. All the LilyPad components are washable, including the microcontroller.

REFLECT AND SHARE: LET'S TALK!—30 MINUTES

As a final activity, which can be used as an assessment, distribute the "Self-Reflection on My ElectriciTee" worksheet (the questions are reprinted next). Ask youths to fill these out individually and to take some time to think about what they now know and understand about circuits and systems from the experience of designing their ElectriciTees.

1. How many systems are *nested* in your shirt? Describe what they are.

2. How do those systems interact and work together?

3. What is the *goal* of your ElectriciTee?

4. What role does conductive thread play in helping the circuit to meet its goal?

5. What one thing could you change about a component in your ElectriciTee that would make a *huge* difference in the system's dynamics?

6. What one thing could you change about a component in your ElectriciTee that would make a *tiny* difference (or no difference at all) in the overall goal of your system (or the appearance and functionality of your T-shirt)?

Use responses to lead a group discussion on the ways that ElectriciTees contain nested systems. Note that the questions that youths are asked to think about are very similar to those that they discussed after completing Parts 1 and 2. There are two reasons for this repetition: first, the task of designing and completing an ElectriciTee can be so engrossing that youths can lose track of some of the systems thinking ideas; this activity serves to bring those ideas back to the forefront. Second, in the process of visualizing and realizing their designs, they will have opportunities to experience for themselves the ways that the Modkit, LilyPad, circuit, and T-shirt design, as well as the interactions with the body, are interconnected. This design activity might bring up new and more sophisticated understandings that will be realized when reflecting on the nature of systems.

WHAT TO EXPECT

Anticipate that the addition of the LilyPad Simple to youths' circuits will bring to the fore some unchecked misconceptions about how circuits work. How currents flow, how loops are made that incorporate the LilyPad Simple microcontroller, how to apply ideas about circuits (parallel and series) to these designs, and the intricacies of stitching circuits are all issues that youths will acquire new perspective about through the process of creating e-textiles. These inevitable misconceptions present opportunities to revisit concepts covered in prior Design Challenges. In addition, youths are going to be learning a host of debugging skills. Though time-consuming to learn, these skills are essential to the development of robust understandings of how circuits work. In terms of systems thinking content, the notion of nested systems is a very simple concept on its surface, and yet it is integral to understanding the domain of e-textiles. Being able to identify the components, behaviors, interconnections, and goals of several different nested systems and the interconnections between these systems is a core objective for this Design Challenge.

	Novice	Expert
Circuitry concepts	• Is unable to launch Modkit Micro without assistance • Is unable to upload a program to the LilyPad Simple using the Modkit programming environment • Is unable to hook up the LEDs or other peripheral devices to the LilyPad Simple to test programs using the alligator clips • Understands that the LilyPad Simple is a programmable microcontroller but has difficulty explaining and naming the various part of the device (i.e., the petal numbers, the plug for the FTDI breakout board, etc.) and what they're used for • Has difficulty remembering and using the essential vocabulary for this Design Challenge (e.g., code, scripts, blocks, hardware, etc.). • Is able to assemble simple scripts on the Modkit Micro Cards but is unable to modify the scripts successfully and with purpose • Has difficulty understanding how to place lights both in parallel and in series to the LilyPad Simple in their designs • Is unable to create a circuit diagram incorporating the LilyPad Simple • Is unable to create a working ElectriciTee incorporating the LilyPad Simple, LiPo battery, and at least two LEDs • Seeks help from others to debug their project without first trying to troubleshoot their project themselves	• Is able to launch Modkit Micro without assistance • Is able to upload a program to the LilyPad Simple using the Modkit programming environment • Is able to hook up the LEDs or other peripheral devices to the LilyPad Simple to test programs using the alligator clips • Understands that the LilyPad Simple is a programmable microcontroller and can explain and name the various part of the device (i.e., the petal numbers, the plug for the FTDI breakout board, etc.) and what they're used for • Has a command of the essential vocabulary for this Design Challenge (e.g., code, scripts, blocks, hardware, etc.). • Has a command of the Modkit Micro programming language and can modify or edit simple scripts successfully and with purpose • Understands how to place lights both in parallel and in series to the LilyPad Simple in their designs. • Is able to create a circuit diagram incorporating the LilyPad Simple • Is able to create a working ElectriciTee incorporating the LilyPad Simple, LiPo battery, and at least two LEDs • Is comfortable engaging in a series of debugging steps to figure out a problem (either with his or her own project or with a peer's)
Systems thinking concepts	• *(Complete novice)* Continues to struggle to describe either LilyPad or Modkit as a system • *(Gaining expertise)* Can explain that LilyPad and Modkit are systems, but struggles to think about the two systems as being "nested" • Has difficulty understanding that the reconfiguration of components in a system does not create an entirely different system, but rather different outcomes for the same system	• Can convey an understanding that both LilyPad and Modkit are systems that function based on interconnections among the behaviors of their elements • Can explain how the two systems are nested; that is, how making a change in one system affects the behavior of another system • Understands that the way that the components are structured has effects on the way a system operates, leading to different outcomes for the same system

DESIGN CHALLENGE 3, PART 5

POSTING YOUR ELECTRICITEE

Use this worksheet to help plan what you will say about your ElectriciTee.

GIVE YOUR PROJECT A NAME

• What will you call your ElectriciTee? Give it a unique and inspiring name!

WRITE A PROJECT DESCRIPTION

• What inspired you?

• List the materials that you used to create your T-shirt, including all the circuit components.

• Describe how your ElectriciTee works and why.

PHOTO SHOOT PLANNING

What should the photo(s) look like online? Sketch them or write down a description of what they should look like, below. (Example: "Photo 1 should be the ElectriciTee with the LEDs turned on; Photo 2 should be me wearing my ElectriciTee.") Should there be a video of someone modeling an ElectriciTee for the chosen site? If so, what should show in the video? **Note:** Be aware of safety issues online; you might want to have students pose wearing their T-shirts with their faces averted or cropped out for any Internet postings.

DESIGN CHALLENGE 3, PART 5

SELF-REFLECTION ON MY ELECTRICITEE

1. How many systems are nested in your shirt? Describe what they are.

2. How do those systems interact and work together?

3. What is the goal of your ElectriciTee?

4. What role does conductive thread play in helping the circuit to meet its goal?

5. What one thing could you change about a component in your ElectriciTee that would make a *huge* difference in the system's dynamics?

6. What one thing could you change about a component in your ElectriciTee that would make a *tiny* difference (or no difference at all) in the overall goal of your system (or the appearance and functionality of your T-shirt)?

OPTIONAL ACTIVITIES FOR THE ELECTRICITEE

Check out these two ideas for adding more creativity and saving money on e-textiles: DIY battery holders and switches! Show youths how they can create their own battery holders and switches using fabric instead of hardware!

DIY 3V BATTERY HOLDER

Purchasing large lots of battery holders can be expensive. However, youths can create their own unique battery holders with this simple craft project, which is both fun and money-saving. Note that there are multiple ways to create a simple battery case; use the tips here to get youths started, and then they can get creative to make their own unique battery holders.

For this do-it-yourself (DIY) battery holder, youths will need a small piece of felt or thick fabric (felt is easy to cut, doesn't fray, and will insulate the battery), small pieces of conductive fabric, a small piece of conductive Velcro, and a hot glue gun and glue sticks. To make the holder, perform the following steps:

1. Cut a rectangular piece of fabric for the battery holder, sized a little longer than two 3V batteries laid out end-to-end.

2. Fold the fabric in half to create a square, or mark the center line of the rectangle with chalk or a marker. This will guide the placement of the next step.

3. Cut two small holes in the center of each side of the rectangle (creating a domino shape with one circle on each side).

4. Cut two small squares of conductive Velcro (use the softer loop side of the Velcro).

5. Stitch or glue the conductive Velcro so that each piece covers the holes and the soft fibers poke through the felt. Fluff the material because those fibers must be able to touch the battery on the inside of the holder, making a secure connection.

6. Fold the material in half with the holes facing in, and stitch the felt on two sides with *nonconductive* thread. Be careful to leave one side open where you can insert the battery.

7. Cut two pieces of conductive fabric (long thin rectangles work well).

8. Sew a piece of conductive fabric (or glue it, being careful not to insulate the connection) onto the Velcro on the outside of the battery.

9. Mark one strip with a "+" to note the positive end, and then sew your homemade battery holder into your project's circuit using *conductive* thread.

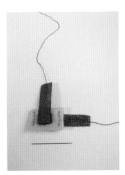

10. Insert the battery, turning it so that the positive side faces the positive fabric strip.

Congratulations! You have finished your homemade battery holder!

Are youths having issues getting your circuit to turn on? If so, they should press down on the holder to make sure that it has a firm connection with the battery. They can use a rubber band or some other means of pressing the circuit components firmly together.

DIY SWITCHES

A switch is simply a purposeful break in the circuit that can be formed and unformed easily. While there are several prefabricated switches (like the push-button switch or slide switch), it is also easy (and fun!) to build your own switch. Play with different materials to make your own switches. Some materials that you can use to make switches are conductive Velcro, conductive fabric, conductive thread, aluminum foil, metal springs, and metal beads. Use your imagination and whatever is lying around to experiment! Here's an example switch to get things going, a DIY Velcro Switch.

1. To get started making a DIY Velcro switch, grab a piece (about 2" x 4") of thick fabric (like felt) and fold the material in half (youths will be cutting two identical pieces).

2. Draw the desired shape on the fabric, or create a pattern from paper. Make sure that the shape is at least half an inch larger around than a coin-cell battery. Note that youths always can trace something like a large heart, star, or flower button. In this example, we created a heart-shaped switch.

3. If youths created a paper pattern, lay it on the folded felt or fleece material and pin the pattern to material with straight pin(s).

4. Use regular sharp scissors (for a straight edge) or pinking shears (for a zigzag edge) to cut out the shape.

5. Next, work on adding conductive Velcro to the switch. To get started, cut top and bottom pieces of conductive Velcro that are approximately ½" wide.

6. Pin one piece of the Velcro on one shape and one on the other, using straight pins.

7. Stitch the conductive Velcro ends down with regular thread. Don't sew all the way around; just sew the ends!

8. Stitch the top shape to the project using *nonconductive* thread. Youths can use a running stitch.

9. Next, add a connecting ribbon to link the two shapes.

10. Choose a color of nonconductive ribbon. Cut a piece of ribbon that is about three times the length of the shape.

11. Glue one end of the ribbon under the conductive Velcro on the shape attached to the project.

12. Slip the other end of the ribbon under the conductive Velcro on the bottom shape and beyond. Youths will want to create a folded-over tab for opening and closing the switch. Glue the end of the fold under the Velcro as well.

13. Note: At this time, one of the shapes is attached to the project, while the other is hanging free, held by the ribbon. The next step is to pass the circuit that has been created for the project through the switch.

14. Sew one of the lines of the conductive thread in the circuit to the conductive Velcro on the shape that is attached to the project.

15. Sew the other line of conductive thread, beginning at the bottom of the attached shape and down the ribbon (*not* attaching it to the project), and then to the other shape and conductive Velcro. Be careful that the two thread lines don't go to the same piece of Velcro—or your switch always will be on!

16. Test your circuit by folding up the dangling shape and sticking it to the other shape with the Velcro. Is the circuit complete (for example, did the lights turn on)? Then congratulations—you've created your own Velcro switch!

DESIGN CHALLENGE 4
SOLAR-POWERED BACKPACK

Total time: 490 minutes

OVERVIEW

Continuing prior explorations of *limited* (energy) *resources in systems,* youths learn about alternative energy sources through the creation of a backpack embedded with a flexible *solar panel.* Batteries with long lifespans often relegate conversations of energy as a limited resource to the background; however, powering objects with alternative energies—like water, wind, and solar—allows for a view into the systemic nature of *energy,* where it comes from, and how it can best be preserved. Youths explore the concepts of *stocks and flows* and *dynamic equilibrium* in play-based activities before the creation and sharing (in class and online) of their solar-powered backpacks.

Note   Due to the complexity of the "make" activities in this Design Challenge, we suggest completing earlier Design Challenges before this one.

PRODUCT

The deliverable for each youth will be a solar backpack designed with a flexible solar panel, programmable microcontroller, and light-emitting diodes (LEDs). The backpack then can be shared and posted to an online community. Consult our website at digitalis .nwp.org/gnl for suggestions, but you also may want to consider Instructables.com, DIY.org, or another venue for sharing your work.

TARGETED SYSTEMS THINKING CONCEPTS

Almost all systems have limited resources, in which a stock is depleted slowly by an outflow. With battery-powered circuits, the stock of energy drains over time as it powers a load. With rechargeable batteries, however, we can affect the system with an inflow of new energy to recharge the battery. The longevity of a system is determined by balancing stocks and flows, putting them into dynamic equilibrium. This necessitates identifying and manipulating different parts of the system (e.g., how the energy is coming in, and where it is being used) to find the optimal use of energy.

PARTS

PART 1: STOCKS AND FLOWS AND PAPER AIRPLANES

First, youths are introduced to the idea of energy flow and its relationship to renewable energy. Then they engage in an embodied activity where they role-play a paper airplane supply chain, highlighting how important systems ideas, including stocks, flows, and dynamic equilibrium, actually play out in practice. A broader discussion following the activity formally introduces these systems ideas, and then youths connect them to the context of circuitry and energy they've been exploring in the situations that they've been exploring, as well as where they exist in the world more broadly.

Time: 80 minutes

PART 2: TESTING SOLAR PANELS

The purpose of this activity is to support youths' thinking about stocks and flows in the particular context of the solar panels that they will be using in their backpack designs. They will test the current and voltage of their solar panels in different kinds of light, and with the panels in series or parallel, so they can think about how the "stock" of energy is accumulated in different light sources and in different circuit configurations, as well as how this stock relates to the "flow" of energy.

Time: 105 minutes

PART 3: DESIGNING THE SOLAR-POWERED BACKPACK

Just as with all previous activities, youths will want to think about how to design their solar-powered backpack strategically with the circuitry and power in mind. In this case, the solar panels need to be able to be exposed to light, which makes the design potentially more challenging.

Time: 270 minutes

PART 4: WRAP UP!

Youths will share and reflect on their solar-powered backpack designs with their local peer group, as well as sharing them with a distributed online community such as those suggested at the Interconnections website (**digitalis.nwp.org/gnl**). Finally, they will reflect on their experience and connect their systems thinking understanding to the core systems thinking concepts in this Design Challenge.

Time: 90 minutes

KEY DEFINITIONS

SYSTEMS THINKING

Stocks and flows. Stocks are an accumulated amount of something within a system (like money in a bank account, fish in a pond, trees in a forest, or jobs in an economy), and flows are the rate at which stocks in a system change either through increasing or decreasing (money comes in and out of a bank account due to wages paid, interest, and purchases. Fish come in and out of a pond due to birth rates, death rates, and fishing rates, etc.). Stocks are always nouns: they're the "stuff" of systems, while flows are always verbs: they're the "movement" of systems. Understanding stocks and flows gives someone an insight into how different parts of the system change over time.

Limited resources. In any system, it is important to understand which resources are finite, ones that will run out at a certain point. Keeping in mind which resources are limited helps people make decisions about how best to maximize resources.

Dynamic equilibrium. A state in which stocks and flows are balanced so the system is not varying widely, but still has internal dynamic processes that are continually in flux even though the system is stable overall. For example: in economics dynamic equilibrium might be used to talk about the constant flux of money movement in otherwise stable markets; in ecology, a population of organisms stabilizes when birth rate and death rate are in balance.

CIRCUITRY

Amp. A unit of measure of the number of electrons flowing through a wire (thread) per unit of time.

Current. A flow of electric charge through a medium; e.g., wire, conductive fabric, or a light-emitting diode (LED).

Debugging. The iterative process of identifying and removing errors from hardware or software designs.

e-Textiles. Also known as electronic textiles or smart textiles, these are everyday textiles and clothes that have digital components and electronics embedded in them.

Lead. A wire that conveys electric current from a source to a component in the system, or that connects two points of a circuit.

Load. A device (like a lightbulb or motor) that requires electric current passing through it to give it power.

Parallel circuit. When components are wired in parallel within a circuit, the electric current divides into two or more paths before recombining to complete the circuit. The current flows through three LEDs wired in parallel, and the electric current is split equally among the three of them. **Note:** The evenness of the split is contingent on the three LEDs being the same type and/or color.

Series circuit. When components are wired in series within a circuit, electric current flows sequentially through those components in a continuous loop. This means that as the current travels from the battery through each LED, it loses some of its original electrical charge or energy (also known as *voltage*) such that the amount of voltage available for each subsequent LED decreases with each one it passes through.

Solar panel. A thin, semiconductor wafer specially treated to form an electric field when struck by light (with a positive charge on one side and a negative one on the other). When activated, electrons are knocked loose from the atoms in the material. If conductors are attached to the positive and negative sides, forming a closed circuit, the electrons can be captured in the form of electric current.

Volt. A unit of measure of the amount of voltage in a circuit.

Voltage. The force that causes electric current to flow through a circuit. Increasing the voltage in a circuit without changing the resistance increases the current that flows through the circuit.

MODKIT AND LILYPAD

Blocks. A puzzle piece shape that is used to create programs in Modkit. Blocks connect to each other like a jigsaw puzzle, preventing common programming syntax errors. In Modkit, there are six categories of blocks: Setup, Output, Input, Operators, Control, and Variables.

Code. Language that describes the instructions or program used in software; in this challenge, code is created in Modkit, through simplified blocks, to tell the LilyPad Simple how to behave.

Microcontroller. A small computer on a circuit board, containing a processor core and memory, which can be programmed for various types of hardware like LEDs, speakers, and other devices like temperature and light sensors.

Programming. The act or process of writing sequences of instructions that are designed to be executed by a computer.

Script. An automated series of instructions carried out in a specific order. In this Design Challenge scripts will be created in Modkit Micro and carried out by the LilyPad Simple.

COMMON CORE STATE STANDARDS	NEXT GENERATION SCIENCE STANDARDS
• R.6–12.7 (anchor standard)	• 3-PS2–3
• RI.7.4	• MS-PS2–3
• W.6–12.2 (anchor standard)	• 4-PS3–2
• W.7.6	• 4-PS3–4
• W.8.6	• MS-PS3–2
• RST.6–8.3	• HS-PS3–3
• RST.6–8.4	• 3–5-ETS1–1
• RST.6–8.7	• 3–5-ETS1–2
• RST.6–8.9	• 3–5-ETS1–3
• WHST.6–8.4	• MS-ETS1–1
	• MS-ETS1–2
	• MS-ETS1–4

MATERIALS OVERVIEW

Find electronics at **www.sparkfun.com/Interconnections**. Each youth will need the following to create a solar-powered backpack:

• Backpack (new or recycled)

• Powerfilm flexible solar panel (MPT6–75)

• Two or more LilyPad LEDs (white and/or colored)

- LilyPad Arduino Simple

- LilyPad LiPower

- LiPo battery (lithium polymer ion battery: 110 mAh recommended, to provide about a 3-hour charge)

- Mini-USB cables

- LilyPad FTDI Basic Breakout board

ADDITIONAL MATERIALS

- Digital projector

- 50–100 sheets of plain 8.5" x 11" paper

- Colored markers (and possibly other art supplies, such as glitter glue, crayons, etc., at the facilitator's discretion, which are used to decorate planes)

- Tokens that can act as game currency (such as paper circles, buttons, Popsicle sticks—anything that can be easily found and distributed as play "wages")

- Plenty of alligator clips

- Standard LEDs

- Conductive thread

- Clear nail polish, fabric glue, or low-temperature hot glue (to secure knots)

- Multimeters (to measure current and voltage and to test for continuity in conductive stitching lines)

- Sewing needles

- Scissors

- Tweezers

- Painters' tape

- Stiff poster board

- Decorative duct tape

- Conductive fabric

- Regular, nonconductive thread

- Computer with Modkit Micro software available

- Digital camera(s) with photo and video capabilities and USB cord(s) to download material to the computer

- *Optional*: Felt (for supporting the back of the flexible solar panel)

- *Optional*: Decorative items, including buttons, felt shapes, puffy paint, textile paint, and colored and patterned duct tape and fabrics of varying textures, colors, and sizes

- *Optional*: Needlenose pliers (to pull needle through fabric if it gets stuck)

- *Optional*: Glass beads (to decorate as well as insulate thread when needed)

- *Optional*: Conductive tape (for quick but temporary repairs)

- *Optional*: A scanner (to scan drawings and diagrams)

HANDOUTS

- "Solar Panel Testing"

- "Testing Solar Panels with LEDs"

- "Sample Solar Backpack Diagram"

- "Diagram Your Solar-Powered Backpack"

- Modkit Micro Cards (from Design Challenge 3)

- "Posting Your Solar-Powered Backpack"

- "Self-Reflection on My Solar-Powered Backpack"

OVERALL CHALLENGE PREPARATION

- Setting up a word wall can be helpful for integrating essential vocabulary into the activities in each Design Challenge. Refer to the vocabulary often and keep the word wall highly visible and clutter free. You can add new vocabulary in each unit to the terms already in use from previous Design Challenges.

- You might want to hold a community collection drive for backpacks, totes, or other types of bags to recycle older backpacks for this Design Challenge. Any type of bag made of soft fabrics that can be sewn easily will do.

- If you haven't already done so, create and review the Modkit Micro Cards.

- If you haven't already done so, set up Modkit Micro (**modkit.com**) on all computers and test them with a LilyPad Simple. **Note:** As a bonus feature for those who purchased this book, Modkit has provided a special help area on their website (**modkit.com/softcircuits**), where you can find instructions for the version of Modkit used here, additional guides, videos of others creating projects from this book using Modkit, and other features.

- Create a working backpack prototype with a flexible solar panel, LilyPad Simple, LiPower, and LEDs to serve as a model.

- Consider using tweezers to peel the solar panel plastic away from the tips of the leads in advance, to prepare them for testing with the multimeters. Youths can damage the solar panels easily if they're not careful. For younger age groups or limited time frames, you may want to consider creating the solar panels used in Parts 2 and 3 before the activity.

- Using your multimeter, pretest the panels in the sun shade, and even indoors to obtain various readings. This will both enhance your expertise and ensure that none of the panels are damaged. Voltage readings should max out at around 6.5V. If it's significantly less than that even in full sunlight, then the panel is damaged.

- Note that the terms *petal* and *pin* are used interchangeably, but *pin* is used most commonly in the context of Modkit software.

CAUTION

With repeated bending and use, wires can break at their connection points without some sort of protection. To minimize wear and tear, put a protective coating of hot glue around the points on your LiPo battery where the wires meet the battery and where the wires meet the plug connector. Encourage youths to be careful pulling these out of the LilyPad connection—they should use needlenose pliers to pull on the *connector*, not the wires.

glue

glue

PART 1: STOCKS AND FLOWS AND PAPER AIRPLANES

In this activity, youths first are introduced to the idea of energy flow and its relationship to renewable energy. Then they engage in an embodied activity where they role-play a paper airplane supply chain, highlighting how important systems ideas, including stocks, flows, and dynamic equilibrium, actually play out in practice. A broader discussion following the activity formally introduces these systems ideas, and then youths connect them to the context of circuitry and energy in the situations that they've been exploring, as well as where they exist in the world more broadly.

Time: 80 minutes

STUFF TO HAVE HANDY

- 50–100 sheets of plain 8.5" x 11" paper

- Colored markers (and possibly other art supplies, such as glitter glue, crayons, etc., at the facilitator's discretion, which could be used to decorate planes)

- Tokens that can act as game currency (such as paper circles, buttons, Popsicle sticks—anything that can be easily found and distributed as play "wages")

- Scissors

RESEARCH: ENERGY FLOW—10 MINUTES

The first activity in this part involves getting youths thinking about the idea of energy flow. This was discussed briefly in Design Challenge 1, when they started to think about the potential energy in batteries running out. Here, we want to build on that frustrating experience, both to create a need for them to understand how that system works and also to help them appreciate the potential usefulness of solar panels. Although you may not choose to get into the subject here, this idea extends easily into ideas about preserving energy—a topic with which many youths might already be familiar. You might have some shared experiences with youths about batteries that you want to capitalize on in this discussion; if not, the following discussion prompts might be useful to guide this conversation:

- Has anyone ever had the experience of a battery running out just when you needed it?

- What can you do when that happens?

- What actually happens when a battery runs out? Where is the energy in the battery coming from? Where does it go? **Note:** This question is preparing youths to start to think about stocks and flows.

- Is there another kind of power source that we could use instead that doesn't have such a limited supply? **Note:** A potential misconception is that electricity cannot run out, as that likely will be the experience that youths have had in their use of electricity at home. You might want to be prepared to have a brief discussion about how electricity is produced and the kinds of proposed action plans that are under way to prevent us from running out of our current resources.

- Has anyone ever heard of solar energy? What about wind energy? How do those sources of energy work?

- Does anyone know anything about challenges to bringing these sources of energy into mainstream use? **Note:** Use this question to draw attention to how the *rate* at which these sources are able to supply energy for mainstream use currently is limited compared to nonrenewable sources like fossil fuels. There are several reasons for this that are both technological and infrastructural, but the key here is that these challenges are important from the perspectives of systems, stocks, and flows.

Explain to youths that next, they will role-play how energy *flows,* specifically how it sometimes increases and decreases and then increases again in such a way that the energy is considered *renewable.*

PLAY: EXPERIENCING STOCKS AND FLOWS—45 MINUTES

In this activity, youths will learn more about systemic stocks and flows through the creation of a mini supply chain where, by manipulating various levers, the facilitator can make evident how stocks, flows, and dynamic equilibrium play a key role in systems. *Stocks* are an accumulated amount of something within a system. In contrast, *flow* is the rate at which a stock changes. The relationship between stocks and flows is always intertwined—the amount of a stock over time always depends on rates of flow within a system. Importantly, flow is measured in two directions: the rate of flow into a stock (*inflow*) and the rate in which a stock depletes itself (*outflow*). When the inflows and outflows are approximately equal, a system exists in a state of dynamic equilibrium.

Examples of Stocks and Flows

Stock	Units of Stock	Inflow	Outflow
Population	Persons	Births, immigration	Deaths, emigration
Water in a bathtub	Gallons	Water pouring in	Water pouring out
Bank account	Dollars	Deposits, interest	Withdrawals

This section provides an overview of a mini–supply chain activity that will model stocks and flow in a paper airplane production activity. To build off youths' emerging ideas, the formal concepts of stocks and flows should be introduced *after* the activity has concluded.

10–20 players

For larger groups, create two supply chains, each with about 10–15 players.

Youths will work at one of the three stations of the supply chain to make it function. They will be paid for their work and receive occasional breaks, during which they can spend their "wages" at the airplane store (should they want to purchase paper airplanes—because that's the only thing that will be sold). The facilitator will act as "factory boss" throughout. Youths need to work collaboratively to understand how stocks and flows balance to achieve dynamic equilibrium so that the business model is sustainable. In the system, the stocks and flows are arranged as shown here:

Stock	Units of Stock	Inflow	Outflow
Paper airplanes	Paper, decorative materials, etc.	Number of paper airplanes produced	Sales of paper airplanes
Wages of workers	Currency	Shifts depending on rate of airplane sales at the store	How much it costs to make an airplane store purchase

When the system is in balance, the stocks flow (in and out) in such a way that there is the right amount of supplies (paper) for the paper airplanes to be made without backup, enough workers to keep the system flowing, and sufficient wage earning and expenditures to keep the system going.

SETUP

Set up four stations, each serving as part of a paper airplane supply chain, as follows:

1. A *boss station,* where the instructor/facilitator gives instructions and holds and distributes the supplies

2. A *folding station,* where the paper airplanes get folded

3. A *design shop,* where the folded airplanes get decorated

4. An *airplane store,* where the finished products are bought and sold

Station	Role of Employees at This Station
Boss station (Instructor/ facilitator)	This is where the materials (paper, art supplies, and wages) are located, all of which are distributed by the "factory boss."
Folding station (About 1/3 of the group)	Youths at this station fold the paper airplanes. They can be subject to various sorts of demands from the "factory boss" at various points, (e.g., pressure to speed up production when there's a big inflow of paper resources, to get creative with resources when paper supplies run low, etc.).
Design shop (About 1/3 of the group)	Youths at this station receive folded airplanes from the folding station and are equipped with markers, scissors, and various other supplies for decorating the planes. Just as with paper at the factory station, the shifting amount of art supplies available at a given point in time is controlled by the facilitator.
Airplane store (About 1/3 of the group)	Youths at this station receive completed (decorated and folded) paper airplanes from the decorating station and have to sell the planes to other youths, who buy them with the game currency. Youths at this station should use their judgment to determine the prices, but they should be prepared to justify their pricing.

Before the game begins, prepare "role slips," each one containing information about one of the four stations. Each youth will be given a role slip when the game begins, informing him or her of the starting station and the role of the employees there. Alternatively, the facilitator can just explain what role youths at each station will play.

RULES

- Every station must have workers, although the number at each station is up to the facilitator; at some points, not as many participants will be at a station, or some stations might not be active at all, especially at the start of the game. This can highlight how different parts of the system change over time.

- All workers at each station are paid by the factory boss for their work, although the amount paid is regulated by the factory boss, and payment is distributed informally over the course of the work period.

- Workers must be able to take breaks, which is when they can buy paper airplanes. Again, the factory boss can regulate how often breaks occur and how many people from each station may take a break at the same time. It's best to keep this informal. You can experiment with giving whole stations breaks at the same time to have youths see what happens to the system when you do so.

- As the activity unfolds, the facilitator modulates and is able to change the system's dynamics in a variety of ways. For example:
    - Workers might be laid off or given a break just when more paper floods the factory, creating a backlog in the production chain.

- Some workers might get raises, but they also get fewer breaks to spend their money.

- At the design shop, art supplies might run out (or be put in storage by the facilitator to be saved for later) just as a lot of folded planes come in to be decorated.

- All of these events, determined by the facilitator, should be both visible to the participants and *felt* by them, in terms of how they affect what the participants are able to accomplish in the system. This creates an experience and context where clear interconnections, dynamics, and patterns of changes are made clear to youths.

GAME PLAY

1. At the start of the activity, explain that today, they'll be forming a "paper airplane supply chain." See if anyone in the group knows what a *supply chain* is. Explain the overall structure of the game: the various stations and their role, your role as "factory boss" (feel free to "ham it up," playing the benevolent boss or harsh task-master), how employees will get breaks and wages, but could be reassigned or even fired depending on their performance.

2. Make sure that everyone understands the requirements at each station. In the event that not all youths know how to make a basic paper airplane, do a quick demonstration at the start, or have one of them do so.

3. Assign youths to the three stations (folding, decorating, and store). Remember to tell them that their station assignments may change, so they should not get too attached to what they're doing at the moment! As a modification, you can let youths choose their own stations, and if they end up unevenly distributed, let the activity run as planned, but have them see what happens as a result of the uneven distribution of labor. Likewise, you might ask the youths in each station if they want to spend a minute to plan a strategy for completing their work most efficiently (or even coordinating across stations, if they think of it).

4. Explain that as they participate in the activity, they should keep two questions in mind:

   - How are things interconnected, and what sorts of patterns form as a result?

   - How do things change over time in the supply chain?

5. Once everyone is ready, let the supply chain begin! As the role play proceeds, it's important that the facilitator shifts the quantities of certain components of the system, including:

   - **Wages** (these can increase or decrease in amount, frequency of distribution, consistency/inconsistency across stations, etc.)

- **Amount of paper** fed into the system over time (play with "flooding" and "draining" the supply, justifying through claims that there are surpluses or shortages in the market for these raw materials)

- **Amount of art supplies** fed into the system over time (play with "flooding" and "draining" the supply, justifying through claims that there are surpluses or shortages in the market for these raw materials)

- **Number of workers** at each station

- **Frequency of breaks** for workers to spend their wages

Note   Running this activity well is mostly about actively engaging and tweaking the system so that youths can see how the decisions that you make as the "boss" affect the way that the system plays out and the patterns that form over time. There is no single way that this activity can unfold or an "exact" right way to run it—part of the fun, and part of the lesson, is that the scenario will play out differently every time due to the ways that connections and patterns form and groups adapt and use their creativity. Mostly, it's important to be attentive, creative, and flexible as the activity unfolds.

MOD THIS ACTIVITY

You can take this activity in a number of different directions depending on the context in which it's going to be used. A few easy modifications include the following:

- As opposed to having all the participants involved in the various stations of the supply chain, create a "fishbowl" in which a subset of participants (about two-thirds) are working at the stations, with the rest observing and taking notes about what happens to the system as each of the various events occur and how it changes over time. While the observing participants don't get to experience the dynamics themselves, they might be able to observe them more easily since they're not "swept up" in the activity. Adjust the debriefing accordingly.

- Break the participants into three to four different supply chains and treat each one differently, but in a consistent way within that chain. Shift participants from one supply chain to another so that they can see how the system operates differently when different components of the system are treated differently by the factory boss. Adjust the debrief discussion accordingly.

- Replace paper airplanes with another item, like greeting cards, that's easy to make quickly, if you're worried that participants (such as younger age groups) might be distracted by the paper airplanes and it might cause a disruption in the space.

- Assign certain youths to be "assistant managers" in the supply chain, responsible for helping to make decisions about how things operate, as well as helping to distribute things like wages, arts supplies, and paper as these parts of the system change over time.

SHARE: LET'S TALK—25 MINUTES

After the activity is complete, use a follow-up discussion to orient the participants to the big ideas of stocks, flows, and dynamic equilibrium, how they were at play in the activity, how they exist within the context of circuitry, and where we see them in systems that we find in the world.

The following questions can guide the early part of the discussion, which should aim to orient youths to some of the dynamics that occurred during the activity:

- Was the supply chain a system? Why do you think so? (*Answer: It is a system, with the goal of producing and selling paper airplanes. The components of the system are paper, decorating materials, the number of workers at each station, the rate that workers are paid, the number of breaks that workers can take, and the price of the airplanes. These components, through their behaviors, work together to produce a functional supply chain.*)

- When did you believe that the chain was "working" best? When did you believe that the opposite was true?

- When did the biggest changes to the supply chain happen? Why?

- What would have happened if more paper, more workers, fewer art supplies, and other elements had been present in the system?

- What were some cause-and-effect relationships in the system? How were different components and activities connected to one another?

- Based on how the activity played out in your unique situation, ask a number of "what if" questions, prompting youths to make predictions about how different changes would have played out in the system.

Note By this point in the discussion, the participants should have discussed, either implicitly or explicitly, how stocks and flows were at play in the chain (though not in that language, of course). This is a good point to introduce the terms *stocks, flows,* and *dynamic equilibrium*:

Stocks are an accumulated amount of something within a system (money in a bank account, fish in a pond, trees in a forest, jobs in an economy, and so on). A stock is always a *noun*; it forms the "stuff" of systems.

Flows are the rates at which stocks in a system change, either through increasing or decreasing (for example, money comes in and out of a bank account due to wages paid, interest, and purchases; and fish come in and out of a pond due to birth rates, death rates, and fishing rates). A flow is always a *verb*; it is the "movement" of systems. Understanding stocks and flows gives an angle into how different parts of the system change over time.

Dynamic equilibrium is a state in which stocks and flows are balanced so that the system does not vary widely and is stable overall, but it still has internal processes that are continually in flux. For example, in economics, this term might be used to talk about the constant flux of money movement in otherwise stable markets; in ecology, a population of organisms stabilizes when birth rate and death rate are in balance, thus having dynamic equilibrium.

Continue the group discussion, now specifically engaging these formal concepts within the context of the game experience:

- What were the stocks in the paper airplane supply chain? (*Answer: The paper, the wages, the airplanes, the art supplies, the workers, etc.*)

- What were the flows in the paper airplane supply chain? (*Answer: The rate that paper went into the factory, how frequently and how much workers got paid, how quickly the airplanes moved from station to station, the price at which they were bought, etc.*)

- How did the various stocks and flows interact in the activity? [*Answer: the amount of stock available directly impacts the potential rate of flow; if there isn't enough paper, (stock) it can't be given to the factory (flow)*]

- Did any of the stock-flow interactions lead to a state of dynamic equilibrium? **Note:** You can mention any time that the system was functioning at an equilibrium and point to the things that were keeping it at that equilibrium: workers working at a regular or fast pace, paper being fed into the factory regularly, etc.

- Were there any clear moments when the system was definitely *not* at dynamic equilibrium? Were there any "peaks" in the airplane supply chain, when productivity was greatest? Did this occur when the system was in equilibrium or not? Were there "valleys" when productivity was down? How did that relate to dynamic equilibrium?

- How did time play a role in the ways stocks, flows, and dynamic equilibrium played out in the system?

Note If it's useful, feel free to create a diagram of the stocks and flows in the airplane supply chain on the board to help map out the relationships in the system during this part of the discussion.

In the final part of the discussion, connect the ideas of stocks, flows, and dynamic equilibrium to the context of circuitry, as well as to systems with which youths might already be familiar. The following questions can be used to guide the final part of the discussion:

- In what way is this activity connected to what we've been doing with circuitry? (*Answers can vary, but students should start to notice that the paper airplane factory is a system with components, behaviors, interconnections, etc.*)

- Are there stocks in the circuitry projects that we've been working on? (*Answer: Yes; examples are the amount of energy in the battery and the number of LEDs.*)

- Are there flows in the circuitry projects that we've been working on? (*Answer: Yes; examples are the rate that the battery's energy is used, the rate at which LEDs use electricity to light up, and the rate at which LEDs burn out.*)

- How might a solar cell help to keep a circuitry project in dynamic equilibrium? (*Answer: The solar cell, by regularly recharging unlike a normal battery, can better keep the circuit system functioning at an equilibrium with the power that it needs.*)

- Where might we see stock and flow dynamics out in the world? (*Answers:* populations and their rates of change, national debt and rate of spending, climate change and the amount of CO_2 in the air and the rate at which it's being added into the air, etc.).

WHAT TO EXPECT

These are new concepts that might take some time to make sense; youths will have had personal experiences with stocks and flows, of course, but connecting stocks and flows to other situations, particularly systems that are sustainable (unlike a traditional battery), might be a challenge. Try to encourage them to think about stocks and flows as describing relationships or interconnections in systems. Youths who are still struggling with systems thinking language will have a more difficult time integrating the language of stocks and flows into their description of systems, of course.

	Novice	Expert
Systems thinking concepts	• Cannot explain fully how components in a system interconnect to produce the goal or behavior of a system • Struggles to identify specific components of a system that are particularly influential in affecting an aspect of the system's behavior (for example, identifying which components are considered stocks and which are considered flows)	• Understands that the way that components of a system work together affects the ultimate behavior of the system • Can identify specific components of a system that are particularly influential in affecting an aspect of the system's behavior (for example, identifying which components are considered stocks and which are considered flows) • Can extend the idea of stocks and flows both to the specific designs that youths have already created and to other instances in the world that they know about (for example, a bathtub filling up), but likely have not thought about before in these terms

PART 2: TESTING SOLAR PANELS

The purpose of this activity is to support youths' thinking about stocks and flows in the particular context of the solar panels that they will be using in their backpack designs. They will test the current and voltage of their solar panels in different kinds of light, and with the panels in series or parallel, in order to think about how the stock of energy is accumulated in different light sources and in different circuit configurations, as well as how this stock relates to the flow of energy.

Time: 105 minutes

STUFF TO HAVE HANDY

- Flexible solar panels (PowerFilm MPT6–75)
- Standard LEDs
- Alligator clips
- Multimeters
- Tweezers
- Stiff poster board
- Painters' tape
- Needles
- Decorative duct tape
- Conductive fabric
- Regular, nonconductive thread

HANDOUTS

- "Solar Panel Testing"

RESEARCH: HOW DO SOLAR PANELS WORK?—5 MINUTES

In this part of the activity, youths will explore solar panels, relating their experiences with battery polarity to the positive and negative sides of this new energy source.

1. *Orient youths to the solar panel:* The PowerFilm MPT6–75 is a solar panel designed to absorb the sun's rays for generating electricity.

   - Point out the two leads on the panel. (A *lead* is a wire that conveys electric current from a source to a component in the system, or that connects two points of a circuit.)

   - On the PowerFilm solar panel, the leads are not wires; rather, they are *metallic strips* at the edges of the panel. Note that a protective coating is covering the strips and leads, which needs to be peeled back carefully on the corners that will be used in the activity to create a connection with the alligator clips.

	Flexible solar panel	A thin, semiconductor wafer, specially treated to form an electric field when struck by light (with a positive charge on one side and negative on the other). When activated, electrons are knocked loose from the atoms in the material. If conductors are attached to the positive and negative sides, forming a closed circuit, the electrons can be captured in the form of an electric current. In this project, the solar panel charges a separate battery, although running electricity directly from the solar panel is also possible. PowerFilm 6V 50mA Flexible Solar Panel MPT6–75. Million Solar Roofs—700–50060–00
leads	Copper tape lead	These are the positive and negative leads (conductive pads) on the solar panel. The lines that run across the panel from one lead to the other resemble an uppercase letter *E*. The long back of the *E* faces the positive (+) lead, and the tips of the E point toward the negative (–) lead. **Note:** some leads are now tin-coated.

- It is extremely important to know which is the positive and which is the negative end of your solar panel. The positive and negative ends of the solar module are shown in the following diagram. Notice at the inner lines look like uppercase letter *E*s? The backs of the *E*s point toward the positive end of the panel.

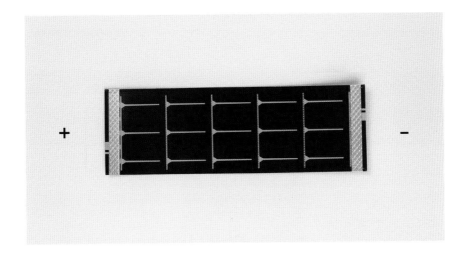

2. *Share background information on solar energy:* The sun is constantly emitting matter called *radiant energy,* which makes its way to the earth (which is measured in photons). In a single year, the amount of radiant energy reaching the earth's surface is about twice as much as *ever* will be obtained from all of the earth's nonrenewable resources of coal, oil, natural gas, and mined uranium combined.[1]

   - One of the methods used to convert energy from the sun into a flow of *electrons* is *photovoltaics.* The solar cells used to do this are made up of layers of silicon that are heated to extreme temperatures and mixed with these two chemicals:

     - Phosphorous (which provides the negative charge).

     - Boron (which provides the positive charge).

- Light excites these electrons into a higher state of energy, allowing them to act as charge carriers for an electric current to power a load.

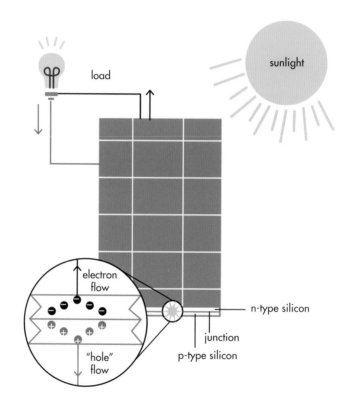

SOLAR PANEL DIAGRAM

load

sunlight

electron
flow

n-type silicon

junction

p-type silicon

"hole"
flow

RESEARCH: TESTING THE CURRENT (AMPS) AND VOLTAGE—5 MINUTES

In this part of the activity, youths will learn how to use their multimeters in a new way: to measure the amount of energy being produced by the solar panel. They will do this first with single solar panels and then with two panels placed in series and in parallel.

1. Let youths know that they will use multimeters to test the current coming out of their solar panels under different conditions. The output of current that they will be reading will be measured as the number of amps flowing through the circuit at a particular time. An *amp* is a unit of measurement that measures the number of electrons flowing through a wire (or conductive thread) per unit of time.

2. From the PowerFilm solar module with tin-plated copper tape leads, an adult should remove a small piece of the clear coating that is on top of the metallic tape to ensure good contact between the probes of the digital multimeter and the metallic tape. This can be done with a pair of tweezers to pull back the plastic coating gently. Do this just in the upper corners of the solar panel at this point. It is better for an adult to do this in advance to prevent youths from accidentally damaging the solar panel.

3. Pass out the solar panels and multimeters and begin the activity by giving youths these instructions:

   • To obtain the current measurement, turn the multimeter dial to 200mA.

   • Attach one alligator clip to the positive lead and one alligator clip to the negative lead. **Note:** Make sure that the clip on the positive side is red and the clip on the negative side is black.

   • Attach the other side of the positive (red) clip to the multimeter's red probe and the other side of the negative clip to the black probe.

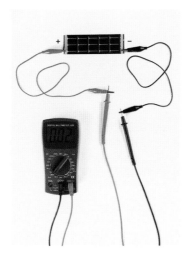

Testing current output (in amps) inside under low-light conditions.

4. Relate the solar panel to batteries and to the airplane supply activity by stating the following points:

   • Remember that a *volt* is the unit of measure of the force of electricity in a circuit. The voltage will determine how much power your solar panel is producing at any one time.

- In earlier Design Challenges, we tested two different batteries with different voltages and ran the system structure experiments. We'll do the same with this solar panel.

- How does the way a solar panel work mimic what happened with stocks and flows in the airplane activity? (*Answer: A solar cell stores energy, and that energy depletes and needs to be stocked up again, just like the paper resources in the airplane activity were depleted and had to be stocked up again.*)

5. To test the voltage, turn the multimeter dial to 20V. Then follow the directions about the alligator clips and probes in step 3.

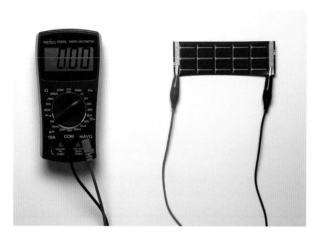

Testing volts inside under low-light conditions.

6. *Connect solar panels in series:* Next, youths will place two power sources in series for the first time. To place two solar panels in series, attach one side of an alligator clip to the positive lead of one panel and the other side of the clip to the negative lead of the other panel.

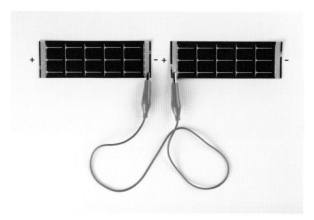

7. To test the current and voltage of the solar panels in series, follow steps 3 and 5, but ensure that the alligator clip attached to the red probe is placed directly on the outward-facing positive lead, and the alligator clip attached to the black probe is placed directly on the outward-facing negative lead. Keep the orientation of the panels the same as depicted in step 6. Here, the red alligator clip in step 6 is replaced by the white one depicted at the top of the panel. Do not put a probe where the two leads face each other in the middle.

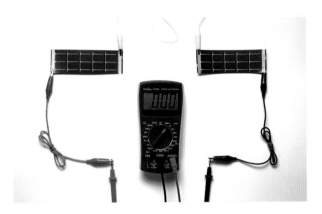

8. *Connect solar panels in parallel:* Now we will put the two solar panels in parallel. For this, we will need two alligator clips. Attach one to the positive leads of both panels, and attach the other to the negative leads.

9. When testing the current and voltage of the solar panels in parallel, it does not matter which panel the probes are attached to, so long as the red probe is attached to a clip that leads to the positive lead and the black probe is attached to a clip that leads to the negative lead. See the picture here for one possible configuration.

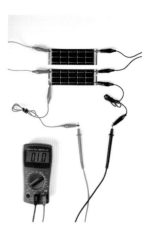

PLAY: TESTING, TESTING!—45 MINUTES

Once youths know how to test the current in their solar panels, the actual testing of the solar panels under different conditions can begin. First, they will test different types of light conditions to see how the panels are powered, and then they will test how well the panels provide power to light electric components.

LIGHT TESTS

1. *Choose the light testing method:* There are a couple of ways that you can run the next play-testing activity. Organize youths into small groups, and choose whether you will have all the groups test the same kinds of light. Or you can choose to assign different "testing conditions" (as described next) to specific groups. In either case, and then have each group share their findings with everyone.

2. Define the light tests that groups will conduct:

- Test the panel inside: Lights on, off, by the window, and away from it.

- Test the panel outside: In full sunlight, partial, and overcast.

- Test the panel while shading part of it with your hand: Does it matter how much it is shaded (one-quarter, one-half, or three-quarters)?

- Test the angle of the panel in relation to the light source: Does it make a difference?

- Test two panels in series and then in parallel in varying light conditions: How does that affect current and voltage? Is the effect consistent?

IMPORTANT TIPS FOR THIS ACTIVITY

- *Caution!* Folding, tearing, and puncturing can damage the flexible solar panel.

- To make testing of the panels in different conditions more consistent, you may want to have youths use painters' tape to tape the panels to a large poster board as pictured here. Make sure that the tape runs only on top of the parts of the leads still covered with plastic and does not cover any of the panel itself.

- When testing indoors, youths will have to ensure that each configuration of panels is receiving the same amount of light from the same angle. With the weaker light sources available indoors, this will usually require moving the board so that each configuration is directly under the light source before testing.

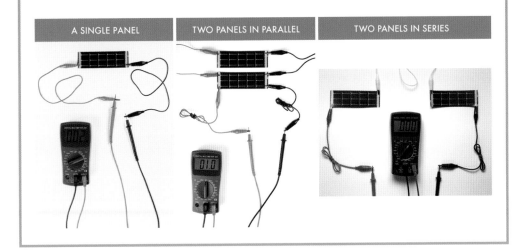

| A SINGLE PANEL | TWO PANELS IN PARALLEL | TWO PANELS IN SERIES |

WHAT TO EXPECT FROM THE SOLAR PANEL LIGHT TESTS

The table below gives a rough estimate of the light intensity under various environmental conditions. **Note:** Intensity is rated as a percentage of the full intensity of direct sunlight.

Condition	Panel Position	Intensity (% of full sunlight)
Full sunlight	Panel square to sun	100
Full sunlight	Panel at 45-degree angle to sun	71
Light overcast		60–80
Heavy overcast		20–30
Indoor lighting		0.2–1.3

POWER TESTS

Now groups will connect an LED to the solar panel(s) to test how well that it powers electric components. Remind youths to use alligator clips to connect the positive lead of the panel to the positive leg of the LED and the negative lead to the negative leg.

1. Ask the following questions to guide exploration:

- How bright does the LED shine in various light conditions?

- How about when the panels are in series? In parallel?

- Try more than one LED. Connect LEDs in series and parallel to the panels and see what happens.

- Do any conditions actually *burn out* an LED?

- Which condition allows you to light the maximum number of LEDs?

2. Here are some additional testing tips:

- Youths can test voltage and current across the LEDs.

- You can try to leave the multimeter at 20V and 200 mA, as you did when testing the solar panels, but if you find that you keep getting readings of 0, turn the multimeter to the next lowest setting.

- To measure voltage through an LED, simply touch the multimeter's red probe to the positive (longer) leg of the LED, and touch the black probe to the negative (shorter) leg.

- To measure current through the LEDs, however, you must disconnect the circuit and put the multimeter in series with the circuit with the help of two additional alligator clips.

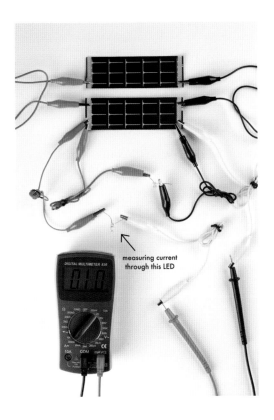

measuring current
through this LED

WHAT TO EXPECT FROM THE LED TESTS

Here are some general patterns that youths should encounter as they test current and voltage:

- They probably will expect that current and voltage for the solar cells will be the highest outdoors in full sunlight, with the panels aimed right at the sun. What may surprise them, however, is *how very much higher* the current measurements will be in sunlight than they are in indoor light. Even overcast skies will yield much higher current measurements than will most indoor lights. This illustrates that the sun provides much more energy than we could ever hope to generate ourselves.

- Sunlight streaming through windows produces lower current and voltage measurements than does sunlight outdoors because most windows are designed to block some of the sun's high-energy ultraviolet (UV) rays.

- Putting two solar panels in series should double the voltage flowing through them, but leave the current unchanged. Putting two panels in parallel should double the current flow but leave the voltage unchanged.

- The number of LEDs that can be lit by the solar panels, as well as the voltage and current measurements across the LEDs, will vary based on the LEDs' type and color. To simplify matters, especially for younger youths, you may wish to provide only one type and color of LED.

  - LED type: Standard versus superbright.

  - LED color: Colors at the higher end of the spectrum (e.g., blue and violet) require more energy to be lit and thus pull greater current. Youths should find that they cannot light as many blue LEDs as they can red or yellow from the same solar panel configuration.

- When LEDs are wired in series, the current should remain at the same level through each LED as it was before LEDs were connected to the circuit. However, when LEDs of the same type and color are wired in parallel, the current should be divided equally among each of them.

VOICES FROM THE FIELD

When I tested the solar panels' current and voltage for the first time, I was astonished by how much higher the measurements were outdoors in daylight—even in overcast conditions!—than they were indoors. It gave me a new appreciation for the sun's energy, and how human-made sources of energy simply cannot compete. This is a great opportunity for discussion with youth about the potential benefits solar power could provide.

—SOPHIA BENDER, GRADUATE RESEARCH ASSISTANT, INDIANA UNIVERSITY

SHARE: LET'S TALK!—5 MINUTES

After youths have finished their testing, bring them together for a group discussion. You might want to ask questions like the following:

- What was the lowest reading that your group measured on the solar panel test? What do you think caused the low reading?

- What was the highest reading that your group measured on the solar panel test? What do you think caused the high reading?

- What other variables affect the output of the solar panel? (*Answers: The direction in which the cell is pointed, weather, time of day, shady or not, series or parallel, etc.*)

- How did those variables affect the brightness and the number of LEDs that you could light?

- It's not very useful to be able to light something only when it's in the light, is it? How could you use a solar-powered system at night, when the sun isn't shining where you are? That is, how can you use solar power to make a light shine in the dark? (*Answer: You need a device to store the electricity—i.e., a battery.*)

CREATE: CONSTRUCTION OF THE SEWABLE SOLAR PANEL LEAD EXTENSIONS—45 MINUTES

Next, prepare the flexible solar panels to be stitched into youths' e-textile projects. **Note:** For younger age groups or projects with time constraints, you may want to assist youths and do these next few steps for them in advance of constructing the solar-powered backpack, as the flexible solar panel can be easily damaged:

1. Distribute flexible solar panels, tweezers, conductive material, decorative duct tape, needles, and nonconductive thread. Introduce items as needed. Be sure to introduce the key term *lead*, as it will be important for youths' understanding of the next few directions. (*Reminder: A lead is a wire that conveys electric current from a source to a component in the system, or that connects two points of a circuit.*)

2. To make contact with the positive and negative metallic leads, the thin plastic cover on the solar panel needs to be peeled back carefully along the two ends. Tweezers will help in peeling back the plastic layer. Leave the plastic protective cover on top of the solar grid. Be careful not to puncture or damage the metallic lead or solar panel.

3. Continue pulling back the plastic cover carefully, without removing, cutting, or tearing, for the entire length of the solar panel until the full metallic lead is exposed. Do not cut or tear off the plastic, as it will be needed later.

4. Repeat for the opposite lead.

 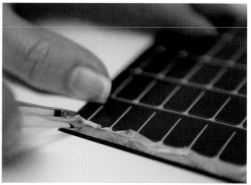

5. Cut two strips—one for each lead—of conductive fabric, approximately 5/8" x 3". Be sure that you are using conductive fabric because the project won't work with regular fabric.

6. Place the conductive fabric on top of the lead and cover it with the loose plastic cover that you just peeled back.

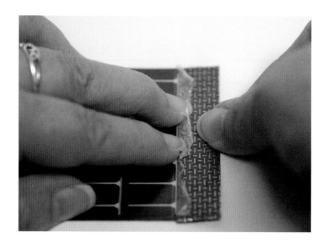

7. Cut two strips of decorative duct tape, approximately 3/8" x 3".

8. Place one piece of duct tape over the loose plastic cover and conductive fabric. (The duct tape will secure the top of the solar panel to the conductive fabric.)

9. Repeat steps 6 and 8 on the opposite lead. You are well on your way to making a sewable solar panel!

10. Using regular (nonconductive) thread, thread a small needle and knot it. With a running stitch placed approximately 1/4" from the solar panel, stitch through the duct tape and conductive fabric, being careful not to puncture the solar panel. This will secure the top of the conductive fabric and solar panel together.

conductive fabric

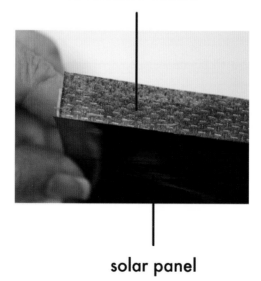

solar panel

View from the back of the solar panel, with the running stitch right along the end of the solar panel.

11. Repeat step 10 on the opposite lead of the solar panel.

12. Congratulations! Your sewable solar panel construction is complete!

DESIGN CHALLENGE 4, PART 2

SOLAR PANEL TESTING

Use this worksheet to record your findings when you test solar cells under different conditions.

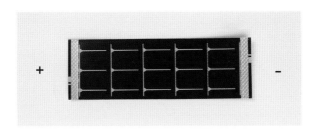

Condition	Panel Position	Panel Configuration (Single-Panel, Series, or Parallel)	Voltage (V)	Current (mA)
Full sunlight	Panel square to sun			
Full sunlight	Panel at 45-degree angle to sun			
Light overcast				
Heavy overcast				
Inside single-pane window				
Inside double-pane window				
Indoor overhead light				
Indoor desk/table light				

What do you notice? When are current and voltage the highest? When are they the lowest?

DESIGN CHALLENGE 4, PART 2

TESTING SOLAR PANELS WITH LEDS

Use this worksheet to record your findings from testing your solar cells with LEDs hooked up to them under different conditions.

Draw your circuit configuration here, and label its parts, including the color of the LEDs.	Light condition	Voltage (V) Also indicate whether you're measuring voltage across the solar panel(s), an LED, multiple LEDs, etc.	Current (mA) Also indicate whether you're measuring current across the solar panel(s), an LED, multiple LEDs, etc.
	Full sunlight		
	Light overcast		
	Heavy overcast		
	Indoor overhead light		

When measuring current and voltage with LEDs, keep the following in mind:

- For voltage, let probes touch each leg (or the outer legs if joined in parallel).
- To measure current, you must disconnect the circuit and put the multimeter in series with the circuit.

Note   If you have the same type of LEDs in parallel, the current will be split equally among them. In series, they will all have the same current flowing through them.

PART 3: DESIGNING THE SOLAR-POWERED BACKPACK

Just as with all previous designs, youths will want to think about how to design their solar-powered backpacks strategically with the circuitry and power in mind (which is much larger with the solar panels). In this case, the solar panels need to be exposed to the light, which makes the design potentially more challenging.

Time: 270 minutes

STUFF TO HAVE HANDY

Each youth will need the following to create a solar-powered backpack:

- Backpack (new or recycled)
- Sewable flexible solar panel constructed in Part 2 of this Design Challenge
- Two or more LilyPad LEDs (white and/or colored)
- LilyPad Arduino Simple
- LilyPad LiPower
- LiPo battery (lithium polymer ion battery: 110 mAh recommended, to provide about a 3-hour charge)
- Mini-USB cables
- LilyPad FTDI Basic Breakout board

ADDITIONAL MATERIALS

- Plenty of alligator clips
- Conductive thread
- Clear nail polish, fabric glue, or low-temperature hot glue (to secure knots)
- Sewing needles
- Scissors
- Regular, nonconductive thread
- Computer with Modkit Micro software available (1 per youth)
- *Optional:* Felt (for supporting the back of the flexible solar panel)
- *Optional:* Decorative items, including buttons, felt shapes, puffy paint, textile paint, colored/patterned duct tape and fabrics of varying textures, colors, and sizes

- *Optional:* Needlenose pliers (to pull needle through fabric if it gets stuck)
- *Optional:* Glass beads (to decorate as well as insulate thread when needed)
- *Optional:* Multimeters (to test for continuity in conductive stitching lines)
- *Optional:* Conductive tape (for quick but temporary repairs)

HANDOUTS

- "Sample Solar Backpack Diagram"
- "Diagram Your Solar-Powered Backpack"
- Modkit Micro Cards (from Design Challenge 3)

IMPORTANT TIPS FOR THIS ACTIVITY

- The LilyPad Simple may overload (and potentially damage the unit) if the voltage or current is too high. This is why we are using the LiPower as a voltage regulator instead of sewing the PowerFilm MPT6–75 Photovoltaic solar panel directly to the LilyPad Simple.

- *Optional:* We strongly suggest that youths use the "buried knot tail" technique when sewing during this activity, in order to prevent possible short circuits from knot tails that fray or are long enough to reach nearby sewn lines. To bury knot tails when tying them, do the following:

  - First, make sure that you're using thread much longer than you need to stitch your line and tie a knot at the end.

  - Stitch the line and double-knot at the end as you normally would.

  - Then thread the knot tail again, and sew it back through the same holes you just made.

  - Finally, tie a double knot when you run out of thread and hold the knot in place with nail polish, fabric glue, or hot glue.

CREATE: DIAGRAMMING YOUR SOLAR-POWERED BACKPACK — 45 MINUTES

In this section of the activity, youths will learn about the new components in their system, look at a sample solar-powered backpack diagram, and then make one of their own.

1. Pass out the "Sample Solar Backpack Diagram" worksheet and materials for the solar-powered backpacks, including the flexible solar panels created in Part 2 of this Design Challenge, alligator clips, the LilyPad Simple, LilyPad LEDs, and the LilyPad LiPower. At this point in the activity, youths will be using these materials to help plan the backpack designs and to draw diagrams of their circuits.

2. Take some time to introduce the various components. First, point out the petals (called *pins* in Modkit) on the LilyPad Simple and the LilyPad LiPower. These silver petal shapes that line the outside of LilyPad components can be programmed independently within Modkit to send signals to a particular input or output device, like an LED.

	Alligator clips	An electrical connector (named for its resemblance to the jaws of an alligator) attached to an electric cable for making a temporary connection to a battery or other component. Also called *alligator test leads*. SparkFun—PRT-11037
	Flexible solar panel	A thin, semiconductor wafer, specially treated to form an electric field when struck by light (with a positive charge on one side and negative on the other). When activated, electrons are knocked loose from the atoms in the material. If conductors are attached to the positive and negative sides, forming a closed circuit, the electrons can be captured in the form of an electric current. In this project, the solar panel charges a separate battery, although running electricity directly from the solar panel is also possible. PowerFilm 6V 50mA Flexible Solar Panel MPT6–75. Million Solar Roofs—700–50060–00
	LilyPad Simple	Wearable, washable e-textile technology whose large connecting pads can be easily sewn into clothing or other textiles. The LilyPad Simple has a built-in power supply socket for a LiPo battery and on/off switch. SparkFun—DEV-10274
	LilyPad LiPower	A sewable input unit, about the size of a quarter, that connects a LiPo battery to an e-textile circuit. Attach a single-cell LiPo battery, flip the power switch, and you will have a 5V supply to power your project. This unit helps to protect your project from any short circuits from potential power surges from your solar panel and is good up to 150mA. SparkFun—DEV-08786

	LilyPad LED	An LED is a small device that lights up when an electric current passes through it. It is frequently used as an indicator lamp in many everyday devices. LilyPad LEDs are designed with a built-in resistor and can be purchased in a wide array of colors, including blue, pink, red, white, yellow, and green. Note that the LED petals are labeled to indicate the positive and negative ends. LilyPad LEDs: SparkFun—e.g., DEV-10081
	LiPo battery	LiPo batteries are small, light, and rechargeable and can be plugged directly into the LilyPad Arduino components. We suggest the 110mAh LiPo battery, which supplies about 3 hours of charge. SparkFun—PRT-00731

3. Also, pay particular attention to these points when introducing the LilyPad LiPower:

- The LiPower is a new component being added to our system to help keep the LilyPad Simple from overloading (and potentially damaging the unit) if the voltage or current coming from the flexible solar panel is too high.

- This is why we are using the LiPower as a voltage regulator instead of sewing the PowerFilm MPT6–75 Photovoltaic solar panel directly to the LilyPad Simple.

Note: The high voltage range is 5.5V for the LilyPad Simple; it should not be exceeded.

4. Direct youths' attention to the LiPower's petals, including the two (–) petals, the one (+) petal, and the two new petals, C and B, which are as follows:

- The C stands for "charge." (This connection allows the solar panel to charge the rechargeable battery that is plugged into the LiPower.)

- The B petal will not be used in this project.

Also, point out that there is a separate on/off switch on this component that will need to be in the off position when the solar panel is charging the battery.

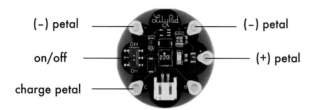

5. Using the "Diagram Your Solar-Powered Backpack" worksheet and the alligator clips and LilyPad materials, invite youths to mock up their designs and diagram their proposed backpack design incorporating the following elements:

- Flexible solar panel
- LilyPad Simple
- LiPower
- LiPo battery pocket **Note:** youths will have to construct one out of scrap materials
- Two or more LilyPad LEDs (white and/or colored)
- Other components or decorative components

6. Make sure that youths include the circuit connections in the drawing (connections sewn with conductive thread to LilyPad petals, positive, and negative lines). The following is a generic overview of the connections; use these or create your own.

SOLAR PANEL TO LIPOWER CONNECTIONS

- Positive (+) solar panel lead extension to C (charge)
- Negative (–) solar panel lead extension to negative (–) LiPower petal

LIPOWER TO LILYPAD CONNECTIONS

- Positive (+) LiPower petal to positive (+) LilyPad petal
- Negative (–) LiPower petal to negative (–) LilyPad petal

POSSIBLE IDEAS FOR LED CONNECTIONS

- Negative (–) LilyPad LEDs to one another (parallel format) and to negative (–) LilyPad petal
- Positive (+) LilyPad LED to a LilyPad petal #5–11 (*if* programming LEDs to exhibit individual behaviors)
- Positive (+) LilyPad LEDs to one another (parallel format) and to one LilyPad petal #5–11 (*if* programming LEDs to exhibit the same behavior)

Here are two sample designs and the completed backpack. The first one is also illustrated on the "Sample Solar Backpack Diagram" worksheet.

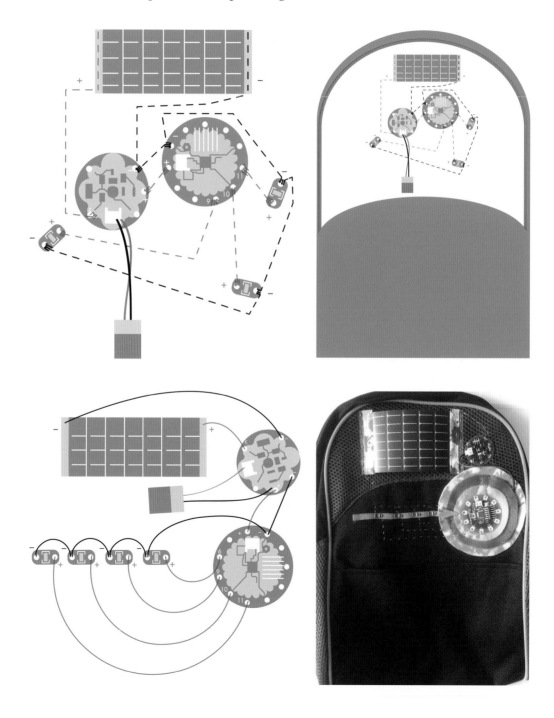

7. Once youths have completed their designs, have a partner double-check their work and that the LiPower is located near enough to the solar panel, as well as to the LilyPad Simple. (*It's important that these connections don't have to travel far because you want as secure a connection as possible with the power source in your project.*)

8. Feedback from other participants should begin with "warm" feedback (positive comments) then "cool" feedback with suggestions on how it might improve the final product. **Note:** All "cool" feedback should come with suggestions for improvement. See more on warm and cool feedback in the "Introduction" to this book.

9. Youths who finish early can set about programming their LilyPad Simple with behaviors, or reusing a program that they created in Design Challenge 3.

ITERATE: PROGRAMMING—30 MINUTES

Youths now will need to program the LilyPad using Modkit Micro. The following is a brief recap of the instructions included in Design Challenge 3. Be sure to look at Design Challenge 3 if you're in need of additional information. In addition, it might be useful to have a few stations set up in your space for youths to revisit the programming of their LilyPad as needed. This step also can be performed once the backpacks are constructed, but it's probably useful to think through the coding behavior before finalizing the back-pack designs.

1. Remember that youths will need access to the LilyPad FTDI Basic Breakout board and a mini-USB cable to program their LilyPad. In addition, you may want to have the Modkit Micro Challenge Cards from Design Challenge 3 available for this activity to help guide youths.

	LilyPad FTDI Basic Breakout board	E-textile-customized hardware that enables communication between a computer and the LilyPad—one side connects to the USB port and the other connects to your LilyPad pins. SparkFun—DEV-10275
	Mini-USB cables	Mini USB cables connect many cellular phones and personal digital assistants (PDAs) to the USB port on a computer. This cable connects the computer to the FTDI Basic Breakout board. It has USB Type-A male to Type-B-Mini 5-pin male connectors. SparkFun—CAB-00598

2. *Caution!* Youths do not need the LiPower, the LiPo battery, or the solar panel connected to their system at this time. Instruct them *not* to sew any circuits until they have programmed the LilyPad Simple. **Note:** *If any circuit is already sewn down, have youths put all of the on/off switches in the circuit in the off position.*

3. Have youths launch Modkit Micro, and then, using the alligator clips, LilyPad, LEDs, and any additional components, they should create the physical mock-up of their planned circuits based on their earlier backpack diagrams.

4. Perhaps building on some of the code that they created in Design Challenge 3, have youths develop code to manage the components that they've selected for their solar-powered backpack.

5. Remind youths to test their programs to be sure that the LEDs and/or other components exhibit the desired behaviors. If not, have them work to debug their projects. Allow them to have some time to debug, and avoid pointing them to the solution directly. If they continue to struggle, you might want to give them some direction, including the following suggestions:

    • Talk me through what you're trying to do and what you've tried so far.

    • Are all of your blocks nested in a forever loop?

    • Do you have just one stack of blocks or multiple stacks? (Remember that LilyPad Simples can handle only one stack at a time.)

    • Have you checked the way that your LEDs are hooked up to the LilyPad? Do the (–) ends connect to the ground or the (–) petal/pin on the LilyPad?

    • Have you checked the petal numbers or LED numbers to make sure that they match what you intend?

6. Once youths have programmed the LilyPad in a manner that they're happy with, be sure to have them upload the program to the LilyPad and save the program to edit or debug it later if there are problems.

7. To avoid confusion with other projects, it's useful to remind youths to create a file name with their name or initials, as well as the particular project that the program will be used for (e.g., Louis H: Backpack).

CREATE: CONSTRUCTION TIME—120 MINUTES

It's time to start e-sewing and placing all the solar-paneled backpack components in place. For more tips on e-sewing, see Design Challenge 2 and the "Toolkit" in this book.

1. *Optional:* If your solar panel is to be sewn into a mesh material, it's best to line the interior of the mesh area with a piece of felt. That provides a firmer surface on which to sew (see step 6 for an illustration). Simply cut a piece of felt about ¼" larger (on all four sides) than the solar panel construction.

2. Thread a needle with conductive thread, knot it, and secure the knot with clear nail polish, fabric glue, or low-temperature hot glue. Give it time to dry.

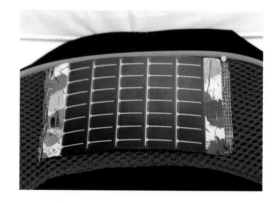

3. Start sewing at the bottom of the solar panel by stitching into the conductive fabric extension on the negative side.

- Stitch through the conductive fabric, the backpack, and the felt backing, if you have one. **Note:** Sewing through all three layers will create support for your solar panel.

- Continue to use a running stitch for the entire length of the conductive fabric extension until you reach the top. **Important note:** Be careful to not puncture the solar panel, but stitch only on the conductive fabric extension.

- This sewing not only will secure the conductive fabric to the backpack, but also it will help press the metallic lead and the conductive fabric together for a strong connection.

4. *CRITICAL STEP:* When at the top of the solar panel's conductive fabric extension on the negative side, continue stitching to connect to the negative (–) petal on the LiPower. Then knot and clip the thread. Be mindful of your stitching, and be sure to situate the LiPower close to your solar panel, so that the electricity generated from the solar panel doesn't have too far to travel. Also, be sure to loop through the petals three times to ensure a solid connection with the conductive thread.

5. Repeat the previous step, but for the solar panel's conductive fabric extension on the positive (+) side. When the entire length of the positive conductive fabric extension has been stitched, continue to stitch to connect to the C petal on the LiPower. Then knot and clip the thread. (The C connection allows the solar panel to charge the rechargeable battery that is plugged into the LiPower.)

6. At this point, this is what the stitching on the inside of the backpack, opposite the solar panel construction, will look like if you used a felt backing.

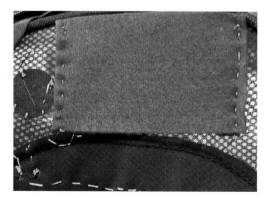

7. *CRITICAL STEP:* Again, be sure to situate the LilyPad Simple close to the LiPower so that the electricity from the LiPower battery doesn't have too far to travel.

   • Be sure to stitch through each petal/pin three times to ensure a solid connection with the conductive thread. **Note:** Lacking a solid connection with the power source will be one of the most common causes of problems in the solar-powered backpack.

   • Also, remember that the LilyPad will be running from the LiPower (not from the solar panel directly) while operating.

8. Stitch the negative (–) LiPower petal to the negative (–) LilyPad Simple petal, and the positive (+) LiPower petal to the positive (+) LilyPad Simple petal.

9. Stitch negative (–) LED terminals using one continuous thread that connects to the negative (–) petal on the LilyPad Simple. (See stitching above the arrow in the picture that follows.)

10. Stitch positive (+) LED(s) to appropriate LilyPad petals (petals #5–11) per youths' designs. (See stitching below the arrow.) Which petal to use will be determined by the design—for example, which petal is closest to the LED or which petal avoids a crossover sewing line.

11. At this point, this is what the underside of the circuits on the backpack looks like.

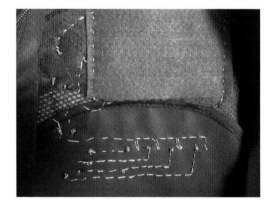

12. Charge youths' solar-powered backpacks in sunlight or another bright light source, and then test them to see if they work. Note that there are two on/off switches in this system: one on the LiPower and the other on the LilyPad SImple. When youths are charging the LiPo battery from the solar panel, both the LilyPad and the LiPo should be turned off. When the battery is charged, both switches should be turned on to power the project.

13. The batteries should come precharged, but if you're unsure of whether the battery is full, remove the LiPo battery from the LiPower and plug it directly into the LilyPad Simple. Then use the mini-USB cord and LilyPad FTDI Basic Breakout board to connect the LilyPad Simple to the computer to recharge the battery quickly.

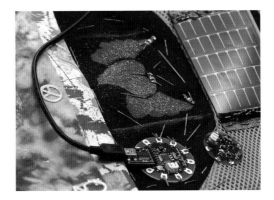

If it does work, congratulations—you've created your first e-textile with a renewable energy source! If not, don't worry—debugging is a natural part of any electronics project. The next part will take you through some easy debugging steps to double-check in your project.

IMPORTANT TIPS FOR THIS ACTIVITY

- *Caution!* Folding, tearing, or puncturing can damage the flexible solar panel.

- When starting a new thread, always start with the knot (secured with clear nail polish, fabric glue, or low-temperature glue) on the inside of the bag.

- Tie knots on the inside of the bag (and again, secure them with clear nail polish, fabric glue, or low-temperature glue). This will improve the appearance of the bag, but it also will insulate the conductive petals from the tails of the conductive thread, preventing unwanted shorts.

- Trim tails off the knots to prevent unwanted shorts in the design. Be sure to seal the knots with nail polish, fabric glue or hot-temperature glue before doing so!

- When connecting to LilyPad petals and/or LilyPad parts, always try to sew through the hole three times, if possible, to secure a good circuit connection.

- If the (–) petal on the LilyPad is blocked or in an inconvenient place from an aesthetic standpoint, you can convert any petal to a (–) petal by using Modkit. Here's how: Drag the "Digital Write" command block into your scripts area and insert it as one of your first blocks in your script. Choose the petal number that you want to set to (–) (e.g., "pin 10") and change the value to LOW. (In electronics, "LOW" means (–) or ground, and "HIGH" means (+) or power).

- If negative and positive conductive threads must cross in the design, you can use glass beads on one of the stitches to insulate one of the conductive threads (thereby not allowing the threads to touch and short).

- The LiPo batteries can be charged at any time in the project by plugging them into the LilyPad Simple and then using the FTDI Basic Breakout board and mini-USB cable to connect to your computer. The LiPo is charging while the orange light on your LilyPad is illuminated. Once the orange light turns off, the LiPo is fully charged, and you should unplug the LiPo or else it may overheat. Alternatively, you can experiment with using separate chargers to charge the LiPo batteries. Once the solar panel is connected successfully to the LiPower, however, youths can recharge their batteries independently in light, without the external power source.

- When debugging projects, the multimeter's continuity test settings can be useful if you're unsure of whether there is a break or a short in one or more of the lines (i.e., if you're unsure whether the current is flowing through the LED, you can place one end of the multimeter on either side of the LED and test for continuity). Before testing for continuity, turn both switches off and remove the battery.

- The silver in the conductive thread can slowly corrode over time. Puffy paint can be used to insulate the thread and ensure the conductivity of the project over time.

- Having trouble? Refer to the "Stitching Tips" section of the Toolkit in this book for troubleshooting guidance and additional techniques for working with conductive thread.

VOICES FROM THE FIELD

If you have any trouble with Modkit, don't hesitate to contact the Modkit team! We've found them very responsive and easy to work with, and they are always willing to work with educators to find solutions that will work for all parties."

—SOPHIA BENDER, GRADUATE RESEARCH ASSISTANT, INDIANA UNIVERSITY

ITERATE: DEBUGGING—60 MINUTES

Here are a few helpful hints to start debugging the project. Because of the complexity of the project, plan for some debugging time with the youths.

DEBUGGING STEPS

- Check to make sure that the battery is fully charged and has a firm connection with the LiPower (and make sure that the battery is not connected to the LilyPad).

- Check the inside of the backpack for any loose or messy stitching. Start by checking the connections between the solar panel and the LiPower, as well as the connections from the LiPower to the LilyPad. Most problems will stem from these areas. Make sure that each thread has a solid connection and that connections are all sewn correctly without touching any of the other lines in the circuit.

- Check to make sure that no two lines of conductive thread are crossed in the design, as this will cause a short.

- Make sure that the (+) sides of the LEDs are oriented toward the LilyPad Simple petals.

- Make sure that the (−) sides of the LEDs are connected to the (−) petal/pin on the LilyPad Simple.

- Check to make sure that each component has a solid connection (i.e., the conductive thread has been sewn around the component three or more times) and is not dangling from the backpack.

- Check to make sure that none of the LEDs have been sewn through (i.e., that the stitching stops at each sew hole and is knotted and cut).

- Check to make sure that none of the stitching has been cut accidentally or has frayed. If there are any questions about whether the stitching is still good in portions, check it with the multimeter in Continuity mode (just remember to remove the battery before testing).

- Make sure that the LEDs are sewn in parallel from one of the petals, not in series.

- Check the back of the backpack to make sure that there are no long tails on the knots or any threads that make unnecessary loops. If there are, affix any dangling pieces so that they are out of the way.

- Check to make sure that the solar panel is not damaged by testing its voltage with a multimeter. Remember that its voltage should max out at around 6.5V.

VOICES FROM THE FIELD

With the use of the Modkit cards, youth can explore the program and troubleshoot the light behaviors on their own with little to no help. In one case, a 10-year-old girl was so determined to finish her LilyPad Arduino LED programming that when her father arrived to pick her up from the after-school setting, she asked if he could come back in an hour to pick her up. She explained to him what she was trying to accomplish, and he smiled and said she could stay. She continued to diligently work on the programming, and perfect the timing of the light behaviors. Upon her father's return, she proudly showed him the coding blocks and played the program that she had fixed on her own. Her father smiled and told her how proud he was of her accomplishment. It was a wonderful moment to witness!"

—DIANE GLOSSON, GRADUATE RESEARCH ASSISTANT, INDIANA UNIVERSITY

SHARE: GALLERY DISPLAY—15 MINUTES

Once they've completed their designs, invite youths to share what they have been working on, allowing for a critique-like model as follows:

1. Each youth may share his or her design drawing, talk about how it changed, and then show off the backpack and point out where all the circuitry components are located, as well as how each component fits together to work as a system.

2. Have youths model their backpacks and take pictures for later posting. **Note:** Be aware of safety issues online; you might want to have students pose wearing their backpacks with their faces averted for any Internet postings.

EXAMPLE PROJECT

DESIGN CHALLENGE 4, PART 3

SAMPLE SOLAR BACKPACK DIAGRAM

This is a sample solar-powered backpack diagram that can help you create your own. Notice that the components added to the system are (a) the flexible solar panel and (b) the LiPower. Also, note the placement of the LiPo battery (it is connected to the LiPower instead of the LilyPad Simple). This is so that the battery can be charged from the solar panel. In addition, note that the LilyPad cannot be run directly from the flexible solar panel. To charge the battery, be sure to have the LilyPad built-in slide switch turned off. The remaining components (the LilyPad Simple and LEDs) should be familiar, as they are the same as those used in Design Challenge 3.

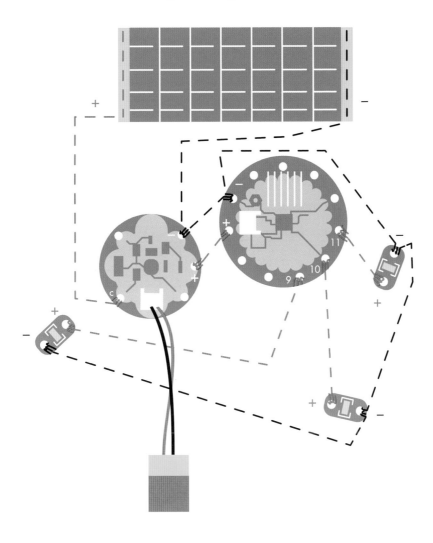

DESIGN CHALLENGE 4, PART 3

DIAGRAM YOUR SOLAR-POWERED BACKPACK

Use the back of this worksheet to sketch out your backpack design incorporating the following components:

- Flexible solar panel

- LilyPad Simple, with some ideas for activity programmed from Modkit Micro

- LiPower

- Two or more LilyPad LEDs (white and/or colored)

- Other components or decorative elements

    Be sure to include the circuit's interconnections in the diagram. The following is a general overview of the connections:

SOLAR PANEL TO LIPOWER CONNECTIONS

- Positive (+) solar panel lead extension to C (Charge)

- Negative (−) solar panel lead extension to negative (−) LiPower petal

LIPOWER TO LILYPAD CONNECTIONS

- Positive (+) LiPower petal to positive (+) LilyPad Simple petal

- Negative (−) LiPower petal to negative (−) LilyPad Simple petal

POSSIBLE IDEAS FOR LED CONNECTIONS

- Negative (−) LilyPad LEDs to one another (parallel format) and to a negative (−) LilyPad Simple petal

- Positive (+) LilyPad LED to a LilyPad Simple petal #5–11 (*if* programming LEDs to exhibit individual behaviors)

- Positive (+) LilyPad LEDs to one another (parallel format) and to one LilyPad Simple petal #5–11 (*if* programming LEDs to exhibit the same behavior).

VOICES FROM THE FIELD

If you'd like to try out some additional LilyPad sensors and components, the ProtoSnap LilyPad Development Board (SparkFun—DEV-11262) is a great place to start. Besides a LilyPad Simple, LEDs, and a buzzer, it also has two types of switches, a tricolor LED, a vibe board, light sensor, and temperature sensor. I've had excellent success programming a light sensor in Modkit to change the pattern of LEDs flashing on a shirt based on the light level in the room!

—SOPHIA BENDER, GRADUATE RESEARCH ASSISTANT, INDIANA UNIVERSITY

PART 4: WRAP UP!

In this part, youths will share and reflect on their solar-powered backpack designs with their local peer group, as well as sharing them at an online community. Finally, they will reflect on their experience and connect their systems thinking understanding to the core systems thinking concepts in this Design Challenge.

Time: 90 minutes

STUFF TO HAVE HANDY

- Computer with active Internet connection (1 per youth)
- Digital camera(s) with video capabilities and USB cord(s) to download material to the computer
- Youths' finished solar-powered backpacks
- *Optional:* Youths' original plans or diagrams for their solar-powered backpacks
- *Optional:* A scanner (to scan drawings and diagrams)

HANDOUTS

- "Posting Your Solar-Powered Backpack"
- "Self-Reflection on My Solar-Powered Backpack"

PUBLISH: POSTING TO THE WEB—60 MINUTES

Today's youths are becoming both consumers and avid producers of media online. The goal of this part of the activity is to give them time to post their solar-powered backpacks to an online community, which allows people to document and share projects that blend electronics and textiles.

Online crafting communities are ideal for posting e-textile projects like those found in this book. Giving them a few minutes to do this allows youths to post their work and become part of the larger participatory culture.

1. If you haven't already done so, create log-in usernames and passwords (or allow time for youths to create their own logins), and test the firewalls in your computer lab to make sure that you can access the website.

2. Allow youths time to visit the chosen website and briefly explore the projects posted there, leaving comments or "liking" projects as they go (*login required*). It might be useful for them to make notes as they explore about what makes a good post (for example, a great picture, interesting text accompanying the post, an attention-grabbing title, etc.).

3. After they've taken time to view other users' offerings, distribute the "Posting Your Solar-Powered Backpack" worksheet. Ask youths to complete the worksheet and post their projects on the chosen website. Remind them to refer to their notes about what they thought makes a good post as they work on their own writing.

GIVE YOUR PROJECT A NAME

What will you call your solar-powered backpack? Give it a unique and inspiring name! The name also will be the title of your post.

WRITE A PROJECT DESCRIPTION

- What inspired you?

- Describe the materials that you used to create your solar-powered backpack, including all the circuit components.

- Describe how your solar-powered backpack works and any other details that you think are important for others to know about.

PHOTO SHOOT PLANNING

What should the photo(s) look like on online? Sketch them or write down a description of what they should look like. (Example: "Photo 1 should be the solar-powered backpack with the LEDs turned on; Photo 2 should show my solar-powered backpack in action.") Should there be a video of your backpack in action? If so, what should show in the video?

1. Have small groups of youths take turns taking pictures and/or videos of their finished projects. Scanning some of the planning materials would make interesting additions to the posts as well. Remind them to refer to their notes about what they thought makes a good post as they work on their own pictures and videos.

2. Once they have drafted their ideas for their post, have them log in to the chosen site to post their projects.

3. Encourage youths to do the following:

   - Give their project a unique name/title.

   - Tag the project with "Soft Circuits," " Solar-Powered Backpack," or another unique tag for your group.

   - Write a compelling project description.

   - Link to other web materials (like their videos that would need to be posted on YouTube before creating their Interconnections submissions).

IMPORTANT TIPS FOR THIS ACTIVITY

- In order to post videos online, they need to be hosted on a site like YouTube or Vimeo, and a link will need to be copied to the website.

- What makes a good post? Suggest to youths that they photograph their work up close, with few distractions in the background of the image. Encourage them to write a clever title and catchy text that is both informative but to the point, and to think of their audience when describing their project, how it works, and what they used to put it together.

- In a few days, check to see if there are any comments on any of your group's posts and/or encourage them to comment on each other's work, too—reading and responding are important aspects of becoming part of an online community!

- If youths are taking the LilyPad Simple home, each one will need an FTDI Basic Breakout board and mini-USB cable to reprogram the LilyPad, if needed. However, they won't need these items to recharge their batteries since now they can do this with the sun!

REFLECT AND SHARE: LET'S TALK!—30 MINUTES

Once they've completed their designs, ask each youth to complete the "Self-Reflection on My Solar-Powered Backpack" worksheet individually (the questions are reprinted below). Then use those questions to lead a discussion to reflect on the ways that they can think about the production of these backpacks as a system that has both stocks and flows.

As with the ElectriciTee activity in Design Challenge 3, the goal here is twofold. First, this activity serves to bring ideas about systems back to the forefront. Second, the process of visualizing and realizing their backpacks might bring up new and more sophisticated understandings that they will realize when reflecting on the nature of systems. After youths have completed the worksheet, bring them together to debrief about how they are thinking of their backpacks as systems.

In addition, since this is the final debriefing conversation of the module, you might want to bring in some of the language that you have been working with in other Design Challenges. Suggestions for these kinds of questions are included after the questions pasted from the worksheet.

QUESTIONS FROM THE "SELF-REFLECTION ON MY SOLAR-POWERED BACKPACK" WORKSHEET

1. How does your solar backpack work? Describe the electrical system that makes your solar backpack display the programmed behavior.

2. How many systems are included in your backpack? Describe what they are.

3. How do those systems interact and work together?

4. How does having the sun involved change the systems that are incorporated into this project? What changes in the function of the system when we switch from recharging the battery to using a solar cell?

5. What one thing could you change about an element in a system in your backpack that would make a *huge* difference in the way that the system behaved?

6. What one thing could you change about an element in a system in your backpack that would make a *tiny* difference (or no difference at all) in the way that the system behaved?

7. Have you created parallel or series circuits in your backpack (or both)? Why did you choose to design your system in that way?

8. What is the switch in your system? How does it work?

9. What are the stocks and flows in your system?

EXTRA SYSTEMS THINKING QUESTIONS

1. Do you consider your backpack to be a nested system? Why or why not?

2. Are your backpack's systems in dynamic equilibrium? Why or why not? What would happen if they are not in dynamic equilibrium?

3. Do you feel that the systems involved in generating electricity for most of the world are in dynamic equilibrium, with balanced stocks and flows? Why or why not? If more energy were generated by solar power, would that change your answer?

WHAT TO EXPECT

Anticipate that this Design Challenge is going to be difficult for youths but will present a host of opportunities for them to learn a variety of things about more complex circuits and solar energy, and to practice a host of debugging skills. Though time-consuming, these skills are essential to the development of robust understandings of how circuits work. In terms of systems thinking content, the notion of stocks and flows can be challenging. However, in the context of circuits and powering batteries, this helps to make these concepts more salient for them and roots these ideas in their everyday experiences with technology and battery-powered toys and tools. Being able to identify and balance a system with stocks and flows is a core objective for this Design Challenge.

	Novice	**Expert**
Circuitry concepts	• Is unable to launch Modkit Micro without assistance • Is unable to upload a program to the LilyPad Simple using the Modkit programming environment • Is unable to hook up the LEDs or other peripheral devices to the LilyPad Simple to test programs using the alligator clips • Understands that the LilyPad Simple is a programmable microcontroller, but has difficulty explaining and naming the various parts of the device (e.g., the petal numbers, the plug for the FTDI Basic Breakout board, etc.) and what they're used for • Has difficulty remembering and using the essential vocabulary for this and previous Design Challenges (e.g., *solar panel, lead, load, code, scripts, blocks, hardware etc.*) • Is able to assemble simple scripts on the Modkit Micro Cards, but is unable to modify the scripts successfully and with purpose • Has difficulty understanding how to connect lights both in parallel and in series to the LilyPad Simple in their designs • Is unable to create a circuit diagram incorporating the LilyPad Simple, LiPower, and flexible solar panel with correct connections • Has trouble understanding the solar panel's role in the circuit and how a solar panel generally works • Is unable to create a working solar-powered backpack incorporating the flexible solar panel, LiPower, LilyPad Simple, LiPo battery, and at least two LEDs. • Seeks help from others to debug their project without first trying to troubleshoot their project themselves	• Is able to launch Modkit Micro without assistance • Is able to upload a program to the LilyPad Simple using the Modkit programming environment • Is able to hook up the LEDs or other peripheral devices to the LilyPad Simple to test programs using the alligator clips • Understands that the LilyPad Simple is a programmable microcontroller and can explain and name the various parts of the device (e.g., the petal numbers, the plug for the FTDI Basic Breakout board, etc.) and what they're used for • Has a command of the essential vocabulary for this and previous Design Challenges (e.g., *solar panel, lead, load, code, scripts, blocks, hardware etc.*) • Has a command of the Modkit Micro programming language and can modify or edit simple scripts successfully and with purpose • Understands how to connect lights both in parallel and in series to the LilyPad Simple in their designs • Is able to create a circuit diagram incorporating the LilyPad Simple, LiPower, and flexible solar panel with correct connections • Can describe the flexible solar panel's role in the circuit (i.e., to recharge the battery) and can describe in general how a solar panel works • Is able to create a working solar-powered backpack incorporating the flexible solar panel, LiPower, LilyPad Simple, LiPo battery, and at least two LEDs • Is comfortable engaging in a series of debugging steps to figure out a problem (either in his or her own project or a peer's)
Systems thinking concepts	• Cannot explain fully how components in a system interconnect to produce the goal of a system • Struggles to identify specific components of a system that are particularly influential in affecting an aspect of the system's goals (for example, identifying which components are considered stocks and which are considered flows) • Does not understand or cannot explain the idea of a system having "stocks" and "flows"	• Understands that the way that components of a system work together affects the ultimate goals of the system • Can identify specific components of a system that are particularly influential in affecting an aspect of the system's goals (for example, identifying which components are considered stocks and which are considered flows) • Can extend the ideas central to the system of their backpack (such as stocks and flows, interconnections, and components) to other instances in the world that they know about but likely have not thought about before in these terms

DESIGN CHALLENGE 4, PART 4

POSTING YOUR SOLAR-POWERED BACKPACK

Use this worksheet to help plan what you will say about your solar-powered backpack on the Interconnections site.

GIVE YOUR PROJECT A NAME

• What will you call your solar-powered backpack? Give it a unique and inspiring name!

WRITE A PROJECT DESCRIPTION

• What inspired you?

• List the materials you used to create your backpack, including all the circuit components.

• Describe how your solar panel works and why.

PHOTO SHOOT PLANNING

What should the photo(s) look like on online? Sketch them or write down a description of what they should look like. (Example: "Photo 1 should be the solar-powered backpack with the LEDs turned on; Photo 2 should be me wearing my solar-powered backpack.") Should there be a video of the solar-powered backpack in action? If so, what should show in the video?

DESIGN CHALLENGE 4, PART 4

SELF-REFLECTION ON MY SOLAR-POWERED BACKPACK

1. How does your solar backpack work? Describe the electrical system that makes your solar backpack display the programmed behavior.

2. How many systems are included in your backpack? Describe what they are.

3. How do those systems interact and work together?

4. How does having the sun involved change the systems that are incorporated into this project? What changes in the function of the system when we switch from recharging the battery to using a solar cell?

5. What are the stocks and flows in your system?

6. What one thing could you change about an element in a system in your backpack that would make a *huge* difference in the way that the system behaved?

7. What one thing could you change about an element in a system in your backpack that would make a *tiny* difference (or no difference at all) in the way that the system behaved?

8. Have you created parallel or series circuits in your backpack (or both)? Why did you choose to design your system in that way?

9. What is the switch in your system? How does it work?

DELVING DEEPER INTO SYSTEMS THINKING

The significant problems we face cannot be solved at the same level of thinking we were at when we created them.

—Albert Einstein

We are caught in an inescapable network of mutuality, tied in a single garment of destiny. Whatever affects one directly affects all indirectly.

—Dr. Martin Luther King, Jr.

So what is systems thinking, and why is it important? With so little time to cover what seems like so much, why should systems thinking get a seat at the educational table? We find the answer in part by looking at the vast problems in the world around us, which range from environmental degradation to global financial meltdowns, growing inequality to ballooning costs of health care, and so many more issues. At their core, these difficulties are about systems, and all can be linked fundamentally to perspective: people have a tendency to look at things in terms of isolated parts instead of interdependent wholes. In short, to solve these complex problems, we need to view the world as a set of complex systems.

We believe that teaching systems thinking holds promise for supporting the development of a generation of young people who look at things differently, through "new lenses" that will allow them to effectively meet the challenges of a world that is more connected than ever. These lenses involve looking before leaping, an orientation toward understanding the big picture, and the approach of *interpreting* things differently rather than *doing* them differently. After all, change in the ways we *do* things naturally follows from a change in the way we *see* things. Rather than focusing on a narrow analysis of phenomena that we too often assume are standing still, a systems thinking approach always assumes that the world is in constant motion, and that in that world, nothing exists in isolation. So the systems thinker learns to focus on the dynamics that surround, shape, and are shaped by whatever it is that we want to understand, whether it be in the realm of science, sociology, economics, or English literature. Systems thinkers seek to understand the impact of their actions on the often tightly interconnected system of which they are a part.

WHAT MAKES A SYSTEMS THINKER DIFFERENT? IT'S ALL ABOUT PERSPECTIVE!

As mentioned previously, much of systems thinking deals with changing our perspectives on situations and adopting the kinds of perspectives that people aren't often taught. Specifically, several practices are engaged in regularly by someone acting from a systems thinking perspective:

- Looking at the world in terms of integrated and interdependent wholes, as opposed to isolated parts

- Knowing that most complex problems involve dynamic systems that are in motion, rather than static parts that stand still

- Viewing situations from multiple levels of perspective, focusing on the connections between events and the underlying patterns, systemic structures, and assumptions from which those events emerge

- Considering how a particular stakeholder's position within a system will affect his or her ideas and assumptions about a system's function and how it should operate

- Adjusting the sense of time—by expanding the range of time considered when looking at a problem, you can gain insights into how certain actions in a system might have delayed effects

- Identifying the various dynamics, especially circular ones in the form of feedback loops, which lead a system to function in a particular way and move in a particular direction

- Focusing on finding leverage points that can be used to make lasting changes, as opposed to falling back on short-term fixes

- Considering the unintended consequences of intervening in a system

Think about the difference between a person who is able to do the things on that list and one who cannot. In an interconnected world, young people who are trained as systems thinkers have a powerful way of understanding, participating in, and changing the structures that affect their lives and those of people they care about.

WHAT MAKES A SYSTEM A SYSTEM?

A system isn't just a whole bunch of stuff that happens to be lumped together geographically or topically. It's not limited to what we usually call *systems* in our daily lives, such as when we refer to our education or healthcare systems, a computer system, or a heating system in a building (though these definitely *are* systems!). Systems have particular qualities, and knowing and being able to identify them is a key part of being able to look at things systemically.

Here's one definition of system that we like to use: A *system* is a collection of interacting *components* that interact to *function* as a whole, where the whole is always greater than the sum of its parts. If you changed one component, the whole would function differently. All these components are set up in a particular way, interacting in relation to one another, which is called a system's *structure*. The structure of a system determines the specific *behaviors* of different parts and the specific *system dynamics* that result from the interactions among the components. In a designed system, or one with intentional actors, these components work together to accomplish an intentional *purpose* or *goal* that someone brings to the system. But regardless of that intentional goal, a system always will function in a certain way that moves the system toward a certain state. (Note that these terms are defined in great detail in Appendix A.)

Linda Booth Sweeney, a leader in the field of systems thinking, likes to talk about the difference between systems and heaps (Sweeney 2001). Both, she says, contain lots of "stuff," or parts. But a heap won't be changed much if you take away some of its parts. Think of a pile of laundry. Add or take away a couple of shirts or a towel, and you still have a pile of laundry—not really a substantive change. Now think of a washing machine. Try taking off the door handle, adding a slot for detergent that doesn't connect to the rest of the machine, or changing the amount of electricity that feeds into the machine. Good luck getting socks clean! That pile of laundry is a heap, where adding and taking away things won't really affect the pile very much (if at all) in terms of how it functions in the world. But a washing machine is a system—we can't just add, take away, or change components willy-nilly since these often are interconnected in specific ways, often feeding back on one another, and have specific roles or behaviors that allow the system to function in a particular way.

A SYSTEM'S GOAL, PURPOSE, AND FUNCTION: NOT ALL ARE CREATED EQUAL

One of the tricky things about systems is the fact that there's often a difference between the way that a system is *actually* working (its *function*) and how we *want* it to work (its *goal*). This is why so many of us try to intervene in existing systems—because they're not working well (or maybe they're working well for *some*, but not for all).

There are many cases where a system is functioning exactly as it was intended to by someone designing or intervening in it. Let's take the example of a game. A game can be considered a system because how the game is played and how the game play unfolds are the results of multiple interactions among different components. The *function* of the system (the experience of playing the game) might be really difficult—and a designer might have meant it to be so (her *goal* might have been to create a difficult game). On the other hand, sometimes the overall function of a system is *at odds* with the intended goal that someone has for the system. For instance, from one perspective, the *goal* or purpose of a car is to take someone from point A to point B; but when the car's transmission gives out, the car will not *function* as a system to meet that goal.

It's important to be able to reflect not only on how a system might be functioning currently, but also on how a designer might have intended it to operate (or intended to change it). A given system might have multiple goals that are at play simultaneously, but come into conflict. The person who designed the washing machine has a pretty straightforward goal: get clothing clean (without destroying it in the process). Many systems are more complex than a washing machine, however, and have a less straightforward purpose. For example, the educational system has many components (e.g., teachers, stud, school buildings, assessments, and educational standards), all of which, presumably, are meant to work together in order to … do what? Well, that question is actually a matter of some dispute. Like many other systems, such as health care, social services, economies, businesses, and communities, the educational system has more than one person who acts as a "designer"—that is, there are multiple actors bringing varying goals and purposes to the design of a given system and contributing to the way that it is configured.

In the case of the educational system, some people believe that the purpose of being educated is to develop a population that is well prepared to engage in the project of democracy (this was Thomas Jefferson's view), while others see its purpose as preparing young people to compete in the global economy. These are only two possible goals, and while there might be some overlap of goals, we probably can agree that an educational system that aims at only one of the goals likely would look different from one that aims at the other. Knowing that any given system can have different stakeholders working toward different goals sometimes can help us understand why a system is not functioning as well as it could be. After all, not all goals are compatible.

Often, though, the way that systems actually operate is more organic than intentional. Many environmental issues involving the interaction of human behavior with natural ecosystems can be described as the result of systems whose functions are completely unintended. Global warming, for instance, results from the interaction of many components (human fossil fuel emissions, carbon dioxide's capacity to retain heat, the particular makeup of the Earth's atmosphere that captures certain gases, etc.), which all create a system that functions to increase global climate over time. Obviously, this was not anyone's intention, but it points to the fact that while many systems are designed and have intended goals or consequences (like that washing machine), others have their own logic and function that is driven by an emergent system structure (like economies and ecosystems).

SYSTEM STRUCTURE

The way that a system's components are set up in relation to one another, known as the *system structure,* is another important factor in understanding systems. On their own, components don't do very much. However, once they're connected to one another, they start to take on specific behaviors and roles within a system. These behaviors aren't a given, though; they depend on the way that the system is structured. For instance, if I take apart a car, lay out all the parts, and then put them back together in a different way, it's unlikely that the car will work the way that it did before or that the parts will exhibit their original behaviors. The relationships between the car parts are contingent on how they're structured.

Circuits offer a great example of this concept, and in Design Challenge 2 of this book, which addresses this idea of system structure, youths consider how a collection of the same components in a circuit, set up in different ways, result in very different systems. Specifically, they experiment with various circuitry components to see the differences between parallel circuits and series circuits.

In a *series circuit,* components (for example, light-emitting diodes/LEDs) are connected "in series," or one right after another, along a single path. When they are connected to a battery to form a closed circuit, the flow of electrons travels along one pathway in a continuous loop. Energy flowing from the battery travels sequentially through each of the LEDs along the circuit. As the current travels from the battery through each LED, more and more of the original electrical charge or energy (also known as *voltage*) is lost, and so the amount of energy available for each subsequent LED decreases. Depending on the voltage of the battery, the single current may not carry enough energy to light all the LEDs in the circuit.

On the other hand, in a *parallel circuit,* components are connected "in parallel," as opposed to one right after another. That is, rather than having one continuous loop, each LED is wired to the battery on a separate loop. This allows the same amount of energy or voltage to reach each LED.

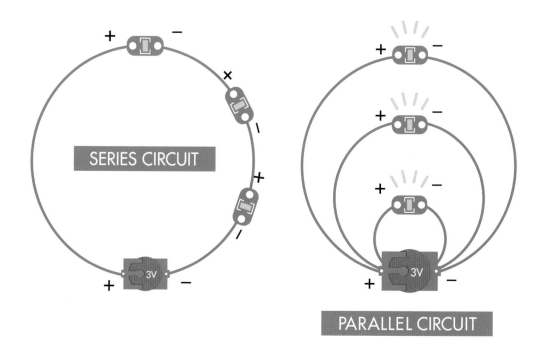

The key difference between the two types of circuits concerns *electron flow*. In a series circuit, there is only one pathway for energy to travel from the battery: As energy passes from the battery to the first LED, energy is used up, so less energy is available to the next LED in the circuit, and then the next gets even less, and so on. On the other hand, in a parallel circuit, energy is able to travel directly from the battery to each individual LED, allowing each to receive the same amount of energy.

This example of parallel versus series circuits can highlight for youths the important role that structure plays in the ways that systems function. A simple change in how a circuit is set up can mean the difference between lighting all the LEDs or only some.

STOCKS, FLOWS, AND LIMITED RESOURCES

Another set of ideas concerns the "stuff" of systems and how it moves across a system. The stuff of systems is called *stocks.* Stocks are an accumulated amount of something within a system (money in a bank account, fish in a pond, trees in a forest, jobs in an economy, and so on). A stock is always a *noun,* and it can accumulate or decrease. In circuitry, the amount of energy in a battery is a stock.

Flow is the rate at which a stock changes. Money comes in and out of a bank account due to wages paid, interest, and purchases. Fish come in and out of a pond due to birth rates, death rates, and fishing rates. A flow is always a *verb*, and it describes the rates of actions that influence stocks in a system. Flows describe "movement" within a system. In circuits, the rate at which a battery's energy is depleted when attached to an LED is a flow.

Understanding how the stocks and flows of a system operate is important due to a basic truth about systems: the concept of *limited resources.* In any system, the resources (stocks) are finite, meaning that at a certain point, they will run out. Many decisions about how to design and intervene in a system are based on trying to make the best use of that system's limited resources. Returning to the example of circuits, in an electronic circuit that involves a battery, the battery contains only a limited amount of energy, so when we design circuits (or any system, in fact), we must be aware of how the stock/flow dynamics work so that those limited resources aren't wasted.

LEVERAGE POINTS: INTERVENING AND CHANGING SYSTEMS

Understanding how systems work is all well and good, but if that insight isn't used to actually do something in the world, then it's just an academic exercise. Our vision of teaching systems thinking is rooted in the idea that young people eventually will become designers of new systems and redesigners of the systems that they inherit from us, and so some of the core ideas that we focus on are those related to how to change and intervene in systems.

When we think about changing systems, we think about *leverage points.* What makes a leverage point unique and powerful is that it's a place within a system where "a small change in one thing can produce big changes in everything," as activist and systems theorist Donella Meadows says. In a now-foundational book in the systems thinking world called *Leverage Points: Places to Intervene in a System* (1999), Meadows outlines different ways we can think about possible leverage points that range from less effective (e.g., changing the amount of "stuff" associated with certain parts of a system or changes to the structures that handle the movement of this "stuff") to more effective (e.g., changing the rules that govern a system, or better yet, the mindset that leads to things like rules, goals, and structure). While we won't go through all of the leverage points that Meadows outlined, we want to stress that focusing on leverage points isn't like generating any old solution to a problem; they are designed not just with mindfulness of the system's structure, but aim to take advantage of these structures so that a little change can go a long way.

In a wonderful example of leverage points at work, Meadows shares the story of the Toxic Release Inventory, which required every factory that released air pollutants to document and report data on these pollutants publicly. When the inventory was instituted in 1986 by the US government, toxic emissions were reduced dramatically. The inventory didn't levy fines or make the process of releasing these chemicals into the air illegal—it simply made the information public. By 1990, toxic emissions in the United States dropped by 40 percent. Factory owners did not want to be known publicly as polluters, so they changed their practices. The availability of information to different stakeholders within a system (in this case, citizens) changed the way that this system operated. The Toxic Release Inventory targeted a leverage point: It didn't aim to remake the whole system to prevent pollution; rather, it just added one small part that wasn't there before. It was a minor change, but it had a big effect.

In the world of electronics and circuitry, we might think about a change to the structure of a system—as we mentioned earlier about parallel versus series circuits—as a leverage point. Nothing is being added or taken away from the system, but through a simple rewiring, the whole system functions differently and is more able to meet its goals.

One type of leverage point that comes up regularly when working with circuits is a *balancing feedback loop.* Balancing feedback loops are processes put in place to help move a system toward its goals or keep it at a desired state of equilibrium. Usually, balancing feedback loops stabilize systems by limiting or preventing certain processes from happening. Think about the way home heating systems work. A thermostat detects when the temperature drops below a preset level and reacts by turning on the heat. It continues to monitor the temperature, and once it reaches the preset level again, it turns off the heat. Eventually heat escapes (maybe because the temperature outside drops), and the process starts over. This is a good illustration of a balancing feedback loop, with the thermostat acting as the balancing mechanism.

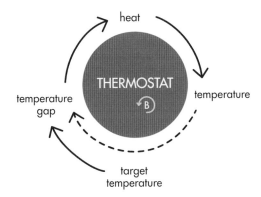

Balancing loops are sometimes harder to notice because, well, they're everywhere. Most systems contain many balancing feedback loops in order to continue functioning. Coolant in a car engine serves a "balancing" function by preventing the engine from overheating. Bathtubs have drains, which create balancing loops that prevent the tub from overflowing. Families who find themselves with a bunch of knickknacks hold yard sales (or these days, maybe they sell things on the Internet) to create more space. A human's or animal's body gets low on energy, so it sends hunger signals to the brain, which prompts eating to satisfy hunger (and keep nutrients and energy coming into the body) so that it can continue to function. In general, balancing feedback loops aim to keep or move a system toward some state of equilibrium that allows it to continue to meet its goals.

But people often try to create new balancing loops after things have gone very, very wrong. Think about bank runs—people fear that their money isn't safe in a bank, which causes them to remove the money they have. This weakens the bank because it has less capital to operate with and is less able to do things like make loans that keep it solvent. Other customers see this weakness, fear for their money, go and withdraw it, and start the whole cycle again until the bank collapses. This cycle is an example of a different type of dynamic: a *reinforcing feedback loop,* one that gets out of control and can derail a system from meeting its goal. We don't have bank runs in the United States these days because after the Great Depression (when they were common) the government created the Federal Deposit Insurance Corporation (FDIC), a balancing mechanism. If a bank is a member of the FDIC, all deposits are insured by the government for up to $250,000. This check on the system eliminates the possibility of bank runs because people don't need to fear that their money will be lost (so long as people have faith in the government's financial standing, anyway!). The presence of the FDIC created a balancing feedback loop, preventing the runaway situation of bank runs.

In the world of circuitry, balancing loops are also ubiquitous. The most common way that they're used as a leverage point in a system is through the inclusion of *switches*. Think about the way that a simple circuit (consisting of a battery, wires, and an LED) operates. If everything is connected, the light is always on, meaning that the very finite amount of energy in the battery will be depleted continuously—even when we don't need it. Enter the switch. The switch acts as a balancing mechanism to regulate when the light is on and when it's off. This allows the system to meet its goals in two ways: First, we can control when the light is on and when it's off (as with most lights, the goal is not to *always* have a light on). Second, the scarce energy resources in the system are conserved so that the system can better meet the goal of functioning and providing light when needed.

We find an even more powerful example of a balancing mechanism when we consider solar-powered cells (see Design Challenge 4). In contrast to a regular battery, which will eventually run out of energy and then fail to power an electrical system, a solar cell battery can be charged continuously by the Sun's energy. Using a solar cell creates a balancing loop that keeps an electrical system at its desired state: having power to function.

HANDLE WITH CARE: FIXES THAT FAIL AND UNINTENDED CONSEQUENCES

Part of the challenge of making a change in a system is that systems are complex, and we usually don't know how they'll respond when we introduce new factors into them. Often, people try to go for simple solutions to problems not amenable to easy fixes and play into one of the common challenges associated with trying to change systems: inadvertently creating *fixes that fail.*

We're unfortunately all too familiar with these "solutions." Someone tries to pay off credit card interest by opening up a new credit card, only to find himself or herself with more interest to pay. A company tries to save money by cutting down on maintenance costs, but the machine malfunctions that result lead to more costs than they would have had in the first place. Traffic jams lead people to demand more roads, but when these new roads are built, they create more incentives to use cars instead of public transportation, and so congestion stays the same or even increases. Most of these involve a mode of thinking that's both short term (in terms of the time scale it envisions) and narrow (in terms of how it frames the problem).

Related to fixes that fail are *unintended consequences,* where one problem might be fixed, but it causes something else to happen in another part of a system that no one planned or even guessed would happen. For instance, in an effort to control cane field pests in Australia, cane toads were introduced, but not only did they fail to fix the pest problem, they became a serious problem in and of themselves. In another instance of unintended consequences Down Under, a law making bicycle helmets mandatory resulted in fewer young people cycling overall because they found it unfashionable, with counterproductive effects for the overall net health of that demographic. In international politics, counterterrorism analysts note the phenomenon of "blowback," where covert military operations meant to fight terrorism result in increased terrorist activity. One infamous instance of this, of course, was the covert US funding of the mujahideen forces that fought the Russian occupation of Afghanistan in the 1980s. The funding of the mujahideen eventually led to the rise of the Al Qaeda terrorist network, which was responsible for the September 11, 2001, attacks on the World Trade Center and the Pentagon, among other catastrophic attacks all over the world.

The ideas of leverage points and balancing loops can empower us to think about ways that we can make big changes, while the concepts of fixes that fail and unintended consequences point to how careful we need to be when we try to intervene in systems. Ideally, a systems thinker keeps both sides of this coin in mind, understanding how important it is to be deliberate and conscientious when interacting with systems, but not shying away from acting within them when intervention is needed.

GLOSSARY OF KEY TERMS

SYSTEMS THINKING

Identifying a system.   Identifying a system and distinguishing it from other kinds of things that aren't systems. Specifically, a system is a collection of two or more *components* and processes that *interconnect* to *function* as a whole. Speed and comfort in a car for example are created by the interactions of the car's parts and thus are "greater than the sum" of all separate parts of the car. The way a system works is not the result of a single part but is produced by the *interaction* among the components and/or individual agents within it. A key way to differentiate things that are systems from things that aren't is to consider whether the overall way something works in the world will change if you remove one part of it.

Identify the way a system is functioning.   The function of a system describes the overall behavior of the system—what it is doing or where it's going over time. A system's function might emerge naturally based on interconnections among components, or it might be the result of an intentional design (in which case, we might also call refer to the function of a system as its goal). Regardless, the function of a system is the result of the dynamics that occur among components' interconnected behaviors.

Distinguishing the goal of a system.   The goal of the system is what a system that was intentionally designed is intended to do. Sometimes this might be the same as the *functioning* of the system … other times the goal and the *function* are not aligned.

A given system might have multiple goals or purposes that are at play simultaneously, and come into conflict. Being able to understand a system's purpose or goal gives a sense of the ideal state of a system from a particular perspective.

Identifying components.   Components are the parts of a system that contribute to its functioning. *Components* have certain qualities and/or *behaviors* that determine how they *interconnect* with other components, as well as define their role in the system. Without being able to effectively identify the parts of a system, it's hard to understand how a system is actually *functioning* and how it might be changed.

Identifying behaviors.   Behaviors are the specific actions or roles that a component of a system displays under various conditions. Being able to identify behaviors becomes important when we change systems, as often a component will look the same after the change, but its behavior will be different.

Identifying interconnections.   Interconnections are the different ways that a system's parts, or *components,* interact with each other through their *behaviors,* and through those interactions, change the behaviors of other components.

Considering the role of system structure.   Understanding how a system's *components* are set up in relation to one another gives insight into the *behavior* of a component. A system's structure affects the behaviors of its components and the overall *dynamics* and *functioning* of a system. For instance, how a city's highway system is structured affects overall traffic patterns and car movement within it. Being able to see a system's structure gives insights into the mechanisms and relationships that are at the core of a system, which can be leveraged to create systemic changes.

Make systems visible.   When we learn to "make the system visible"—whether modeling a system on the back of a napkin, through a computer simulation, a game, a picture, a diagram, a set of mathematical computations, or a story—we can use these representations to communicate about how things work. At their best, good pictures of systems help both the creator and the "reader" or "audience" to understand not only the parts of the system (the components), but also, how those components work together to produce a whole.

Balancing feedback loops.   Feedback loops are circular, cause-and-effect processes that create stability by counteracting or dampening change. These processes keep a system at the desired state of equilibrium, the system goal. Usually, balancing feedback processes stabilize systems by limiting or preventing certain processes from happening.

Having a sense of how balancing feedback loops operate can give a person a sense of what will make a system stable.

Stocks & flows. Stocks are an accumulated amount of something within a system (like money in a bank account, fish in a pond, trees in a forest, or jobs in an economy), and flows are the rate at which stocks in a system change either through increasing or decreasing (money comes in and out of a bank account due to wages paid, interest, and purchases. Fish come in and out of a pond due to birth rates, death rates, and fishing rates, etc.). Stocks are always nouns; they're the "stuff" of systems, while flows are always verbs; they're the "movement" of systems. Understanding stocks and flows gives someone an angle into how different parts of the system change over time.

Limited resources. In any system, it is important to understand which resources are finite, ones that run out at a certain point. Keeping in mind which resources are limited helps people make decisions about how best to maximize resources.

Nested systems. Systems that are a smaller part of other systems. Almost all systems are nested within larger systems. With nested systems, a larger system will affect the way that a subsystem behaves, and the subsystem will affect the way that the larger system behaves. Having a sense of nested systems helps people keep an eye on how systems interconnect and are always part of bigger pictures.

Dynamic equilibrium. A state in which stocks and flows are balanced so the system is not varying widely, but still has internal dynamic processes that are continually in flux even though the system is stable overall. For example: in economics dynamic equilibrium might be used to talk about the constant flux of money movement in otherwise stable markets; in ecology, a population of organisms stabilizes when birth rate and death rate are in balance.

Designing a system. Creating a system through engaging in an iterative design process, one that entails cycles of feedback, troubleshooting, and testing. One of the most effective means of developing systems thinking is to regularly create and iterate on the design of systems.

Leverage points. Particular places within a system where a small shift in one thing can produce big changes in everything. Leverage points are difficult to find because they often lie far away from either the problem or its obvious solution. It is because of the multitude of cause-and-effect relationships, feedback loops, and system structures that a seemingly small change can be amplified, often in unexpected ways. Not every place in a system is a leverage point—sometimes changing one thing in a system creates only small effects that aren't felt throughout the system.

CIRCUITRY

Amp. A unit of measure of the number of electrons flowing through a wire (thread) per unit of time.

Battery. An energy source that converts chemical energy into electrical energy.

Conductivity. The degree to which a material transmits electricity. Conductivity is inversely related to resistance.

Conductor. A material through which electric current flows easily.

Current. A flow of electric charge through a medium; e.g., wire, conductive fabric, or a light-emitting diode (LED).

Current flow/flow. The rate at which an electric charge passes through a point in the circuit.

Debug. The iterative process of identifying and removing errors from hardware or software designs.

e-Textiles. Everyday textiles and clothes that have electric components embedded in them; also known as *electric textiles* or *smart textiles.*

Electronic circuit/circuit. An unbroken path capable of carrying an electric current (i.e., a *loop*). Typically, an electric circuit contains a source of power (e.g., a battery).

Lead. A wire that conveys electric current from a source to a component in the system, or that connects two points of a circuit.

Load. A device (like a lightbulb or motor) that requires electric current passing through it to give it power.

Multimeter. A handheld device with a negative and a positive probe, which is designed to measure electric current, voltage, and resistance to help determine whether a material or artifact is conductive or not.

Parallel circuit. When components are wired in parallel within a circuit, the electric current divides into two or more paths before recombining to complete the circuit. The current flows through three LEDs wired in parallel, and the electric current is split equally among the three of them. **Note:** The evenness of the split is contingent on the three LEDs being the same type and/or color.

Resistance. A measure of how difficult it is to "push" current through a circuit. A *resistor* is a component in a circuit that limits, but doesn't stop, the flow of electric current.

Series circuit. When components are wired in series within a circuit, electric current flows sequentially through those components in a continuous loop. This means that as the current travels from the battery through each LED, it loses some of its original electrical charge or energy (also known as *voltage*) such that the amount of voltage available for each subsequent LED decreases with each one it passes through.

Short circuit (or "short"). A low-resistance connection between the two sides of the battery that causes the energy of a battery to drain or terminate completely.

Solar panel. A thin, semiconductor wafer specially treated to form an electric field when struck by light (with a positive charge on one side and a negative one on the other). When activated, electrons are knocked loose from the atoms in the material. If conductors are attached to the positive and negative sides, forming a closed circuit, the electrons can be captured in the form of electric current.

Switch. A component that controls the flow of current by opening and closing a circuit.

Volt. A unit of measure of the amount of voltage in a circuit.

Voltage. *Voltage* is the force that causes electric current to flow through a circuit. Increasing the voltage in a circuit without changing the resistance increases the current that flows through the circuit.

MODKIT AND LILYPAD

Block. A puzzle-piece shape that is used to create code and programs in Modkit. Blocks connect to each other like a jigsaw puzzle, preventing common syntax errors.

In Modkit, there are six categories of blocks: Setup, Output, Input, Operators, Control, and Variables.

Code. Language that describes the instructions or program used in software; in the examples in this book, code is created in Modkit to tell the LilyPad Simple how to behave.

Microcontroller. A small computer on a circuit board, containing a processor core and memory, which can be programmed for various types of hardware like LEDs, speakers, and other devices like temperature and light sensors. One example of a microcontroller is the LilyPad Simple.

Petal. A silver shape that lines the outside of the LilyPad Arduino and other LilyPad components. Each petal can be programmed independently within Modkit to send signals to a particular input or output device, like an LED. (Also called *pins* in Modkit.)

Programming. The act or process of writing sequences of instructions that are designed to be executed by a computer.

Script. An automated series of instructions carried out in a specific order, created in Modkit Micro and carried out by the LilyPad Simple.

STORYTELLING

Character. A real or imaginary person represented in a story.

Character trait. A distinguishing feature or specific quality of a character that influences a character's actions.

Context. The circumstances in which an event occurs; a setting.

Narrative. An often-chronological sequence of real or fictitious events in a story, consisting of a context (or setting), a narrator, characters, or both; and an event sequence that has a beginning, middle, and end and includes a conflict and resolution.

Narrative conflict. Inherent incompatibility or tension between the goals of two or more characters or forces.

Narrator. A person who tells a story or gives an account of something.

Plot. The main events of a story, rendered by the writer as an interrelated sequence.

Resolution. A literary term; the goal of a narrative/story.

Script. A map or outline that a director or artist uses to create a movie, play, comic book, television show (or in the examples in this book, a shadow puppet show).

Shadow play. A theatrical entertainment using silhouettes thrown by puppets or actors onto a lighted screen.

Shadow puppet. A cut-out figure or object held between a source of light and a translucent screen.

Storyboard. A panel of sketches that depict a sequence of action. Storyboards contain frames, and within each frame is a depiction of an important moment in the storyline. Storyboards often are used to plan out the sequence and composition of a movie, video, or animated film.

Appendix B

Here is a selection of videos, links to other resources, and inspirations that you might use in your classroom to help students better understand electric circuits. You also can search online for other similar resources using key terms such as "electric circuits," "electricity," "power source," "switch," "conductivity," "load," "batteries," and "current."

DESIGN CHALLENGE 1

ADDITIONAL INSPIRATION

BRAINPOP: ELECTRIC CIRCUITS AS AN INTRODUCTION

Electrical circuits are mighty important—but how do they work? Includes components of a circuit.

www.brainpop.com/science/energy/electriccircuits/

Video: 3 minutes, 45 seconds
Requires subscription, or sign up for a five-day free trial

BRAINPOP: BATTERIES

They power everything from flashlights to submarines, but how do batteries work?

www.brainpop.com/science/energy/batteries/

Video: 2 minutes, 24 seconds
Requires subscription, or sign up for a five-day free trial

BRAINPOP: ELECTRICITY

Light up my life! General information about electricity.

www.brainpop.com/science/energy/electricity/

Video: 2 minutes, 24 seconds
Requires subscription, or sign up for a five-day free trial

BILL NYE THE SCIENCE GUY: ELECTRIC CIRCUITS

Electricity might seem mysterious, but once you understand the science the light goes on (so to speak).

www.youtube.com/watch?v=rg-XFXdtZnQ

Video: 23 minutes

EXPLORING CONDUCTIVITY: KID CIRCUITS

Video from PBS Zoom. Youths become conductors for a broken circuit by holding hands and using a lemon battery.

www.pbslearningmedia.org/resource/phy03.sci.phys.mfe.zcircuit/
exploring-conductivity-kid-circuits

Video: 3 minutes, 23 seconds

DESIGNING ELECTRIC CIRCUITS: DOOR ALARM

Video from PBS Zoom. Youths use electrical circuits to create door alarms out of a variety of materials.

www.teachersdomain.org/resource/phy03.sci.phys.mfw.zalarm/

Video: 3 minutes, 47 seconds

ENERGY QUEST: CHAPTER ON CIRCUITS

Energy Quest is the energy education web site of the California Energy Commission. It is very thorough and informative.

www.energyquest.ca.gov/story/chapter04.html

Energy Story website, Chapter 4

HOW STUFF WORKS: HOW BATTERIES WORK

Text-based resource with information on how a battery works to create an electrochemical charge.

www.howstuffworks.com/battery.htm

DESIGN CHALLENGE 2

INSTRUCTIONAL RESOURCES

LEDS IN CUFFS AND BRACELETS

Discuss different purposes of having light-emitting-device (LED) lights incorporated into cuffs and bracelets. Consider these examples and explore the different purposes that the LEDs have within these various systems.

FLASHING LED PET COLLARS

dongwes.en.ec21.com/Flashing_Collar--4280830_4399270.html

LED BRACELET

talk2myshirt.com/blog/archives/260

DESIGN CHALLENGE 4

INSTRUCTIONAL RESOURCES

SOLAR PANELS

How to connect solar panels to fabric (sewing)

www.instructables.com/id/How-to-make-a-Heating-and-Cooling-Jacket/step7/Solar-Panel-optional/

How to connect solar panels to fabric (snaps)

www.instructables.com/id/How-to-connect-solar-cells-to-fabric/step2/Positive-and-negative/

How PV Cells Work

fsec.ucf.edu/en/consumer/solar_electricity/basics/how_pv_cells_work.htm

Video: How Photovoltaic Panels Work (from the U.S. Department of Energy)

www.youtube.com/watch?v=x2zjdtxrisc

Video: How Solar Energy Panels Work (from Best Energy Power)

www.youtube.com/watch?v=x4CTceusK9I&feature=related (stop at minute 1.22)

Video: How Solar PV Works (from the Energy Conservation Group)

www.youtube.com/watch?v=k3CSg6gkU0E&feature=related

CARING FOR THE LILYPAD ARDUINO

- Plug the LilyPad FTDI Basic Breakout board into the LilyPad Arduino Simple with the SparkFun name facing down; if the board is flipped, it will damage the LilyPad.

- To wash a solar-powered backpack, perform the following steps:

  1. Remove battery. (Why must you do this? That is a good question for youths to answer.)

  2. Remove the solar panel (if it is attached with snaps or conductive Velcro).

  3. Hand-wash in mild detergent. (Another good question: Why not put it in the washer?)

  4. Dry it on a rack. (Why not use the dryer?)

ADDITIONAL INSPIRATION

BACKPACK CONCEPT

Learn about the Seil bag, a bikers' backpack with flexible LEDs and circuitry applied to the back, which lets you make turn signals with both hands on the handlebars.

www.wired.com/gadgetlab/2010/09/cyclists-backpack-shows-led-turn-signals/

LILYPAD ARDUINO BLINKING BIKE PATCH

Add flashing LEDs to your backpack for fun and safety.

www.instructables.com/id/LilyPad-Arduino-Blinking-Bike-Safety-Patch/

ORIGINAL TURN-SIGNAL BIKING JACKET BY LEAH BUECHLEY

This tutorial will show you how to build a jacket with turn signals that will let people know where you're headed when you're on your bike.

www.instructables.com/id/turn-signal-biking-jacket

GREAT DESIGN DRAWING FOR THE TURN-SIGNAL BIKING JACKET

Step-by-step instructions on making a biking jacket with lights.

www.instructables.com/id/turn-signal-biking-jacket/?ALLSTEPS

VARIATION ON LEAH'S JACKET

A video demonstrating a turn-signal jacket for bicyclists.

mocoloco.com/fresh2/2010/02/11/turn-signal-bike-jacket-by-leah-buechley
.php

TWEET SLEEVE

The tweet sleeve is a wearable item that visually displays the moods of your Twitter stream on your garment. If you've been sending out angry tweets, the LEDs on your sleeve will radiate red. If your spirits suddenly brighten, the colors will shift to a "happy" green.

www.fashioningtech.com/profiles/blogs/tweet-sleeve

RESOURCES

LessEMF.com   Conductive fabrics and thread

SparkFun.com   LilyPad kits and pieces

Aniomagic.com   Aniomagic kits and pieces

MakerShed.com   Kits and books

FashioningTechnology.com   Companion to the book *Fashioning Technology: A DIY Intro to Smart Crafting*, by Syuzi Pakhchyan

Electricfoxy.com Explores the aesthetics of circuitry and the marketability of wearable technology solutions

Talk2myshirt.com A platform to bring together the consumer and the designer of wearable electronic products

Craftzine.com Daily source of craft projects and inspiration

Computationaltextiles.com Growing collection of notable projects and resources

SoftCircuitSaturdays.com Weekend explorations in wearable computing, e-textiles, and the intersection of craft and technology

lilypadarduino.org/?cat=15/ LilyPad Arduino tutorials: Getting Started with LilyPad (including Arduino programming)

Web.media.mit.edu/~emme/e-sewing/ Introductory e-sewing tutorials: Simple soft circuit walkthrough (lights, batteries, and switches only)

www.kobakant.at/DIY/How To Get What You Want (HTGWYW): How to make soft sensors and other fabric electronics

FASHIONING TECHNOLOGY

Fashioning Technology: A DIY Intro to Smart Crafting, by Syuzi Pakhchyan (O'Reilly Media, 2008)

A "DIY introduction to smart crafting."

GETTING HANDS ON WITH SOFT CIRCUITS: A WORKSHOP FACILITATOR'S GUIDE

web.media.mit.edu/~emme/guide.pdf

A workshop guide containing a set of introductory e-sewing activities.

Appendix C

SOFT CIRCUITS FORMAL ASSESSMENTS

Name: _____   Date: _____

You will need to reference the following components to answer some of these questions.

3V battery in holder   Switch   LED   9V battery in holder

1. Use one 3V battery in a battery holder, one switch, and one LED to draw a *working circuit*. **Note:** Draw the components that you see above, or write their names in a box within your circuits—whatever method is easiest for you. Don't forget to draw the connections between the components and mark the positive and negative ends!

2. Use one 9V battery in a battery holder, one switch, and three LEDs to draw a *series circuit.* **Note:** Draw the components you see above, or write their names in a box within your circuits—whatever method is easiest for you. Don't forget to draw the connections between the components and mark the positive and negative ends!

3. Use one 3V battery in a battery holder, one switch, and three LEDs to draw a *parallel circuit.* **Note:** Draw the components you see above, or write their names in a box within your circuits—whatever method is easiest for you. Don't forget to draw the connections between the components and mark the positive and negative ends!

4. Use one 9V battery in a battery holder, one switch, and two LEDs to make a *broken circuit* (i.e., one that will not work.) **Note:** Draw the components you see above, or write their names in a box within your circuits—whatever method is easiest for you. Don't forget to draw the connections between the components and mark the positive and negative ends!

5. What is the relationship between the following three things? You can explain your answer in words or pictures.
(a) studying, (b) grades, and (c) interest in the subject matter
Based on your answer, what do you think would happen to your studying effort and grades if your interest in the subject matter went *down?*

6. David has not been doing well in school this year, and many of the students in David's class make fun of him. This makes David act out, often getting into fights. As a result, he has gotten suspended several times. Being suspended keeps him out of class and causes his grades to drop even further.

What is the best way for David to improve his grades? (Circle one choice.)

(a) Get David a tutor.

(b) Tell the other students to stop teasing David.

(c) Continue to punish David.

(d) Do nothing. The situation will eventually clear up on its own.

Why do you think your answer will work?

7. What is the relationship between the amount of grass that is growing in a field, the number of rabbits that live in the area (rabbits eat grass), and the number of wolves in the area (wolves eat rabbits)? Explain your answer in either words or pictures.

If someone decided to kill all the wolves, what would happen to the rabbits and the grass?

8. There's a rumor spreading around school that Jamie has a crush on Frankie. Jamie is very upset about this. Jamie's friend told her not to worry because by tomorrow, everyone will be talking about something else. She explained that rumors spread quickly because they're interesting and because it's fun to tell "secrets." However, once everyone knows, rumors just aren't interesting anymore because they're no longer secret.

How does this explain why Jamie shouldn't worry?

SYSTEMS THINKING CONCEPT CARDS: SOFT CIRCUITS

The following cards have been included for you to use any way that works well in your setting, such as printing a set for each youth, creating a classroom deck to store in a resource center, or even using them as game cards for a whole-group games or activities (like *Jeopardy!*, *Flyswatter*, *Baseball*, and so on).

01.

IDENTIFYING A SYSTEM

Identifying a system and distinguishing it from other kinds of things that aren't systems. Specifically, a system is a collection of two or more components and processes that interconnect to function as a whole. Speed and comfort in a car for example are created by the interactions of the car's parts and thus are "greater than the sum" of all separate parts of the car. The way a system works is not the result of a single part but is produced by the interaction among the components and/or individual agents within it. A key way to differentiate things that are systems from things that aren't is to consider whether the overall way something works in the world will change if you remove one part of it.

02.

IDENTIFY THE WAY A SYSTEM IS FUNCTIONING

The function of a system describes the overall behavior of the system–what it is doing or where it's going over time. A system's function might emerge naturally based on interconnections among components, or it might be the result of an intentional design (in which case, we might also refer to the function of a system as its goal). Regardless, the function of a system is the result of the dynamics that occur among components' interconnected behaviors.

03.

DISTINGUISHING THE GOAL OF A SYSTEM

The goal of the system is what a system that was intentionally designed is intended to do. Sometimes this might be the same as the functioning of the system... other times the goal and the function are not aligned. A given system might have multiple goals or purposes that are at play simultaneously, and come into conflict. Being able to understand system purpose or goal gives a sense of the ideal state of a system from a particular perspective.

04.

IDENTIFYING COMPONENTS

Identifying the parts of a system that contribute to its functioning. Components have certain qualities and/or behaviors that determine how they interconnect with other components, as well as define their role in the system. Without being able to effectively identify the parts of a system, it's hard to understand how a system is actually functioning and how it might be changed.

05.

IDENTIFYING BEHAVIORS

Identifying the specific actions, roles, or behaviors that a component of a system displays under various conditions. Being able to identify behaviors becomes important when we change systems, as often a component will look the same after the change, but its behavior will be different.

SYSTEMS THINKING CONCEPT CARDS:
SOFT CIRCUITS

06.

IDENTIFYING INTERCONNECTIONS

Identifying the different ways that a system's parts, or components, interact with each other through their behaviors, and through those interactions, change the behaviors of other components.

SYSTEMS THINKING CONCEPT CARDS:
SOFT CIRCUITS

07.

PERCEIVING DYNAMICS

Perceiving a system's dynamics involves looking at a higher level at how the system works. Dynamics in a system are often characterized by circles – patterns that feed back on another. These are called feedback loops. Understanding dynamics gives insights into the mechanisms and re-lationships that are at the core of a system and can be leveraged to create systemic changes.

SYSTEMS THINKING CONCEPT CARDS:
SOFT CIRCUITS

08.

CONSIDERING THE ROLE OF
SYSTEM STRUCTURE

Understanding how a system's components are set up in relation to one another gives insight into the behavior of a component. A system's structure affects the behaviors of its components and the overall dynamics and functioning of a system. For instance, how a city's highway system is structured affects overall traffic patterns and car movement within it. Being able to see a system's structure gives insights into the mechanisms and relationships that are at the core of a system, which can be lever-aged to create systemic changes.

SYSTEMS THINKING CONCEPT CARDS:
SOFT CIRCUITS

09.

MAKE SYSTEMS VISIBLE

When we learn to "make the system visible" – whether modeling a system on the back of a napkin, through a computer simulation, a game, a picture, a diagram, a set of mathematical computations, or a story–we can use these representations to communicate about how things work. At their best, good pictures of systems help both the creator and the "reader" or "au-dience" to understand not only the parts of the system (the components), but also, how those components work together to produce a whole.

SYSTEMS THINKING CONCEPT CARDS:
SOFT CIRCUITS

10.

SYSTEMS DIAGRAM

Is a diagram used to visualize the dy-namics that occur between components in a system, intended to capture how the variables interrelate. One way of diagram-ming a feedback loop uses an "R" with a clockwise arrow around it to indicate a reinforcing feedback loop. A "B" with a counterclockwise arrow around it would indicate a balancing feedback loop, which "counters" something in a system. The plus sign indicates an increase in that amount of a component in a system, and a minus sign indicates a decrease in the amount of a component in a system. There are other ways to create systems diagrams, but the most important thing about a good systems diagram is that it not only shows the components in a system, but is able to show the relationships between the components through the arrows, symbols, and text.

SYSTEMS THINKING CONCEPT CARDS:
SOFT CIRCUITS

11.

FEEDBACK LOOPS

Are relationships between two or more components of a system, where actions by these components interact in a circular fashion – something that component A does effects component B, which then cir-cles back and effects component A. There are two types of feedback loops, Balancing and Reinforcing.

SYSTEMS THINKING CONCEPT CARDS: SOFT CIRCUITS

12.
REINFORCING FEEDBACK LOOPS

Relationships where two or more components of a system cause each other to increase, such as in escalation cycles, or decrease, such in resource drain cycles, in a way that's "out of control" or creates a "snowball effect". Reinforcing loops encourage a system to reproduce certain behaviors, though these behaviors always "exhaust" themselves after the resources fueling the growth or diminishment run out. This is also called "limits to growth". There are two types of reinforcing feedback loops: "vicious" cycles and "virtuous" cycles.

SYSTEMS THINKING CONCEPT CARDS: SOFT CIRCUITS

13.
VICIOUS CYCLES

Reinforcing feedback loops that cause a negative outcome in terms of the perceived goal of the system. One thing to keep in mind is that the same thing might be a vicious cycle to one person, but a virtuous cycle for another person who has different goals.

SYSTEMS THINKING CONCEPT CARDS: SOFT CIRCUITS

14.
VIRTUOUS CYCLES

Reinforcing feedback loops that cause a positive outcome in terms the perceived goal of the system. One thing to keep in mind is that the same thing might be a virtuous cycle to one person, but a vicious cycle for another person who has different goals.

SYSTEMS THINKING CONCEPT CARDS: SOFT CIRCUITS

15.
BALANCING FEEDBACK LOOPS

Relationships where two or more elements of a system keep each other in balance, with one (or more) elements leading to increase, and one (or more) elements leading to decrease. These processes keep a system at the desired state of equilibrium, the system goal. Usually, balancing feedback processes stabilize systems by limiting or preventing certain processes from happening. Having a sense of how balancing feedback loops operate can give a person a sense of what will make a system stable.

SYSTEMS THINKING CONCEPT CARDS: SOFT CIRCUITS

16.
STOCKS & FLOWS

Stocks are an accumulated amount of something within a system (like money in a bank account, fish in a pond, trees in a forest, or jobs in an economy), and flows are the rate at which stocks in a system change either through increasing or decreasing (money comes in and out of a bank account due to wages paid, interest, and purchases. Fish come in and out of a pond due to birth rates, death rates, and fishing rates, etc.). Stocks are always nouns; they're the "stuff" of systems, while flows are always verbs; they're the "movement" of systems. Understanding Stocks and Flows gives someone an insight into how different parts of the system change over time.

SYSTEMS THINKING CONCEPT CARDS: SOFT CIRCUITS

17.
LIMITED RESOURCES

In any system, it is important to understand which resources are finite, ones that will run out at a certain point. Keeping in mind which resources are limited helps people make decisions about how best to maximize resources.

SYSTEMS THINKING CONCEPT CARDS:
SOFT CIRCUITS

18.
NESTED SYSTEMS

Systems that are a smaller part of other systems. Almost all systems are nested within larger systems. With nested systems, a larger system will affect the way that a subsystem behaves, and the subsystem will affect the way that the larger system behaves. Having a sense of nested systems helps people keep an eye on how systems interconnect and are always part of bigger pictures.

SYSTEMS THINKING CONCEPT CARDS:
SOFT CIRCUITS

19.
DYNAMIC EQUILIBRIUM

A state in which stocks and flows are balanced so the system is not varying widely, but still has internal dynamic processes that are continually in flux even though the system is stable overall. For example: in economics dynamic equilibrium might be used to talk about the constant flux of money movement in otherwise stable markets; in ecology, a population of organisms stabilizes when birth rate and death rate are in balance.

SYSTEMS THINKING CONCEPT CARDS:
SOFT CIRCUITS

20.
DESIGNING A SYSTEM

Creating a system through engaging in an iterative design process, one that entails iterative cycles of feedback, troubleshooting and testing. One of the most effective means of developing systems thinking is to regularly create and iterate on the design of systems, and doing so in a way that creates opportunities for students to think about generic systems models that apply across multiple domains and settings.

SYSTEMS THINKING CONCEPT CARDS:
SOFT CIRCUITS

21.
FIXES THAT FAIL

Any kind of solution to a problem that fixes the problem temporarily but fails fix it in the long term, and might even make it worse over time. Fixes that Fail are often put in place quickly, usually without much reflection on what consequences they'll have for the system. They're important to see since they're often the ways that people respond to problems in a system.

SYSTEMS THINKING CONCEPT CARDS:
SOFT CIRCUITS

22.
LEVERAGE POINTS

Particular places within a system where a small shift in one thing can produce big changes in everything. Leverage points are difficult to find because they often lie far away from either the problem or the obvious solution. It is because of the multitude of cause and effect relationships, feedback loops and system structures that a seemingly small change can be amplified, often in unexpected ways. Not every place in a system is a leverage point – sometimes changing one thing in a system will just have small effects that aren't felt throughout the system. Leverage points are important since they let us know where to focus our energies when we try to change systems.

SYSTEMS THINKING CONCEPT CARDS:
SOFT CIRCUITS

23.
UNINTENDED CONSEQUENCES

The unexpected result of an action taken in a system that the actor taking that original action did not want to happen. Unintended Consequences are often the result of fixes that fail or someone aiming to find a leverage point in a system but not considering long-term implications to those actions — someone failed to keep in mind time horizons. Having a good sense of potential unintended consequences means that someone will carefully consider before too hastily intervening in a system.

SYSTEMS THINKING CONCEPT CARDS:
SOFT CIRCUITS

24.

CONSIDERING HOW MENTAL
MODELS SHAPE ACTION IN A SYSTEM

The ability to consider the assumptions, ideas, and intentions that a given actor might have in relation to a system, and how these affect that actor's behavior within the system. Mental models are often correct about what components are included in a system, but frequently draw wrong conclusions about a system's overall behavior.

SYSTEMS THINKING CONCEPT CARDS:
SOFT CIRCUITS

25.

LOOKING AT A SYSTEM
FROM MULTIPLE PERSPECTIVES

The ability to understand that different actors in a system will have different mental models of the system and consider each of these perspectives when engaging in action within a system. This is also called "thinking across the table."

SYSTEMS THINKING CONCEPT CARDS:
SOFT CIRCUITS

26.

CONSIDERING MULTIPLE LEVELS
OF PERSPECTIVE

The ability to move fluidly between different levels of perspective within a system, from events, to patterns to system structures, to mental models. The most visible level of systems are events, visible instances of elements interacting in a system. Using the metaphor of a system as an iceberg, events are "above the waterline" – they're easy to see. When we start to think "below the waterline," we start to see three other levels of perspective: patterns (recurring sets of events), structures (ways the elements are set up in a system which give rise to regular patterns), and mental models (which shape systems structures). Switching between different levels of perspective when looking at a system deepens understanding of how a system operates.

SYSTEMS THINKING CONCEPT CARDS:
SOFT CIRCUITS

27.

TIME DELAYS

Are the time lag between an action in a system and the evidence of its effects. For example, there's a long delay between the point when you plant a seed in the ground and the appearance of a fruit-bearing tree.

SYSTEMS THINKING CONCEPT CARDS:
SOFT CIRCUITS

28.

TIME HORIZONS

Are the overall period of time that you look at something in order to understand it. For example, if we only look a complex system like an economy for a short period of time, we might misunderstand how it's behaving and miss the effects of actions taken far into the past.

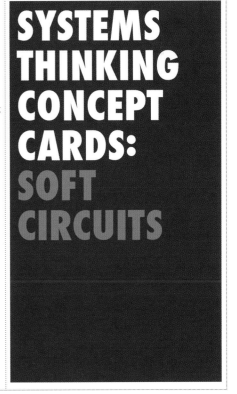

SYSTEMS THINKING CONCEPT CARDS: SOFT CIRCUITS

UNDERSTANDING SYSTEMS:
DIGITAL DESIGN FOR A COMPLEX WORLD

SOFT CIRCUITS CHALLENGE CARDS

Soft Circuits challenge cards offer a series of jumping-off points for the creation of projects using micro-electronics and found materials. The cards in this deck allow budding designers of all levels to combine circuitry and physical materials to create many different kinds of open-ended projects. Challenges are rated from easy to hardcore and come with some hints to help get things started. All can be modified to include alternative materials so let your imagination run wild!

LEVELS

⬤ EASY
✚ MEDIUM
✵ HARD
❄ HARDCORE

WHERE TO GO FOR MATERIALS

Radio Shack
radioshack.com

SparkFun
sparkfun.com

Jameco
jameco.com

Adafruit LED tutorial:
http://tinyurl.com/7ssqzgv

Lessons in Electric Circuits:
http://tinyurl.com/3bvvjs

SOFT CIRCUITS CHALLENGE CARDS

OVERVIEW

This deck contains 5 different categories of challenges from which to pick:

CATEGORIES

MINI-CHALLENGES
If you're just warming up, or need a bit of a challenge, these activities will get your brain working and test your knowledge of circuits and components.

HACK IT!
Give your old electronics new life by hacking them apart and using the components inside for your own projects!

EXPLORE COMPONENTS
Components are the building blocks of circuits. If you don't understand them, you won't get far! These challenges look more closely at the components you've used in Short Circuits.

SCIENCE (FICTIONAL) DEVICES
Time to use your imagination! The future is here—and you're the engineer. Design the world of tomorrow today!

MICROCONTROLLER CHALLENGES
These activities will use a micro-controller that will allow you to use sensors and switches to create complex circuits with ease! You'll also need a computer to do some programming.

TIPS

SAFETY TIPS

Put your safety goggles on. Cutting metal and plastic can result in small flying bits of material. Soldering irons "spit" sometimes as well.

Never use a sharp tool without someone else around.

Never use a tool you haven't used before, or which you are uncomfortable using. Ask someone for help.

Never use a damaged tool. If a tool is damaged, stop using it and tell an adult. If no adult is present, then mark the tool so you or someone else won't use it later.

Make sure that the path around you is clear when using sharp tools or soldering irons. It is important that people do not bump into you. It's easy to be injured or injure someone else who isn't paying attention.

SOLDERING TIPS

Never touch the end of the soldering iron. It is about 600 degrees and will burn you!

Hold wires to be heated with tweezers or clamps, not your hands. Wires get hot, too.

Always return the soldering iron to its stand when not in use. Never put it down on your workbench.

Work in a well-ventilated area. Avoid breathing any smoke or fumes by keeping your head to the side of, not above, your work.

Make sure to throw out any solder, wires, or bits of metal in the trashcan. Don't leave it sitting around.

Be sure to wash your hands after soldering. Don't even think about putting them near your mouth until you do!

---

01 PINCUSHION BREADBOARD

LEVEL

HARD

CATEGORY

MINI-CHALLENGES

Create a pincushion that doubles as a breadboard!

EXPLANATION

Breadboards are great for making prototypes of circuits. Find out how they connect components and conduct electricity by making one of your own.

HINTS

Make sure to use conductive fabric with fusible interfacing, or you'll need to sew very small pieces of fabric.

COMPONENTS

Conductive fabric and regular fabric, stuffing, scissors, an iron, regular thread, and needle. Electronic components to play with: LED's, momentary push-button switches, resistors, 3V coin cell batteries, wire

SYSTEMS THINKING SPOTLIGHT

designing a system,
component relationships

---

02 BOOKMARK LIGHT

LEVEL

MEDIUM

CATEGORY

MINI-CHALLENGES

Create an LED book light that doubles as a bookmark when it's turned off.

EXPLANATION

The light will only shine when the bookmark is "closed." When open, the circuit isn't connected.

HINTS

Be careful not cross thread from the positive and negative sides of the battery as you sew the circuit into the bookmark.

COMPONENTS

3V battery, felt and fabric, conductive thread, Lilypad LED

SYSTEMS THINKING SPOTLIGHT

component relationships,
considering a system's purpose or goal

03
CONTINUITY TESTER

LEVEL

MEDIUM

CATEGORY

MINI-CHALLENGES

Create a simple continuity tester with a few cheap components and a battery.

EXPLANATION

e-Crafters need a good continuity tester. In this challenge, the circuit tries to pass a small current through the item being tested and the LED will light brightly, dimly, or not at all according to the resistance of the item.

HINTS

Be sure to unclip the battery or attach the leads to cardboard to stop them from touching when not in use — or you'll drain your battery if they accidentally touch!

COMPONENTS

390 ohm resistor, LED, 9V and battery clip, alligator clips, breadboard

SYSTEMS THINKING SPOTLIGHT

component relationships, role of system structure, system dynamics/interconnections

---

04
FLASH 555

LEVEL

HARD

CATEGORY

MINI-CHALLENGES

Create a flashing light with an LED, a 555 timer, and a few cheap components.

EXPLANATION

Use the timer to help control the on and off flashing of an LED light.

HINTS

Make sure the 555 chip is facing the right direction. Look at the little notch at one end. That is the top of the chip. Directly to the left of that notch is pin number 1.

COMPONENTS

NE555 Bipolar Timer, LED, 470K resistor, 1K resistor, 1uF capacitor, 9V battery

SYSTEMS THINKING SPOTLIGHT

balancing feedback loop; system dynamics/interconnections, designing a system

---

05
CONDUCTIVITY CHALLENGE

LEVEL

EASY

CATEGORY

EXPLORE COMPONENTS

Using a multimeter and your favorite room, find five conductive surfaces.

EXPLANATION

Multimeters have two leads, and can be placed on a surface to see if it is conductive or a component that will transmit electricity.

HINTS

You will need to put the multimeter in Continuity Mode, and it should beep or light up when you touch both leads to a conductive material.

COMPONENTS

Multimeter, various surfaces and materials

SYSTEMS THINKING SPOTLIGHT

component relationships; system dynamics/interconnections

DR. RESEARCH

LEVEL

MEDIUM

Using a variety of coin cell batteries and resistors, light up a multi-colored selection of LEDs.

EXPLANATION

Using an LED, a battery, and a resistor figure out which voltage works best with which LED colors. What about resistors? Can you figure out the resistor names based on the brightness of the LED?

HINTS

Be careful not to use batteries of a high voltage, like 9V, or you may burn out your LED.

COMPONENTS

resistors, LEDs, coin cell batteries (3-5 volts)

SYSTEMS THINKING SPOTLIGHT

component relationships; system dynamics/interconnections, role of system structure

---

SWITCH IT UP

LEVEL

EASY

Use a multimeter to test out different switches and buttons to see how they work.

EXPLANATION

You can use a multimeter to test out the way electricity flows through a button or switch.

HINTS

You will need to put the multimeter in Continuity Mode, and it should beep or light up when there is a connection between both leads.

COMPONENTS

various switches (momentary push-button switches, SPST and SPDT switches), multimeter

SYSTEMS THINKING SPOTLIGHT

identifying components, identifying behaviors, system dynamics/interconnections

---

CONDUCTIVITY EXPERIMENT

LEVEL

EASY

CATEGORY

EXPLORE COMPONENTS

Use batteries to light up a flash-light bulb, using aluminum foil

EXPLANATION

The aluminum foil strip is conductive and makes a path for the energy in the battery to follow. The energy follows the path and lights up the bulb.

HINTS

Start by folding the aluminum foil to make a long strip and figure out how to light up the battery. Now that you've made it light up, can you create a switch?

COMPONENTS

batteries, aluminum foil about 4" x 12", flashlight bulbs

SYSTEMS THINKING SPOTLIGHT

role of system structure, system dynamics/interconnections

09
MODEL RESISTOR

LEVEL

MEDIUM

CATEGORY

EXPLORE COMPONENTS

Create a paper resistor model with layers that show how a resistor functions.

EXPLANATION

Resistors are devices that make use of poor conductors to limit the flow of electricity through a circuit.

HINTS

Be sure to label each part so it is clear how each part of the component works.

COMPONENTS

paper, pencils, markers or colored pencils, tape

SYSTEMS THINKING SPOTLIGHT

modeling a system, component relationships, role of system structure

---

10
MODEL BATTERY

LEVEL

EASY

CATEGORY

EXPLORE COMPONENTS

Create a paper battery model with layers to show how a battery functions on the inside.

EXPLANATION

Batteries turn stored chemical energy into electrical energy.

HINTS

Be sure to label each part so it is clear how each part of the component works.

COMPONENTS

paper, pencils, markers or colored pencils, tape

SYSTEMS THINKING SPOTLIGHT

modeling a system, component relationships, role of system structure

---

11
SWITCH MODEL

LEVEL

MEDIUM

CATEGORY

EXPLORE COMPONENTS

Create a paper model of a switch that will show how the inside of an actual switch works.

EXPLANATION

Switches work by connecting or disconnecting parts of a circuit.

HINTS

Be sure to label each part so it is clear how each part of the component works.

COMPONENTS

paper, pencils, markers or colored pencils, tape

SYSTEMS THINKING SPOTLIGHT

modeling a system, component relationships, role of system structure

12
LEGO®
CIRCUITS

LEVEL

HARD

CATEGORY

EXPLORE COMPONENTS

Find a simple circuit diagram and create a Lego® diagram that mimics it.

EXPLANATION

Circuit diagrams are very specific. Find the right Legos® to represent each component.

HINTS

Can you make a working switch? How about multi-Lego battery with layers?

COMPONENTS

Legos®, circuit diagrams

SYSTEMS THINKING SPOTLIGHT

modeling a system, component relationships, role of system structure

---

13
MISSING
PARTS

LEVEL

EASY

CATEGORY

EXPLORE COMPONENTS

Fill in the blanks on a circuit diagram, drawing in the proper components to complete it.

EXPLANATION

Every circuit must have the right balance of components to function properly.

HINTS

Choose from the bank of listed components to complete the circuit.

COMPONENTS

circuit diagrams, pen or pencil

SYSTEMS THINKING SPOTLIGHT

modeling a system, component relationships, role of system structure

---

14
ELECTRONIC
SYMBOLS
MINI-GAME

LEVEL

EASY

CATEGORY

EXPLORE COMPONENTS

Create flash cards for basic electrical components.

EXPLANATION

Draw the diagram on one side and label the component on the other.

HINTS

If you have space, write a small definition for the component on the back as well.

COMPONENTS

paper, pencils, markers or colored pencils

SYSTEMS THINKING SPOTLIGHT

identifying components, identifying behaviors, identifying a system

15
PAPER POTS

LEVEL

MEDIUM

CATEGORY

EXPLORE COMPONENTS

Create a paper potentiometer with paper and a brass fastener for the paper "wiper."

EXPLANATION

Potentiometers have variable resistance based on the wiper position, so focus on that mechanism.

HINTS

Be sure to label each part so it is clear how each part of the component works.

COMPONENTS

brass fasteners, paper, pencils, markers or colored pencils

SYSTEMS THINKING SPOTLIGHT

component relationships, designing a system, role of system structure

---

16
FIRST STEP

LEVEL

EASY

CATEGORY

MICROCONTROLLER CHALLENGES

Set up your breadboard by running power and ground to both sides.

EXPLANATION

The two long lines that run down the side of each breadboard are bus lines. One is for power, one is for ground. Hooking them up to your Arduinio will allow power to flow — but just to one side. It's up to you to connect the other side!

HINTS

5V is the same as + and GND is the same as — on the Arduino and breadboard

COMPONENTS

Arduino, breadboard, four pieces of wire

SYSTEMS THINKING SPOTLIGHT

designing a system, component relationships

17
LIGHTS ON

LEVEL

EASY

CATEGORY

MICROCONTROLLER CHALLENGES

Get an LED shining bright on your breadboard.

EXPLANATION

Use the power and ground from your Arduino to your breadboard. Then plug in your LED and resistor to light it up.

HINTS

Remember, resistors help limit the amount of current passing through components. Make sure to include it on one side of the LED.

COMPONENTS

Arduino, breadboard, 220 ohm resistor, LED, wire

SYSTEMS THINKING SPOTLIGHT

designing a system, component relationships

18
SWITCH IT UP

LEVEL

MEDIUM

CATEGORY

MICROCONTROLLER CHALLENGES

Use a momentary pushbutton switch to turn on/off an LED.

EXPLANATION

A switch can help you turn on or off an LED, depending on its position. Build the circuit from "Lights On" and then insert your switch on the power or ground side!

HINTS

Make sure the switch is aligned correctly. Feel free to experiment with different pins on the switch until you get it right!

COMPONENTS

Arduino, breadboard, 220 ohm resistor, LED, switch, wire

SYSTEMS THINKING SPOTLIGHT

designing a system, component relationships, role of system structure

---

19
SMOOTH IT OUT

LEVEL

HARD

CATEGORY

MICROCONTROLLER CHALLENGES

Use a potentiometer to fade an LED.

EXPLANATION

Hook up an LED on pin 9. Next, hook up a potentiometer to one of the analog inputs. This will be used to control the brightness of the LED.

HINTS

Look at the AnalogIn example that comes with Arduino for some help and example code.

COMPONENTS

Arduino, breadboard, 220 ohm resistor, LED, 10k potentiometer, wire

SYSTEMS THINKING SPOTLIGHT

designing a system, component relationships, reinforcing feedback loops

---

20
LIVE WIRE

LEVEL

MEDIUM

CATEGORY

MICROCONTROLLER CHALLENGES

Use wire and just about anything conductive to make a custom switch.

EXPLANATION

Make your own switch from wire and other conductive materials. The sky's the limit! Use the "Switch it Up" activity, but forget about a boring pushbutton switch!

HINTS

Try drawing dark lines on a piece of paper with a #2 pencil, but don't have the lines touching! The graphite used to draw is conductive. Attach your wires to the lines with alligator clips. Now, connect the two lines together by drawing a third line. You've just created a new switch. Now, come up with some of your own.

COMPONENTS

Arduino, breadboard, 220 ohm resistor, LED, wire, alligator clips

SYSTEMS THINKING SPOTLIGHT

designing a system, component relationships, role of system structure, system dynamics/ interconnections

NOTES

DESIGN CHALLENGE 1

1. The LilyPad Arduino is a microcontroller board designed for wearables and e-textiles. It can be sewn to fabric and similarly mounted power supplies, sensors and actuators with conductive thread. LilyPad Arduino components can be ordered through SparkFun Electronics.

DESIGN CHALLENGE 2

1. On the 9V battery snap connector, it is important that the tips of the wires are exposed (uninsulated). If this is not the case, use wire strippers to expose the ends of the wires before the start of the activity.

2. Because 3V batteries can short easily, we recommend inserting the 3V battery into the holder before placing it in the zip-closed plastic bag.

3. LilyPad LEDs come in multiple colors, including white, blue, pink, green, red, purple, and yellow. Choosing the color of the LEDs is a great way to personalize the project. Alternatively, you could have youths pack their own e-Textile Cuff Kits so that they can choose the color of the LEDs themselves.

DESIGN CHALLENGE 3

1. The "Soundie" is a hoodie sweatshirt computationally enhanced with iron-on conductive fabric that detects electrical conductivity when the wearer touches it. When the wearer places her hands on each sleeve, her body creates a closed electrical circuit that causes the sweatshirt to emit light and sound. The garment lights up corresponding LEDs and "sings" different pitches depending on how much the wearer touches the conductive fabric. Note that the "soundie" uses a non-LilyPad buzzer and uses Arduino programming instead of Modkit.

2. Note that the pocket would need to be made by the youths using a scrap piece of fabric and affixed with fabric glue, needle and nonconductive thread, or hot glue.

3. Note that youths can change the petals to which they attach their LEDs, buzzer, or both, but they will have to change the pin assignment in Modkit's Hardware tab to reflect this revision. Reassigning petals/pins may come in handy for aesthetic reasons or to prevent thread lines from crossing.

REFERENCES

Baafi, E., and A. Millner. 2011. Modkit: A Toolkit for Tinkering with Tangibles & Connecting Communities, Upcoming in Proceedings of Tangible, Embedded, and Embodied Interaction. TEI. doi:10.1145/1935701.1935782

Brown, A. L. 1992. Design experiments: Theoretical and methodological challenges in creating complex interventions in classroom settings. *Journal of the Learning Sciences* 2 (2): 141–178.

Brown, Gordon S. 1990. The genesis of the system thinking program at the Orange Grove Middle School, Tucson, Arizona. Personal report. 6301 N. Calle de Adelita, Tucson, AZ 85718: March 1.

Buechley, L. 2006. A construction kit for electronic textiles. In *2006 10th IEEE International Symposium on Wearable Computers*, 83–90.

Colella, V. 2000. Participatory simulations: Building collaborative understanding through immersive dynamic modeling. *Journal of the Learning Sciences* 9 (4): 471–500.

Colella, V. S., E. Klopfer, and M. Resnick. 2001. Adventures in modeling: Exploring complex, dynamic systems with StarLogo. Williston, VT: Teachers College Press.

Danish, J. A., K. Peppler, D. Phelps, and D. Washington. 2011. Life in the hive: Supporting inquiry into complexity within the zone of proximal development. *Journal of Science Education and Technology* 20 (5): 454–467.

Draper, F. 1989. Letter to Jay Forrester. Personal communication, Orange Grove Junior High School, 1911 E. Orange Grove Rd., Tucson, AZ 85718. May 2, 1989.

Goldstone, R. L., and U. Wilensky. 2008. Promoting transfer by grounding complex systems principles. *Journal of the Learning Sciences* 17 (4): 465–516.

Hmelo-Silver, C. E., and M. G. Pfeffer. 2004. Comparing expert and novice understanding of a complex system from the perspective of structures, behaviors, and functions. *Cognitive Science* 28 (1): 127–138.

Hmelo-Silver, C., R. Jordan, L. Liu, and E. Chernobilsky. 2011. Representational tools for understanding complex computer-supported collaborative learning environments. *Computer-Supported Collaborative Learning Series* 12 (Part 1): 83–106. doi:10.1007/978-1-4419-7710-6_4

Kafai, Y. B. 2006. Constructionism. In Cambridge Handbook of the Learning Sciences, ed. K. Sawyer, 35–46. New York: Cambridge University Press.

Lenhart, A., and M. Madden. 2007. Social networking websites and teens: An overview. Washington, DC: Pew Internet and American Life Project.

Lyneis, D. 2000. Bringing system dynamics to a school near you: Suggestions for introducing and sustaining system dynamics in K-12 education. International System Dynamics Society Conference. Bergen, Norway.

Maloney, J. H., K. Peppler, Y. Kafai, M. Resnick, and N. Rusk. 2008. Programming by choice: urban youth learning programming with scratch. *ACM SIGCSE Bulletin* 40 (1): 367–371.

Meadows, D. 1999. Leverage points: Places to intervene in a system. The Sustainability Institute.

Papert, S. 1980. Mindstorms: Children, computers, and powerful ideas. New York: Basic Books, Inc.

Papert, S., and I. Harel. 1991. *Constructionism.* New York, NY: Ablex Publishing Corporation. http://www.papert.org/articles/SituatingConstructionism.html.

Peppler, K. A., and Y. B. Kafai. 2007a. From SuperGoo to Scratch: Exploring creative digital media production in informal learning. *Learning, Media and Technology* 32 (2): 149–166.

Resnick, M., J. Maloney, A. Monroy-Hernandez, N. Rusk, E. Eastmond, K. Brennan, et al.,and Y. Kafai. 2009. Scratch: Programming for all. *Communications of the ACM* 52 (11): 60–67.

Rusk, N., M. Resnick, and S. Cooke. 2009. Origins and guiding principles of the Computer Clubhouse. In The Computer Clubhouse: Constructionism and creativity in youth communities, ed. Y. Kafai, K. Peppler, and R. Chapman. New York: Teachers College Press.

Salen, K. 2008. Toward an ecology of gaming. In The Ecology of Games: Connecting Youth, Games, and Learning, ed. K. Salen. Cambridge, MA: The MIT Press.

Salen, K., R. Torres, R. Rufo-Tepper, A. Shapiro, and L. Wolozin. 2010. Quest to learn: Growing a school for digital kids. Cambridge: MIT Press.

Sweeney, L. 2001. When a butterfly sneezes: A guide for helping kids explore interconnections in our world through favorite stories. Waltham, MA: Pegasus Communications.

Wilensky, U. 1999. NetLogo [Computer Program]: Center for Connected Learning and Computer-Based Modeling. Northwestern University, Evanston, IL.

Wilensky, U., and M. Resnick. 1999. Thinking in levels: A dynamic systems perspective to making sense of the world. *Journal of Science Education and Technology* 8 (1): 3–19.

SPARKFUN PHOTO CREDITS

The following photographs of electronic components found in this volume are the creative copyright of Sparkfun Electronics (sparkfun.com/):

9V Battery: SparkFun Electronics, Juan Pena, Product SKU-10218

9V Snap Connector: SparkFun Electronics, Juan Pena, Product SKU-00091

Alligator Test Leads: SparkFun Electronics, Juan Pena, Product SKU-11037

Coin Cell Battery, two views: SparkFun Electronics, Juan Pena, Product SKU-00337

Conductive Fabric: SparkFun Electronics, Juan Pena, Product SKU-10056

Conductive Thread: SparkFun Electronics, Juan Pena, Product SKU-11791

Diagonal Cutters: SparkFun Electronics, Juan Pena, Product SKU-08794

Digital Multimeter, two views: SparkFun Electronics, Juan Pena, Product SKU-09141

Electrical Tape: SparkFun Electronics, Juan Pena, Product SKU-10689

Hook-up Wire: SparkFun Electronics, Juan Pena, Product SKU-08023

LED Superbright: SparkFun Electronics, Juan Pena, Product SKU-08285

LED-Basic Blue: SparkFun Electronics, Juan Pena, Product SKU-11372

LED-Basic Red: SparkFun Electronics, Juan Pena, Product SKU-09590

LilyPad Arduino Simple Board: SparkFun Electronics, Juan Pena, Product SKU-10274

LilyPad Button Board: SparkFun Electronics, Juan Pena, Product SKU-08776

LilyPad Buzzer: SparkFun Electronics, Juan Pena, Product SKU-08463

LilyPad Coin Cell Battery Holder: SparkFun Electronics, Juan Pena, Product SKU-10730

LilyPad FTDI Basic Breakout: SparkFun Electronics, Juan Pena, Product SKU-10275

LilyPad LED White: SparkFun Electronics, Juan Pena, Product SKU-10081

LilyPad LiPower: SparkFun Electronics, Juan Pena, Product SKU-11260

LilyPad Slide Switch: SparkFun Electronics, Juan Pena, Product SKU-09350

Mini Power Switch: SparkFun Electronics, Juan Pena, Product SKU-00102

Needle-Nose Pliers: SparkFun Electronics, Juan Pena, Product SKU-08793

Polymer Lithium Ion Battery, two views: SparkFun Electronics, Juan Pena, Product SKU-00341

Rotary Potentiometer: SparkFun Electronics, Juan Pena, Product SKU-09939

Sewing Snaps: SparkFun Electronics, Juan Pena, Product SKU-11347

USB Mini-B Cable: SparkFun Electronics, Juan Pena, Product SKU-00598

Wire Strippers: SparkFun Electronics, Juan Pena, Product SKU-08696

INDEX

INTERCONNECTIONS CURRICULA SUMMARY SHEET:
SOFT CIRCUITS

WHAT IS THE INTERCONNECTIONS CURRICULA?

Interconnections: Understanding Systems through Digital Design is a collection of curricula that support students to develop critical 21st century skills—systems thinking and digital design—by engaging in rich project-based learning using the latest technologies.

WHAT'S SYSTEMS THINKING, AND WHY IS IT IMPORTANT FOR MY STUDENTS?

As the world gets more complex and interconnected, we need to help our kids to understand and positively impact the dizzying number of systems around them. Systems thinking is a set of ideas and practices that allow kids to see through the "lens" of systems: how to take a "big picture" view of complex social structures and technologies, how to see the patterns and dynamics that drive systems, how to understand that the whole is usually greater than the sum of its parts.

HOW IS DIGITAL DESIGN DIFFERENT FROM OTHER USES OF EDUCATIONAL TECHNOLOGY?

Digital design is all about getting students the skills they need in order to be innovative, creative, and entrepreneurial thinkers. Rather than educational technologies that replicate a consumer mentality around learning, dumping information into students' brains, digital design activities put them in the driver's seat, having them come up with the ways technology can look in the world and preparing them for a world that increasingly expects them to engage in creative processes.

CIRCUITRY AND FASHION DESIGN, REALLY?

There are lots of great reasons we've found in our work to use the combination of physical computing and fashion design as the foundation for a classroom curriculum. Technologies like these are incredibly engaging, are an integral part of youth culture, and can be leveraged to get students excited about entering into some pretty important academic practices: giving and getting feedback, revising drafts, making arguments, problem solving, and more.

DOES THIS ALIGN TO STANDARDS?

Yes! All the Interconnections curricula have been aligned to the Common Core State Standards in areas including language arts, history and science, as well as the Next Generation Science Standards.

HOW MUCH TIME DOES THIS TAKE?

The *Soft Circuits* curriculum is designed to take about 20–30 hours overall, but of course can and will be adapted to fit your students' needs and abilities as well as your school culture. This means that we fully expect that you might take certain parts and extend them, cut other parts, or repurpose them to fit existing units of study.